Masculinity and Power

For Jessica and Daniel

Men themselves were now split into a (female) interior and a
(male) exterior – the body armour. And as we know, the interior
and the exterior were mortal enemies. What we see being
portrayed in the rituals are the armour's separation from and
superiority over the interior: the interior was allowed to flow, but
only within the masculine boundaries of the mass formations.
Before any of this could happen, the body had to be split apart
thoroughly enough to create an interior and exterior that could
be opposed to each other as enemies. Only then could the two
parts re-form 'in peace' in the ritual. What fascism promised men
was the reintegration of their hostile components under tolerable
conditions, dominance of the hostile 'female' element within
themselves. This explains why the word 'boundaries', in fascist
parlance, refers primarily to the boundaries of the body.

Theweleit, *Male Fantasies*

Masculinity and Power

Arthur Brittan

Basil Blackwell

Copyright © Arthur Brittan 1989

First published 1989

Basil Blackwell Ltd
108 Cowley Road, Oxford, OX4 1JF, UK

Basil Blackwell Inc.
432 Park Avenue South, Suite 1503
New York, NY 10016, USA

British Library Cataloguing in Publication Data

Brittan, Arthur
    Masculinity and power.
    1. Men. Sex roles
    I. Title
    305.3′1

    ISBN 0–631–14166–9
    ISBN 0–631–14167–7 Pbk

Library of Congress Cataloging in Publication Data

Brittan, Arthur.
    Masculinity and power.

    Bibliography: p.
    Includes index.
    1. Men. 2. Masculinity (Psychology)
    3. Power (Social sciences). 4. Sex role
    5. Patriarchy. I. Title.
    HQ1090.B75 1989 305.3′1 88–7966

    ISBN 0–631–14166–9
    ISBN 0–631–14167–7 (pbk.)

Printed in Great Britain by TJ Press, Padstow

Contents

Acknowledgements   vi
1 Masculinities   1
2 Masculinity and Identity   19
3 Male Sexualities   46
4 Masculinity as Competitiveness   77
5 Men as a Collectivity?   108
6 True Male Discourse   142
7 Men, Reason and Crisis   178
Bibliography   205
Index   214

Acknowledgements

I would like to thank the students in the feminist theory seminars who made me realize that masculinity is not just another academic topic, but is also dangerous and volatile. My special thanks to Eileen who has had to put up with my particular version of masculinity, and also to Vivienne Taylor who somehow made sense of my typescript.

1

Masculinities

Most discussions of masculinity tend to treat it as if it is measurable. Some men have more of it, others less. Those men who appear to lack masculinity are, by definition, sick or genetically inadequate. Gay men, for example, are often regarded as men who lack a proper hormonal balance, and who consequently are not 'real' men. This assumption – that we can know and describe men in terms of some discoverable dimension is problematic – because it suggests that masculinity is timeless and universal.

My aim in this book is to examine this assumption. My position is that we cannot talk of masculinity, only masculinities. This is not to claim that masculinity is so variable that we cannot identify it as a topic. I am not in favour of a doctrinaire relativism which would make it an almost impossible object of study. It seems to me that any account of masculinity must begin with its place in the general discussion of gender. Since gender does not exist outside history and culture, this means that both masculinity and femininity are continuously subject to a process of reinterpretation. The way men are regarded in late twentieth-century England is obviously different from the way that they were regarded in the nineteenth century. Moreover, versions of masculinity may vary over a limited time scale. In this respect, Ehrenreich (1983) has documented the changes in American men's attitudes to marriage from the fifties to the eighties.

> In the 1950s ... there was a firm expectation ... that required men to grow up, marry and support their wives. To do anything

else was less than grown-up, and the man who willfully deviated
was judged to be somehow 'less than a man'. This expectation
was supported by an enormous weight of expert opinion, moral
sentiment and public bias, both within popular culture and the
elite centres of academic wisdom. But by the end of the 1970s
and the beginning of the 1980s, adult manhood was no longer
burdened with the automatic expectation of marriage and
breadwinning. The man who postpones marriage even into
middle age, who avoids women who are likely to become
financial dependents, who is dedicated to his own pleasures, is
likely to be found not suspiciously deviant but 'healthy'. And this
judgement, like the prior one, is supported by expert opinion and
by the moral sentiments and biases of a considerable sector of the
American middle class. (Ehrenreich, 1983, pp. 11–12)

If the 'breadwinner ethic' has indeed collapsed among
large sections of middle-class American men, then is there
any point in talking about masculinity in terms of a
generalized category? If men are now dedicated to the
cultivation of their own pleasures, does it make much sense
even to attempt to theorize about masculinity? Does the
concept 'masculinity' have any meaning at all when it seems
to change from moment to moment? Surely this is not what
is being suggested by Ehrenreich. The fact that men are
rebelling against their role as breadwinners does not entail
the undermining of their dominance in the political and
economic spheres. Nor, for that matter, does it imply that
they have surrendered authority in the family or household.
What has changed is not male power as such, but its form,
its presentation, its packaging. In other words, while it is
apparent that styles of masculinity may alter in relatively
short time spans, the substance of male power does not.
Hence, men who run away from family involvements are not
signalling their general abdication of power; all they are
doing is redefining the arena in which that power is
exercised.

The fact that masculinity may appear in different guises
at different times does not entitle us to draw the conclusion
that we are dealing with an ephemeral quality which is
sometimes present and sometimes not. In the final analysis,
how men behave will depend upon the existing social

relations of gender. By this I mean the way in which men and women confront each other ideologically and politically. Gender is never simply an arrangement in which the roles of men and women are decided in a contingent and haphazard way. At any given moment, gender will reflect the material interests of those who have power and those who do not. Masculinity, therefore, does not exist in isolation from femininity – it will always be an expression of the current image that men have of themselves in relation to women. And these images are often contradictory and ambivalent.

Masculinity, from this point of view, is always local and subject to change. Obviously, some masculinities are long-lived, whilst others are as ephemeral as fads in pop music. However, what does not easily change is the justification and naturalization of male power; that is, what remains relatively constant in the masculine ideology, masculinism or hetero-sexualism. What I am proposing here is that we must distinguish between three concepts which often tend to be confused in the literature as well as in political and everyday discourse, namely masculinity, masculinism and patriarchy.

Masculinity refers to those aspects of men's behaviour that fluctuate over time. In some cases these fluctuations may last for decades – in others it may be a matter of weeks or months. For example, if we look at the fashion in male hairstyles over the past 20 years or so, we find that they range from the shoulder length vogue of the sixties, to the punk cuts of the late seventies and early eighties. During the same period men have experimented with both macho and androgynous styles of self-presentation. At the same time, we have been bombarded with stories about role reversals in marriage and the home. Men are now 'into' fatherhood. They look after their children, they sometimes change nappies and, in some cases, they stay at home and play the role of houseperson. The speed of these changes, it is sometimes suggested, has led to a crisis in masculinity. The implication here is that male identity is a fragile and tentative thing with no secure anchorage in the contemporary world. Such fragility makes it almost impossible to talk about masculinity as though it had some recognizable substantive basis. And yet, in everyday and academic discourse, we find that men are commonly described as aggressive, assertive, independent, competitive, insensitive and so on. These attributions are based on the idea that there is something about men which transcends their local situation. Men are seen as having natures which determine their behaviour in all situations.

Indeed, the habit of attributing some kind of exalted power to masculinity is so ingrained in our culture that it makes it very difficult to give credence to those explanations which stress its contextuality. This is precisely the point. Those people who speak of masculinity as an essence, as an inborn characteristic, are confusing masculinity with masculinism, the masculine ideology. Masculinism is the ideology that justifies and naturalizes male domination. As such, it is the ideology of patriarchy. Masculinism takes it for granted that there is a fundamental difference between men and women, it assumes that heterosexuality is normal, it accepts without question the sexual division of labour, and it sanctions the political and dominant role of men in the public and private spheres. Moreover, the masculine ideology is not subject to the vagaries of fashion – it tends to be relatively resistant to change. In general, masculinism gives primacy to the belief that gender is not negotiable – it does not accept evidence from feminist and other sources that the relationships between men and women are political and constructed nor, for that matter, does it allow for the possibility that lesbianism and homosexuality are not forms of deviance or abnormality, but are alternative forms of gender commitment.

Masculinism as a Dominant Ideology

However, I am not for one moment suggesting that the connection between masculinism and masculinity is tenuous. This would be absurd. If, for example, we look at the exaggerated politeness of male behaviour in some middle-class contexts, and then we observe the more direct male assertiveness in a working-class environment, this does not entitle us to draw the conclusion that middle-class and working-class masculinity are qualitatively different. Alternatively, if we examine the behaviour of men cross-culturally and discover that the number of ways of 'being a man' appears to be flexible and varied, it is then wrong to assume that this variation undermines male domination. Just as there is a large number of styles and behaviours associated with class relations so there is an almost infinite number of styles and behaviours associated with gender relations. Working-class life in the north of England is not a carbon copy of working-class behaviour in the south. This is not to say that the specificity of working-class life in different parts of Britain cannot be subsumed under the rubric of a more general view of class. Similarly, the fact that men have a multitude of ways of expressing their masculinity in different times and places does not mean that these masculinities have nothing to do with male dominance.

I realize that there are problems in talking about masculinism as a dominant ideology. To assume this is to accept without reservation that a dominant group's ideology is inevitably imposed upon everybody else. In the case of the masculine ideology, this is to claim that men have a collective ideology which they collectively force women to accept as being natural and inevitable. This implies that men constitute a class, and that they maximize their class interest. Now this is a vulgar version of ideology. It proposes that ideology is some kind of monolithic worldview which is used by a ruling group to justify and legitimate its claims to rule. By no stretch of the imagination can men be considered to be a class in this sense. One has only to look at the position of black and white men in Britain, or in the United States, to establish that their membership of a common class is problematic. Of course, it is true that black and white male workers may occupy the same class location, but this does not mean that they constitute a homogeneous class. Furthermore, it may be asked, in what ways do white working-class men have the same interests as black men workers in a country like South Africa? To assert that these men are a class sharing a common ideology poses all sorts of difficulty.

Accordingly, the proposition that masculinism is the ideology that justifies and naturalizes male domination needs to be qualified. Granted that men collectively do not form committees to ensure their continued domination, and that men themselves are exploited and dominated by other men, we can nevertheless still speak of a set of gender relations in which the power of men is taken for granted, not only in the public but in the domestic sphere as well. Masculinism is reproduced and reaffirmed in the household, in the economy and in the polity. Even when there is a great deal of gender and sexual experimentation, as was the case in the sixties and the early seventies, masculinism was never under real attack because gender relations remained relatively constant. The great amount of attention given to the increased participation of men in household chores and the emphasis on 'democratic' family relationships did not, in any marked way, alter these gender relations. Despite the feminist analysis and demystification of patriarchy, the masculine ideology remains intact, as evidenced by the successful counter-campaign of the New Right in the United States and Britain.

Male Natures

It may seem peculiar, after nearly a century of counter-arguments, that there is still strong support for the thesis that human nature is something that can be discovered and measured, that it is knowable. Despite the apparent success of the social sciences in accounting for socialization as a learning and social process, the idea of an original and underlying basis for human behaviour remains a central aspect of much academic and everyday thinking. Moreover, this thesis has been given new life by the emergence of sophisticated biological approaches such as ethology and sociobiology. While the crude social Darwinism of the nineteenth century has long since been relegated to the academic dustbin, this is not to say that its influence is dead. On the contrary, the new evolutionists have re-entered the debate about human nature with new ferocity. In the case of gender, they claim that there is no way in which it can be seen as a social construction. Gender behaviour is rooted in biological imperatives which serve evolutionary purposes. Of course, they are not so naive as to deny the influence of social and cultural factors, but this does not amount to anything more than suggesting that culture is itself a particular kind of manifestation of evolutionary mechanisms (Sahlins, 1976).

Take the example of male aggressiveness. The socialization case is that aggression is learned. It is acquired in a context in which men learn that it is both rewarding and expected to behave in an assertive way. Boys grow up in environments which encourage certain kinds of conduct, rather than others. They learn to be 'men'. Aggression, from this point of view, is a response to specific kinds of experience. Men will only behave aggressively if they have learned it is appropriate to do so. The implication is that a society's proper functioning depends upon the inculcation of aggressive patterns of behaviour in young boys.

> Even as small boys, males are trained for a world of independent aggressive action . . . males are groomed to take the universe by storm, to confront the environment directly. Males learn that society's goals are best met by aggression, by actively wrestling their accomplishments from the environment. Force, power, competition and aggression are the means. Achievement, males are taught, is measured in productivity, resources, and control – all the result of direct action. In the Western world, the importance of self reliant, individual action is systematically inculcated in males. To be masculine requires not only self reliance and self control, but control over other people and resources. (Lipman-Blumen, 1984, p. 55)

Sociobiologists take issue with this. They argue that to talk about aggression exclusively in terms of learning is to fly in the face of evidence from the study of animal populations. While agreeing that human behaviour cannot be explained only in terms of evolutionary forces, they are not too worried about this. Aggression has an evolutionary significance for primate societies – it allows dominant males to pass on their genes to suitable female partners, thus ensuring the survival of the group. What is functional for the baboon or chimpanzee is, therefore, equally functional for human males, provided one accepts the evidence that there is indeed a real continuity between primate and human behaviour.

In this connection the observation that young boys are more aggressive than girls has been used to support this proposition. Now it is certainly true, if you watch small boys playing in a school playground, that the incidence among them of aggressive activity appears to be much higher than among girls of a similar age (Archer and Westeman, 1981). There often seems to be a great deal of gratuitous hitting and bashing going on which looks 'natural' and unrehearsed. Are we to conclude that this behaviour is genetically determined? Certainly, Maccoby and Jacklin seem to think so. Their studies of the difference between male and female aggressiveness have been very influential, although I suspect that they would be dubious about some of the ways in which their work has been used by others (Maccoby and Jacklin, 1974).

One of the key problems in the controversy about aggression is the difficulty of linking individual and group behaviour. In a recent illuminating article, Morgan writes:

> It may be possible to argue that the search for links is doomed from the start, that the level or types of violence are different things altogether and should be treated as such. Such connections as are made, it may be argued, belong to polemic or rhetoric, rather than to analysis. One may have some sympathy with this view, although at this stage it would be unwise to close off this field of exploration prematurely. Nevertheless, such links that do exist must be considerably more complex than assuming that wars are manifestations of masculine violence (or aggression) writ large, just as it would be simplistic to assume that individual manifestations are enactments of ideological or cultural definitions of 'man as warrior'. (Morgan, 1987, p. 185)

But even if we were to grant that individual and collective violence are not the same thing, there still remains a prior problem, namely that the whole discussion of aggression is saturated with unwarranted extrapolations from animal behaviour, especially the fighting behaviour of caged animals (Bleier, 1984, p. 96). The concept 'aggression' is highly loaded. It is a term we use to describe a large number of discrete behaviours, ranging from the threatening gestures of two roosters to the belligerent stance of politicians trying to intimidate their opponents.

> With respect to humans – the inordinate amount of scientific and popular interest in a biological basis for sex differences in 'aggressivity' does not have to do with explaining why women so seldom fight in bars, but rather with explaining differences in achievement in the public world. In such a context, the word is invested with qualities that remain unexpressed and unspecified, such as assertiveness, independence, intelligence, creativity and imagination, which are usually associated with men who are leaders; that is, aggressive. So, by means of semantic flim-flam animal experiments are used to 'prove' that men are naturally, hence inevitably, dominant or superior to women because of hormonal differences. Thus, however exemplary the work itself may be, it lends itself to misuse and misinterpretation when it uses language in ways that are both imprecise and laden with ill-defined, anthropomorphic values and meanings. (Bleier, 1984, p. 95)

It would be easy enough to see the behaviour of Mikhail Gorbachev and Ronald Reagan in terms of an excessive excretion of testosterone. We could then see superpower politics as being nothing more than the interplay of uncontrollable androgens. Put like this, of course, the proposition is absurd, yet versions of this kind of thinking remain very pervasive. For example, the success of Margaret Thatcher as a leader is often attributed to her aggressive masculinity which presumably relates to her *male* hormones. This is not the place to replicate the countless discussions about the relationship between biology and culture. In a sense, nothing more can be said that has not been said before. With respect to aggressiveness, we can spend countless hours reporting the work of this or that researcher who has found a new correlation between hormones and behaviour, and we can equally spend hours refuting his or her evidence. There are certain things we cannot deny. We cannot deny the fact that it is men who rape; we cannot deny the fact that most crimes of violence are committed by men; we cannot deny the fact that men are also the victims of physical violence. Putting all these 'facts' together, and what do we have? We have a picture of some kind of raging beast, untamed by the trappings of social convention and morality. But this picture is not the only one. What about those men who do not rape, who do not engage in acts of violence? Is this a different kind of beast, more gentle and considerate perhaps? If it is a man's 'nature' to be aggressive, then equally it is his 'nature' to be gentle.

It is also a fact that some societies appear to be more violent than others. For example, if we managed to obtain the relevant statistics from South Africa, we would find that the incidence of violent crime is probably higher there than in most other contemporary societies. It is easy enough to draw conclusions from these statistics, and white South Africans do so without much difficulty.

The same kind of conclusions have been drawn about the prevalence of violence among white working-class boys in most of the industrial heartlands of the West. Recently, this discussion has focused on the behaviour of youths at football matches. Popular explanations for this kind of violence range from some watered-down frustration–aggression hypothesis to the crudest biological determinism. Academic theories have looked at class and cultural factors. All these explanations, whether they are popular or academic, implicitly assume that violence is largely a male matter, that women are only peripherally violent. What is certainly the case about football violence is that it is largely directed against other young men. So, we are bombarded with media images of local football tribalism which, supposedly, is a reminder of the primitive atavistic heritage that underpins working-class male behaviour.

It is not only men's aggression which is seen as innate. Their sexuality is given the same kind of treatment. There is supposed to be something in a man's make-up which pushes him into acts of sexual assertiveness. In its extreme form, this view imbues his sexuality with transcendental power which brooks no interference. Men are at the mercy of strong drives over which they have very little control. Such an uncompromising view has not been limited to everyday discourse, but provides the rationale for a considerable amount of academic theorizing.

When sexuality became a topic of inquiry in the nineteenth century, it did so under the auspices of evolutionary thinking. The commonsense view that male sexual behaviour was different from female behaviour was given the legitimation of science. The evidence from the animal world seemed to confirm this. Everywhere, the male of the species was seen taking the sexual initiative; everywhere, females were perceived as being passive and sexually receptive. Inevitably this evidence was applied to human beings. Today it is not very much different. We still find male sexuality described in very much the same terms by experts, and by highly speculative and sensationalized accounts in the media. The 'distinctiveness' of the male sex drive is based upon the myth of the autonomous and independent penis.

> The penis is seen to have a life of its own, leading the man on despite himself. At best the man is seen as the possessor or owner of this object, but it is an object over which he does not have full control. It is the beast below.
>   The idea of the penis, and hence of male sexuality, as separable from the man, forms the basis of stories about male sexuality, especially those with a violent and bestial view of sexual intercourse itself. (Dyer, 1985, p. 31)

Sexuality and Violence

This conflation of sexuality and violence is a very strong strand in the commonsense account of masculinity. It is explicit on television, in the cinema, in novels written by men, being almost a necessary convention. Best-selling novels (and not only best-selling novels) all have the required rape scene, the obligatory episode of sexual violence. But this is not simply a 'cultural' matter. This view is also found in academic texts and journals, where it is given credibility by its location in an evolutionary and naturalistic framework.

As Jeffrey Weeks has noted, the discussion of the biological foundation of sexual behaviour rests upon a number of dubious assumptions (Weeks, 1986, pp. 50–3). First, there is the assumption that 'argues from analogy'. That is, the tendency to construe animal and human behaviour as directly comparable. Because there are pecking orders among chickens, then it is easy enough to transpose this order into a hierarchical human social structure. The point is that evolutionary biologists and other experts see animal behaviour in terms of categories and concepts which only have meaning in a human context. Humans have class systems, animals do not. Men rape, male baboons do not. Men fight wars, they exploit other men, they develop symbol systems, animals do not. Human sexuality and aggressiveness are not simply the expression of impulses rooted in a genetic or biological sub-stratum – they are saturated with meaning. This is not to say that men (and women) do not have the capacity to be aggressive, but this is not the same as saying that this capacity is causal.

Secondly, there is the assumption that 'on average' men behave more aggressively than women, and that their 'sex drive' is far more demanding. Official statistics indicate that most crimes of violence are committed by men, and that rape is a male activity. If only men rape, and if statistics show that the incidence of rape is high in a given population, then the conclusion must be that rape is an expression of their 'natural' desires. But, if it can be demonstrated that the incidence of rape varies both historically and culturally, then presumably the biological case is in difficulty. Surely it would be absurd to claim that those societies with lower rape rates are different biologically from those with higher rates?

While statistical analysis is not necessarily supposed to draw causal conclusions, there is no doubt that it is how statistical averages are regarded by both expert and non-expert. Accordingly, while we know that only men rape, and that rape is prevalent in a great many contemporary societies, we cannot go on to state that rape is a universal feature of male behaviour in all societies at all times. Once we assent to the argument that a particular behaviour is universal, we are thereby proposing that human nature is timeless and unchanging.

Thirdly, it is relatively easy to fall back on biological

explanations. They appear to be so straightforward, parsimonious and scientific. After all, if only men rape, then why should we look for explanations outside biology? Most biological accounts of human behaviour appear to be perfectly logical. In addition, they tend to be consistent with other scientific explanations in which a reductionist 'levels of analysis' approach is deemed appropriate. The 'levels of analysis' approach takes it as gospel that some levels are more basic than others, that they have some kind of causal priority. The implication is that it is no use looking at aggression in terms of events which occur at the cultural or social level because, by definition, these events are all reducible to a lower level, a level at which biochemistry, genes or hormones may be operative. Ultimately, the reductionist strategy is posited on the belief that 'higher' levels are always dependent on 'lower', and that consequently the sciences that study the latter are more capable of explaining the former. In the final reckoning, disciplines like biochemistry take precedence over disciplines such as sociology or psychology. The problem of masculinity, therefore, is a problem in biochemistry, not learning or socialization.

Furthermore, reductionist explanations tend to emphasize the centrality of the individual. Until recently, a discipline like psychology was not really concerned with collective social behaviour, except in so far as individual behaviour shapes social conduct. Thus, if men behave aggressively, the consequences for society are additive, not collective. Wars are fought by men with specific dispositions, not for economic, political or moral reasons. Of course, there are other psychologies with different kinds of theoretical and empirical interest, but their concern is mainly with the level of individual functioning. The social is inevitably a backdrop to, or a by-product of, individual perception, motivation and cognition. Even today, when multi-disciplinary cooperation and integration are fashionable, the temptation is to think in terms of the individual.

To be sure, the kind of crude instinctual thinking associated with early academic psychology is now a thing of the past, but it nevertheless remains true that most psychologists are committed to the primacy of psychological over social process. In rejecting the reductionist thesis about the primacy of biology and psychology, it is, however, not my intention to substitute an alternative social and cultural determinism which treats human beings as if they are the helpless victims of overwhelming external forces. To repeat, men and women do not exist outside history, but at the same time they do not exist outside their bodies. From the moment a child is born, he or she is exposed to a world in which the facts of gender are taken at their face value. A boy's genitals are the first sign of his potential membership of the category male. Such a categorization is not simply a label – it affects the way in which he defines his difference from the category female. The raw sexual features are imbued with symbolic content, but this content becomes a fact of biology. Biology and society are never separate – they mutually constitute each other. Hence, the 'true facts' of biology are never pristine and uninterpreted. They are always mediated. The 'facts' of sexual difference are 'facts' by virtue of the generalized belief (in Western society at least), that heterosexuality is normal and natural. The 'fact' that men and women have different sexual organs is translated into a principle of social organization in which men 'father' and women 'mother'. The 'fact' that men usually are breadwinners is traced back to genetic programming.

Problematic Dichotomies

It is as though we find it almost impossible to think of gender and sexuality except in terms of a dichotomy. We find it difficult to conceive of masculinity without contrasting it with femininity; but more than this, we assume that these definitions reflect a universal trend in nature, departures from which are instances of abnormality and deviance. In the same way, we dichotomize nature and culture, individual and society. We assume that we can separate them into constituent parts, each of which exists independently of the other, although inevitably it is biology and nature which are given priority over society and culture or vice versa. In other words, we take it for granted that there are distinct realities to which the categories 'male' and 'female' refer, and that they are always discoverable by inspection. Behind a social mask, there is a basic man or woman waiting to be let out. The 'natural facts' speak for themselves. Put a boy in an environment controlled by women and he will still express his 'true nature' by playing 'Cowboys and Indians' or other imaginary war games. On the other hand, if he plays with dolls and develops a taste for girls' games, then it is easy enough to see this as being due to hormonal deficiency or genetic abnormality. Alternatively, we may define his deviance in terms of social conditioning or socialization. In both cases, we are attributing a primary level of causation to his behaviour. He behaves like a girl either because of abnormality or social determination. The biological and the social are, by this token, two completely self-contained levels.

In separating the biological from the social we do violence to our understanding of human reality – moreover, we are assenting to a dualism which has underpinned the theorizing and analysis of human behaviour ever since Descartes's time. We assume that there is sharp division between the body and society, between desire and rationality, between the person and context, between man and woman. And because most of us have been exposed to an educational system which naturalizes sexual differences and other dualisms, we tend to accept them without too much trauma and questioning.

The position taken in this book is to question the very basis of this dualism. It is my contention that 'masculinism' provides the underpinning for a particular way of organizing gender relationships which separates biology from culture and ensures the political domination of men and the subordination of women. I do this advisedly because I do not believe that all forms of domination can be subsumed under a common explanatory framework, that is, I reject the claim that domination must always be explained in class terms, *and* I also reject the alternative claim that gender inequality explains class differences. Nevertheless, it would be very naive to suppose that class and gender relationships exist in separate compartments. Both forms of domination are in a state of constant interaction, so that it often becomes difficult to disentangle their separate contribution to a given set of social relations. Moreover, masculinism takes on a distinctive flavour when associated with capitalism.

Certainly, what appears to be paramount in the representation of masculinity in capitalist societies is an obsession with competition and achievement. In other words, masculinism appears to lend itself very nicely to the ethos of industrialism and capitalism. But, if we reject dualism in social and political theorizing, how can we reconcile this with the argument that there are two or more kinds of domination that co-exist in some uneasy alliance? How can we justify the claim that patriarchy should be given a separate status from class? Surely, if we want to understand domination, we should look for a common source for that domination?

When we argue that class cannot be reduced to patriarchy and vice versa, this is not an argument for the inevitability of each. On the contrary, both patriarchy and class only exist in history. What we have to establish is the historicity of domination, not its inevitability. Whether or not patriarchy and class are twin-born seems to me to be irrelevant – what is important is the fact that domination has a history. The key point is that both forms of domination are historically constructed. Yet, this is not to say that this construction is simultaneous. Thus, for Engels, private property was the key concept for any consideration of the historicity of domination. It is its emergence which sets in motion the division of society into those who control the means of production and those who do not. Private property is responsible for the establishment of a class system in which men own the means of production and the services of their women. Patriarchy and class, therefore, have a common origin in a mode of production which is geared to the male appropriation of an economic surplus. So, from this perspective, patriarchy does not exist independently of class, and in various Marxist texts it appears to be dependent on and reducible to class.

Alternatively, we have those views which give priority to patriarchy. Patriarchy is seen as existing long before the emergence of private property and class. The emphasis here is on the way in which the sexual division of labour was turned into a system in which men seized or appropriated the key political positions in the kinship system. Usually this process is linked to the problem of child-rearing. Because women were often incapacitated by the time and energy devoted to the gestation and nurturing of children, they were construed by men as not being able to contribute to political and economic life. Such a construction (for this is what it is) is the essential element in the establishment of male domination. The male perception of a biological fact (the woman's role in child-bearing) is translated into the basic principle of social organization. After a while this construction comes to be regarded as natural and inevitable – it becomes part and parcel of the way in which gender is embedded into social organization and consciousness – the construction, once made, is constantly reproduced. (In addition, the domination of women is seen as the model for all domination. Not only do men oppress women, they also oppress other men.)

In a nutshell, the argument for the independent existence of patriarchy is based upon the social construction of men and women into two separate, but unequal, categories. The implication here is that this construction occurred long before the division of society into economic classes. Hence both class and patriarchy are explained in terms of the interaction of complex social events which do away with the necessity of positing some final biological or psychological cause. In either case the end result is the same – the division of society into those who have power and authority, and those who do not.

Now it is the theme of this book that masculinism naturalizes male domination. Yet I have shied away from calling men a class in the sense that they all share common interests in relation to women. However, it would seem to me that under certain circumstances some men do constitute a class or, to put it more accurately, they are in a class-like situation *vis-à-vis* women. In this respect, I refer to the kind of evidence deriving from Christine Delphy and her associates which describes the family and the household as a terrain in which men act as a class. But male domination is not only about the appropriation of a woman's labour power, it is also about the appropriation of her sexuality, her body. In talking about the masculine ideology, we are therefore not only referring to the economic and political position of men, but also how they define and theorize sexuality and gender. And it is the variability of these theories and definitions, that, to a large extent, constitute the historical specificity of this or that form of masculinity.

It is in this respect that it might be more appropriate to talk about 'hierarchic heterosexuality'. 'While it is possible for other forms of heterosexuality to exist, hierarchic heterosexuality is premised on an inequality of power between women and men. To develop egalitarian heterosexuality would necessarily mean a loss of domination of heterosexuality over other sexualities. In other words, heterosexuality that is not hierarchic undermines heterosexuality (Hearn, 1987, p. 91). Thus, when we talk about the specificity of a masculinity, it is always in terms of its relationship to the hierarchical heterosexual structuring of gender relationships. This structuring is not permanent. My position is that it is always in the process of being reinterpreted and subverted – what gives it the appearance of permanence is the way in which it is taken for granted and reproduced as if it were normal and natural. In the last instance heterosexualism is tentative and problematic. But this does not mean that its proponents are conscious of this. Nevertheless, the past three decades have seen a challenge to its predominance from feminists and gay theorists and activists. Whether in the long run this challenge will be successful is not yet clear. What is clear, however, is that 'hierarchic herterosexuality' is now defending itself more systematically and ferociously. It is in this context that the proliferation of new local masculinities must be evaluated.

Nowhere has the challenge to heterosexualism been more apparent than in the discussion and politics of male gender identity and sexuality. These are the topics of the following two chapters.

2

Masculinity and Identity

My intention in this chapter is to examine the preoccupation with identity in current discussions about gender. To be sure, identity is not only a gender problem; it is also important for 'ethnic politics' and for contemporary accounts of class consciousness. Indeed, identity has infiltrated into every kind of popular and academic discourse. To a certain extent, it has become one of those portmanteau terms which purport to illuminate individual experience, but which, instead, end up in a morass of obscurity. Nevertheless, the fact that identity is a highly contentious and ambiguous concept does not mean that it has no value for any consideration of the relationship between subjectivity and social processes.

In the case of gender identity there are three emphases which are relevant to the 'theorization' of masculinity:

1   the socialization case;
2   masculine crisis theory;
3   the reality construction model.

The Socialization Case

The socialization case emphasizes the internal representations of sexual differences associated with the learning of sex roles. Gender identity is acquired through socialization. Unfortunately, in the literature, there is a great deal of confusion in the use of terms like 'sex role' and 'gender role'. For the purposes of this discussion, I use them as interchangeable concepts, although I realize that there are considerable objections to doing so.

Kessler and McKenna (1978, p. 8) define gender identity as: 'an individual's own feeling of whether she or he is a woman or a man, or a girl or a boy. In essence gender identity is self-attribution of gender.'In short, gender identity is the subjective sense that a man or woman has about his or her masculinity or femininity. It can be conceived of as a person's interpretation and acting out of the generally accepted social definitions of what it is to be a man or woman. Hence, a man becomes a man because he learns the required behaviour associated with the male gender role. He comes to define himself from the perspective of those around him who treat him as male.

In Western society, gender identity is considered to be central to a person's biography. The sexual division of labour ensures that from the moment of his birth a boy is not only differentiated from a girl, but that he is also treated differently. From the cradle to the grave, he is inculcated with expectations, beliefs and values designed to make him conform to extant gender divisions. A boy will be expected to do things that boys do, and not things that girls do – he is not encouraged to play with girls' toys, just as he is not supposed to be timid when playing with other boys. At the same time, he learns about his sexuality and how it differs from a girl's sexuality; he comes to know himself as gendered in terms of the internalization of these differences. At any given moment he can locate himself as a 'male' with a biography which is markedly different from that of a female – he can envisage his past as a boy, he can remember his first experience of desire, he can look forward to a future in which he will still be a man. In other words, he regards his gender, his sexuality, as being a bedrock of his life in the world. His gender identity is experienced as though it is certain and unambiguous.

Now this emphasis does assume that society is organized in such a fashion that the sexual division of labour is natural or, if not natural, is permanent for all practical purposes. It also assumes the universality of heterosexuality. It is easy enough to draw the conclusion that gender identity is to a large degree a reflection of broader sexual divisions. I know I am a man because my parents, my teachers, my friends, my employers, my wife etc. define and treat me as such. And I know these things because I have been exposed to the determining power of socialization processes which give me this knowledge, and also profoundly influence my behaviour.

To be sure I may have exaggerated the socialization case, but there is no doubt that certain versions of role theory come very close to completely encapsulating gender and sexuality in social strait-jackets. The problem with such a view is that it does not enable us ever to be anything other than the roles we have internalized. This means that when I behave like a man this can be accounted for by my identification with some master gender script which lays down the requirements of my role performance – it is assumed that I will conform to these requirements either because not to do so would have negative consequences (I might be punished, ridiculed, ostracized etc.) or because I imitate, model and identify with other men (fathers, teachers, friends etc.). In both instances, the implication is that I experience my maleness, my masculinity, as nothing more than an ensemble of internalized social relationships.

The socialization case assumes that a man's and a woman's body respectively provide *different* foundations on which the social and cultural world builds its gender system. Biological differences are the starting point for the construction of an edifice of gender differences. *Roles are added to biology to give us gender* – and, once this happens, men and women acquire their appropriate gender identities. In a nutshell, the socialization thesis asserts that human beings acquire gender as a result of the social definition and construction of male or female bodies. A man will become a man only when his genitals are defined as having the attributes that belong to men. It is as though he can only testify to his masculinity because others have said this is how he has to be.

Underpinning the socialization case are a number of associated arguments and assumptions. First, there is the assumption that gender and gender identity are acquired in early childhood. Right from the beginning of a person's life there is a systematic attempt on the part of parents and other child-minders to reproduce the existing gender divisions of society. A boy not only has to learn to behave like a boy, he also has to feel like a boy. So, according to the literature, the foundations of gender identity are laid down at a time when the child is flexible and impressionable. In starker versions of this position, the child is literally forced to acquire the appropriate gender because he or she has no defence against the superior power of parents.

Secondly, the socialization thesis assumes that there is a clearly demarcated sexual division of labour which shapes male and female roles. To acquire a firm sense of gender identity presupposes the ability to distinguish oneself from a complementary, but opposing, identity. If men are breadwinners or hunters, and women are mothers and food gatherers, then it is logical to suppose that these differences will be reflected in the way in which men and women define themselves.

Thirdly, it does not allow for deviance, that is, it treats anomalies as if they were irrelevant, or as being due to some biological defect or psychological problem.

Obviously, the socialization thesis is beset by all sorts of difficulty. Is deviance nothing more than an instance of malfunction, a quirk in the operation of the sexual division of labour? Moreover, this image of complete social absorption suggests a society in which there is a perfect fit between the individual and role demands, and this, to say the least, is a dream of social theory, not reality. Where do we find a society where men and women conform to this master stereotype? True, in the nineteenth century it was fashionable for Western anthropologists and colonialists to report back to their European audience on the peculiar sexual behaviour of colonized people, but behind this behaviour they always discovered the 'inevitability' of the sexual division of labour. In the hands of a supposedly more sophisticated social science, the sexual division of labour was described in terms of the inexorable pressure of role expectations and demands. Such a thoroughgoing social determinism makes it impossible to envisage how, for example, we can ever conceive of opposition and resistance to gender ascription and attribution?

Put very simply, if we accept the socialization thesis at its face value, we would have to give up any idea of subverting and changing present gender inequalities. And perhaps equally important, the thesis does not fit the facts – there never have been societies constructed in this way. This point is put nicely by Connell:

> Socialization theory, supposing a mechanism of transmission and a consensual model of what is produced, has been credible to the extent that social scientists have been willing to ignore both choice and force in social life. I would argue, with Sartre and Laing, for seeing them as constitutive. 'Agencies of socialization' cannot produce mechanical effects in a growing person. What they do is invite the child to participate in social practice in given terms. The invitation may be, and often is coercive – accompanied by heavy pressure to accept and no mention of an alternative. (Connell, 1987, p. 195)

In other words, gender acquisition is not smooth, harmonious and consensual. The conventional view of socialization is that children become social to the extent that they absorb and internalize ready-made norms of behaviour. Thus we are bombarded with images of young boys learning to become men in terms of a generally accepted norm of masculinity. Although the literature allows for contradiction in the traditional male sex role, these contradictions are never really decisive. What remains central is the belief that there *is* a 'male sex role' which inevitably ensures the compliance of most men (Solomon, 1982 pp. 45–76). Although the traditional view makes allowance for force, it does not attempt to account for force, except in so far as it may speak of male aggressiveness as being intrinsic to male power, and this, to say the least, is tautological. We cannot say that boys are socialized to be aggressive and assertive, and at the same time claim that they are intrinsically aggressive.

Connell argues that the entire discussion of socialization in the social sciences has been:

> supported by two occupational blindnesses, the inability of sociologists to recognise the complexities of the person, and the unwillingness of psychologists to recognise the dimensions of social power. Both groups have been willing to settle for a

consensual model of intergenerational transfer – playing down conflict and ignoring violence – and for a consensual model of the psychological structure produced. (Connell, 1987, p. 194)

In the case of the male sex role, this has led to a picture of masculinity which is both clear-cut and uncompromising. It is a picture which does not allow for any departure from male gender scripts, nor does it allow for conflict between so-called 'agencies of socialization'. To believe, for example, that there is a degree of consistency between early primary socialization, and the secondary socialization of school and employment, is to argue for a view of social processes which does violence to reality. Although we might agree that in certain historical circumstances socialization appears to work like this (in Nazi Germany for instance), it is also clear that in these circumstances, we are not merely talking about socialization. What we are doing is to highlight the way in which institutions like the state use socialization processes in order to flatten dissent and ensure compliance. Socialization mediates force; it is not coterminous with it. The construction of male gender identity in Nazi Germany, therefore, was not only a matter for socialization agencies. Rather, it was an essential component of state policy.

Yet even in such a totalitarian context, the proposition that all German men were turned into a species of aggressive and intolerant sexists and racists is not in keeping with the evidence. Certainly, German men were strongly invited 'to participate in a social practice' premised on 'strength', 'nationalism' and 'heterosexuality', but this does not mean that they all accepted this invitation, nor does it mean that those who appeared to conform to the Nazi stereotype of masculinity did so without resistance.

The real trouble with the socialization thesis is that it finds it almost impossible to explain the exceptions to the rule. It cannot account for change, either at the individual or the social level. It cannot explain why some men have not accepted the invitation to participate in heterosexuality, nor why others may feel uncomfortable even when playing the game according to the rules.

Masculine Crisis Theory

Masculine crisis theory is founded on the observation that both men and women deviate from the master gender stereotypes of their society. Indeed, this version seems to suggest that gender identity is tentative and fragile, especially in the case of men. Pleck (1981) has analysed and summarized the literature and research findings related to male gender identity which have been dominant in the social sciences since the 1930s. What he calls 'male sex role identity' is a concept which focuses on the crisis of masculinity prevalent in Western industrial societies. The presumption is that this crisis was brought about by the erosion of male power in the workplace and in the home. In the past, men supposedly knew who they were; their roles were minutely specified, and they also knew who women were supposed to be. However, all this has changed – they have lost their gender certainty, their sense of place in a world in which women are challenging them at all levels. Their response has been to over-compensate for this loss of power and authority but, the more they do this, the more acute is their feeling of insecurity and anxiety. Whether or not this is only a phenomenon associated with the emergence of industrial society is not immediately clear. What is certain is that over the past few decades the crisis has apparently increased in severity.

Basically, the problem is that men find it difficult to identify with appropriate male role models. If such models are absent, or partially absent, men suffer from an acute sense of gender confusion. A healthy gender identity requires a proper identification with some kind of father-figure.

Sex role identity is the extremely fragile outcome of a highly risky developmental process, especially so for the male. An individual's sex role identity ideally derives from his or her relationship with the same-sex parent. A man's efforts to attain a healthy sex role identity in this way are thwarted by such factors as paternal absence, maternal over-protectiveness, the feminising influence of the schools, and the general blurring of male and female roles that

is occurring now in society ... the failure of men to achieve
masculine sex role identity is a major problem in our culture, one
obvious expression of which is homosexuality. A man also reveals
his insecurity in his sex role identity by phenomena such as
deliquency, violence, and hostility toward women. If we understand the factors that cause role identity problems in men, then
we can prevent or reduce these problems in the future and perhaps
even provide help now. (Pleck, 1982, pp. 3–4)

In contrast to the socialization thesis, male crisis theory
stresses psychological need as being of paramount importance.
If a man's needs are not met, then he is likely to be socially
and sexually ineffective. In the last instance, the crisis of
masculinity is a problem of male psychology. A society which
does not encourage the development of strong sex role
identities is a sick society.

This argument explains male gender problems in terms of
psychological processes, which have their origin in early or
primary socialization. It is what happens to a boy in infancy
and childhood which determines his sexual and mental
future. His initial interactions with his parents, therefore,
are responsible for his present discontents. The contemporary
family no longer provides a framework in which he can
identify with an appropriate father or male figure due to the
logic of the sexual division of labour. In the past men worked
at home, or in the local community, or they took their sons
hunting, but now they go out to work away from home and
neighbourhood, leaving women with the sole responsibility
for the rearing of children. This is fatal for male gender
identity. What is needed is a family context in which boys
have equal emotional and cognitive access to both parents,
but this is impossible in a world where men are only
marginally concerned with their sons' socialization. The
assertion that boys have a 'need' to identify with their
fathers, and that this need is frustrated in contemporary
society, implies that we can actually describe and identify
this need. But can we? While commonsense accounts of male
gender development presume that those boys who do not
have fathers living with their mothers will inevitably be at a
disadvantage when compared with those boys who have a
'normal' family life, the evidence seems to be much more

ambiguous and contradictory (Pleck, 1981, pp. 56–8). In fact, this evidence indicates that there is not much difference between those boys with, and those without, fathers. So when we say that a boy 'needs' his father we may be echoing popular opinion and ideology, not reality.

The achievement of men who somehow have successfully negotiated the pitfalls of inappropriate gender identifications can be compared to the runners in an obstacle race. The object of this race is to acquire an unambiguous gender identity. The rules are deceptively simple – in order for a boy to become a man he must not allow himself to be attracted to other paths to adulthood – he must stick to the path taken by other men, especially his father. Before modernization and industrialization, the path and obstacles to manhood were well defined and understood, but this is no longer the case. The old certainties about the male sex role, the fragmentation of social life and consciousness means that old rules are no longer of much use because they are continuously rewritten and reinterpreted, so that by the time a boy reaches adulthood, he is not clear in his mind whether or not he has successfully run a race, or even that a race has been run.

Today, if there is a race, then it is no longer a straight run to the finish. Everybody seems to be under different 'starter's orders'. Everywhere there are casualties, everywhere men are nursing bruised egos, everywhere the course is littered with the debris of their unresolved sexual conflicts. However, even when a man does arrive at the finishing post and appears to have overcome all obstacles, there is still something suspect about this. We do not believe that there can be a successful winner of the race because we have accepted, albeit unconsciously, the proposition that male gender identity can only be achieved or acquired when the psychological conditions are favourable. Now, all we can see is the spectacle of countless millions of men experiencing acute gender anxieties. Something has gone badly wrong in the male psyche.

What I am stressing here is that the dominant orthodoxy in the discussion of masculinity has been heavily overladen by psychology. The entire spectrum of social and political problems facing Western civilization is explained by reference to traumas of the male psyche. In previous centuries, the male psyche, although troubled by outbreaks of irrationality, was always brought under control by clearly defined rules and prohibitions. Masculinity was circumscribed by a world in which gender differences were taken for granted. Now, everything is in a state of flux and uncertainty. Instead of the framework which accepted without question the naturalness of heterosexuality, everywhere we see the old regime subverted by other sexualities which make it almost impossible to speak of male identity with any degree of confidence at all. By giving such a heavy emphasis to psychology, the analysis of masculinity moves away from consideration of the social relations of patriarchy by focusing on the subjective experience of men who cannot function properly in the modern world. So men fight wars, engage in the most ferocious competition, play games, rape and live their lives pornographically because they no longer know how to cope with their desires. To be sure, they did all these things in the past, but this was always in the context of an identity which they supposedly experienced as possessing an enduring reality.

Underpinning the research and theoretical arguments of masculine crisis theory is an amalgam of psychoanalytic, role learning and cognitive approaches to gender acquisition. Most of these approaches highlight the extreme vulnerability of masculine identity, although the psychoanalytic version has been most influential in providing the essential ingredient of the thesis, namely that gender identity is the product of a developmental process which has its roots in early childhood. Furthermore, they all, to a lesser or greater degree, assume that gender identity is a necessary dimension of normal personality growth. A person without a gender identity is, by this token, not fully human. As we have already noted, men are more likely than women to be deficient in this respect. Pleck argues that masculine crisis theory retains its influence despite the fact that it has been subject to trenchant criticism. This is due to a number of factors (Pleck, 1981, pp. 156–60).

First is the current preoccupation with fatherhood and the plethora of both academic and media coverage of the father's role in child-rearing. Fatherhood is now back in fashion – a child's mental and physical health is now seen to be crucially dependent on the father's participation in nurturing activities. 'Boys need their fathers' has become one of the dominant themes in psychological discussion of male behaviour. A whole range of 'abnormal' behaviours is attributed to the absence of the father, including homosexuality and delinquency.

Secondly, in blaming the absence of the father for the fragility of male gender identity, the emphasis has switched to the mother as the most significant figure in a boy's psychological development. Both Chodorow (1978) and Dinnerstein (1987) have been in the forefront of this change in emphasis. From different starting points they reverse the orthodox Freudian position about the inevitability (given the right conditions) of a child identifying with the parent of the same sex. For Freud, this process always involved a tremendous psychic battle in which boys overcame their Oedipal fixations on their mothers by internalizing their fathers' threat of castration. The successful resolution of the Oedipus complex meant that they became 'men'. Those boys who did not manage to identify with their fathers (from Freud's perspective) are the reserve army of future neurotics and social misfits. Freud's picture of male gender identity was therefore one in which identity was achieved at the cost of giving up one's mother. Admittedly, this achievement is always problematic and often unstable, but given that Freud was committed to a version of family life in which men always assumed the dominant role, and which he thought was both necessary and almost universal, it is not surprising that he saw father–son relationships as being the foundation stone on which all civilized life is built. The price of civilization is the cost of men giving up their desire for their mothers, even though this meant that they would never feel comfortable with themselves. (For Freud there is no such thing as a fully integrated personality in which the different elements of the psyche co-exist in harmony with each other.) Nevertheless, lurking beneath the surface of the masculine ego is an intense irrational emotionality which must be continuously monitored and repressed. Take away the framework that allows a son to identify with his father and then anything can happen.

Historically, this framework began to collapse with the supposed divorce between home and work. The encapsulation of men and women into public and private spheres, respectively, was the first milestone on the road to the disintegration of the male psyche. The absence of the father became the normal condition of family life. The socialization and disciplining of sons were left to mothers who also acted on behalf of the absent father. In other words, instead of a real father-figure, sons identified with the symbolic representation of the father, a representation interpreted and defined by the mother. Mothers punished their sons if they misbehaved; it was they who were left with the task of turning their sons into men. Moreover, it was mothers who were expected to force their sons to reject any kind of identification with femininity. They were responsible for ensuring the channelling of their sons into the appropriate path defined by the sexual division of labour.

> any society in which a traditional division of labour exists, that is, in just about all societies, a baby boy inevitably identifies first with his mother and then has to struggle to attain an unavoidably elusive 'masculine' identity defined negatively by the society's rigid denunciation of male participation in female work and especially of even a partial return by the male to anything resembling an infant's closeness to the mother. This being the case, the male invariably comes to devalue typically female work and attitudes in order to protect himself against forbidden wishes and at the same time may well come to harbour a repressed hostility to his mother for denying him even temporary return to that once safe port of call, a hostility which he may come to displace on the female sex in general. Since the male is, of course, a male because he finds himself in possession of a penis instead of a clitoris, vagina, womb and breasts, typically male activities will almost invariably come to be associated with the 'power' of the penis. Since in addition the male may well, at either a conscious or unconscious level, resent being thus forced into elusive manhood through the absence of a womb, he may well come to envy women their reproductive capacity which, while denigrating at one level, he will at another level attempt to emulate or even surpass in the performance of certain of his masculine activities. From this point of view, then, a sexual division of labour brings with it the seeds of hostility

and conflict on the part of men towards women and then of reciprocated hostility and conflict on the part of women towards men. (Easlea, 1983, pp. 11–12)

I have quoted from Easlea's text at length because it seems to me to present the kernel of this thesis. Easlea's discussion is based to a large extent on the work of Chodorow. Chodorow herself owes her theoretical position to Freudian object-relations theory. Although there are various schools and emphases in this approach, in general they all tend to focus on the relationship between the mother and child, especially the bonding of emotion and identity that takes place between them in the infant years. The cardinal question here is how do male children identify with, and then break away from, their mothers? Chodorow suggests that from the very beginning mothers engage in an exercise of confirming sexual differences. A mother has literally to coerce the boy into a masculine gender identity. A boy has to give up his mother as an emotional object – he has to reject feminine attributes by becoming something other than feminine, but he can only do this if his mother is there to ensure that he does so (Chodorow, 1978).

So a woman to a large extent colludes in her future oppression. It is she who reproduces the gender system, and it is she who is the creator of an insecure male gender identity. Boys are taught to separate themselves from female tutelage, they are expected to identify with an absent father or, more accurately, the abstract qualities associated with masculinity. In this respect, a mother is the symbolic representative of heterosexuality – the guardian of the gender status quo. Moreover, in Dinnerstein's view, the entire fabric of male–female relationships depends on the overpowering influence that women have in the socialization process. Right from the moment a child is born he is engulfed in maternal care, but this care is always ambiguous and contradictory. It is the mother who has to discipline the child, and it is the mother who is resented because her children cannot come to terms with her power. In the case of male children this means that they spend the rest of their lives trying to escape from the consequences of her awesome

potency. It is a woman's *power* that men resent, not merely
the fact that they have lost their 'safe harbour'. Mothers both
frustrate and meet their needs – it is this single factor that
determines their future hostility to women. Somehow or
other, they will get their own back, not only on their
mothers, but on their wives, their girlfriends, their female
employees. Having been cast out into the world, they make
an alliance with other men who have equally suffered at the
hands of women. Hence, the subordination of women is
guaranteed by the nature of the child–mother relationship
(Dinnerstein, 1987).

What both Chodorow and Dinnerstein emphasize in
different ways, is that the emergence of masculinity is not
simply dependent on the repression of castration anxiety, on
the resolution of the male Oedipal complex, but on the way
in which male infants experience their mothers. In the final
analysis, men are created by women and until such time as
the present child-rearing practices of our society (and most
societies) are changed, it is likely that the present male-
dominated culture will continue to exist. Men have to be
brought back into child-rearing in order to maximize human
potential. By a roundabout route we come back to the
original proposition, namely that male children need their
fathers to achieve a balanced gender identity. The historic
domination of child-rearing by women has led (so the
argument goes) to an asymmetrical dichotomization of
gender. Both sons and daughters internalize the mother as
object, but it is only sons who have to give her up. Their
separation from the mother sets in motion all those
characteristics that we associate with masculinity, characteristics that Simone De Beauvoir and others see leading to the
'male transcendental ego' bestriding history like some out-of-
control leviathan (De Beauvoir 1972). From this perspective,
patriarchy seems to be expressly designed for the purpose of
giving men the power to cope with the powerlessness they
experience when their mothers insist that they become men.

Although masculine crisis theory has been subject to
attack, it still retains a large degree of influence on both the
social science and lay imagination. One reason for this is the
importance given to the role of the father in contemporary

child-rearing practices. The emphasis here is on the need for fathers to become participatory members of the nuclear family in order to help their sons find suitable role models. In the case of girls the problem is not so acute because they still mainly identify with their mothers. Despite the undermining of traditional family structures, women on the whole are more likely than men to achieve a satisfactory gender identity (so the argument goes). Male children, on the other hand, are increasingly faced with the problem of finding an appropriate model. The remedy suggested by expert and everyday opinion is that men should somehow or other be involved in the nurturing process. Not only should they take their turn in looking after their children, but they should also be prepared to take full responsibility for the domestic sphere. What is demanded here is a complete role reversal which would allow women to go out to work full-time, while their husbands stay at home and do all the things associated with mothering. In this way, it is believed, male children will have the opportunity to have empathy with and identify with their fathers. Moreover, fathers will eventually lose their hardness, their assertive male egos, because they will be involved in the nitty-gritty of child care which demands complete emotional commitment. There are two points to be made in this context.

First, it is taken for granted that male children do need to identify with the parent of the same sex, and that if they fail to do so, they will have both gender and personality problems. Secondly, it is also taken for granted that women are somehow to blame for their own oppression, because they have been largely instrumental in defining and reinforcing the masculinity of their sons. Now this might not be the intention of those theorists like Chodorow and Dinnerstein who have been active in deconstructing the patriarchal bias of orthodox Freudian theory, but this is how they are often interpreted by some other critics. For example, Grimshaw writes:

> It is not always clear how far Chodorow sees her thesis about psychological differences between males and females as depending on the existence of a particular kind of child-care or family life,

or how far she sees it as dependent simply on the fact that women have been mainly responsible for the care of infants. I do not think that Chodorow really intends to put forward a thesis about the psychic development of males and females in all historical periods, and she criticises Freud for example, for failing to recognise the historical specificity of the constellation of family relationships that he saw as underlying the Oedipus complex. On the other hand, there are points at which it is not difficult to read Chodorow as arguing that it is simply women's responsibility for child-care which is the crucial factor in the different psychic development of males and females. (Grimshaw, 1986, pp. 57–8)

The problem is, that in claiming that it is a woman's control of child care which is the determining factor in the development of male and female gender identity, there is a temptation to go much further and say that this control is the cause of all our present discontents. Thus Easlea (1981, 1983) sees the present slide into nuclear madness as being a measure of the instability of male gender identity which not only resents women and sees them as objects, but also attempts to dominate nature itself. On the face of it, therefore, it seems to me that child-rearing is elevated into a master psychological and social process, which assumes the same kind of status as the mode of production does in Marxism. In other words, when mothers force their male children out into the world, they not only unleash a terrible potentiality for mass destruction, but they also reproduce the structure of domination. All domination is derived from this basic relationship.

Now to say this, is somehow to go back to a reductionist version of human behaviour. If the basic human relationship is that between a mother and child, and if that relationship determines all others, then domination and oppression are inevitable facts of life. Historical specificity is dismissed as being irrelevant because of the prior assumption that children 'need' their mothers, and mothers 'need' their children. This is to assume that these relationships have always been like this, and will always remain so. Yet, the entire thrust of most feminist and social constructionist critiques of patriarchy and masculinism takes issue with essentialistic and reductionist accounts of gender and social processes. While both Chodorow and Dinnerstein are very much aware of the historicity of child-rearing processes, and are also sensitive to the diversity of family and kinship systems, this does not prevent them from abstracting the mother–child relationship as though it exists independently of time and place.

Perhaps one of the difficulties in any discussion about gender and gender identity is that our terms of reference are already defined for us. I have already noted that most discussions of masculinity are informed and often shaped by masculinism, by the prevalent ideology of gender differences and inequalities. Certainly, the discussion of gender identity is not immune from this, especially the assumption that gender and identity are terms which have some kind of reality, some kind of measurability. But what if we argued to the contrary, namely that gender identity is infinitely negotiable, that the specification of masculine and feminine traits was simply an aspect of a continuing process of interactive relationships in which both men and women mutually construct, confirm, reject or deny their identity claims? Why should we assume that identity is predetermined or made in the crucible of family relationships? Both the socialization model and masculine crisis theory have no doubts about the history of gender identity. They both assume that this history has a beginning, a middle and an end. What happened in childhood determines who and what we are now.

What seems to be clear is that both versions of gender identity acquisition assume that certain things are done to children by their parents and other socialization agencies, and that once done, nothing can reverse or subvert what is done. We say, for example, that 'he' is sexually aggressive because of childhood experiences, or we say that 'he' joined the army because everything in his history makes this inevitable. Not only was his father a war hero, but his mother encouraged him to follow in his father's footsteps. However, in the case of masculine crisis theory, we also assert that a man's present psychosexual insecurity is understandable as a direct result of his ambivalent attitude towards women arising from his relationship with his mother. From this point of view, therefore, the present is always determined by the past.

The Reality Constuction Model

The reality construction model is an alternative to this biographical and developmental view of gender. It argues that gender has no fixed form, and that gender identity is what I claim it to be at this particular moment in time. Although all the indications are that most people do not question the dichotomous view of sex and gender as given, this is not to say that such a questioning does not take place. All that one can say at the present is that I see myself as a 'man', but this may be simply an interpretation of myself in a specific context. Usually such an interpretation is considered to be unproblematic because on inspection I find myself to have the appropriate sexual organs which are associated with 'maleness'. Also, I presumably display secondary sexual characteristics which are taken to be a sign of my membership of the community called 'men'. The point about this is, that in inspecting myself and coming to the conclusion I am a man, I am not simply replicating automatically what everybody else has told and taught me about men, I am also accomplishing or doing 'maleness'. Every time I see myself as a man I am doing 'identity work'. Although, it may appear that I take my masculinity for granted, in reality I only do so because I work at it. Every social situation, therefore, is an occasion for identity work. Of course, it may well be that all the 'identity work' I do will prop up the dichotomous view of gender, but this is merely another way of saying that gender is always a construction which has to be renegotiated from situation to situation.

The idea that gender has to be accomplished, rather than considering it a finished product, runs counter to both the socialization thesis and the masculine crisis theory. Most socialization theories are premised on the assumption that a person's life story can be seen in developmental terms. Hence, gender identity is regarded as being some kind of internal snapshot that men or women may have of themselves at any point in their histories. What the snapshot will show reflects the particular experiences of the individual. In any event, the traditional view is that gender identity is always the result of forces that have entered into its construction. These forces determine, mould, shape and define the gender pictures we have of ourselves. They do not allow us much leeway in the way of experimentation and role reversal.

Take as an example the person who knows he is gay. Such a self-attribution may not be supported by the people he comes into contact with. His family may not know, his co-workers may not know, his friends may not know. Some people may know, perhaps other people who define themselves as gay. The point of this is to suggest that a great deal of work goes into the presentation of an acceptable image of gender. Although everybody else (except those in the know) accepts without question the reality of external manifestations of straightness, a gay person may have to work hard at maintaining and presenting himself as such. Moreover, he may also have to do identity work in the gay community. To be sure, a great deal of the evidence for this perspective comes from the observation and analysis of trans-sexuality, but the conclusions to be drawn are the same. Gender is not static – it is always subject to redefinition and renegotiation.

It may be objected that the evidence used for the claim that gender has to be accomplished comes from atypical instances. What about so-called normal gender identity? Surely a heterosexual male does not have to engage in identity work? Kessler and McKenna argue that what happens in so-called 'violations' of normal gender behaviour may illustrate the operation of identity work in general. They write:

> Garfinkel's assumption (which we share) is that something can be learned about what is taken for granted in the 'normal' case by studying what happens when there are 'violations'. Transsexuals take their own gender for granted, but they cannot assume that others will. Consequently, transsexuals must manage themselves as male or female so that others will attribute the 'correct' gender. It is easier for us to see that transsexuals 'do' (accomplish) gender than it is to see this process in nontranssexuals.

The transsexuals' construction of gender is self-conscious. They make obvious what nontranssexuals do 'naturally'. Even though gender accomplishment is self-conscious for transsexuals, they share with all the other members of the culture the natural attitude toward gender. The ways that transsexuals talk about the phenomenon of transsexualism, the language they use, their attitude about genitals, and the questions they are unable to answer, point to their belief that though others might see them as violating the facts, they, themselves believe that they are not violating them at all. (Kessler and McKenna, 1978, p. 114)

The implication of this is that even though we take our own gender identities for granted, even though we naturalize sexual differences by giving them the status of facts, we are nevertheless always in the business of putting together our sense of gender. What is taken for granted can be subverted and threatened by interruptions and violations which test our confidence in our perceptions and attributions. If I have construed myself as a 'normal' heterosexual male, and then I am confronted by a situation in which all my own certainties appear to be nebulous and insecure, then I may have not only to make adjustments to my behaviour, but also begin partially to redefine my gender identity. For example, a man going into a 'gay' bar might think that the experience could be amusing, but if the 'regulars' begin to treat him as a member of their community he might not only find this uncomfortable, he may begin to understand that his own sexual commitments need some justification. Admittedly, such a justification may not mean that his belief in the security of his gender identity is in any way compromised, but it does put him into the position of having to be reflexive about a reality which previously he thought was inviolate and immutable. What is being suggested here is that this immutable reality is an accomplishment which, like all other human accomplishments, is tentative. Of course, this begs the question why so many people seem to make the same attributions about their own and other people's gender. How is it that most members of our society accomplish gender in more or less the same way? Why do the majority of men and women living in contemporary industrial society (and most other kinds of social contexts) operate on a dichotomous view of gender? Why is masculinity opposed to femininity? In short, why does gender attribution appear to have such long-reaching consequences, so that its everyday accomplishment is never seen as an accomplishment, but is taken for granted as natural and inevitable?

These questions have traditionally been answered in terms of the mechanical interaction of social and biological factors which, together, produce a sense of gender in male and female bodies. Men and women become gendered at the moment they begin to define themselves in terms of sexual attributes. Sexual differences are thus written into the socialization process, so that by the end of infancy the child finds it almost impossible to question his or her gender. So, I 'know' that I am a man because I 'know' there are other people (women) who have different bodies, with different sexual characteristics.

How this all happens, of course, is the subject of various theories of child development but, whatever the theory, the end result is always couched in the language of 'stage irreversibility'. By this I mean that gender is considered to be the product of the intersection of a number of specific inputs which, together, force people into the dichotomous heterosexual world. Gender, from this point of view, is compulsory (with apologies to Adrienne Rich) – there is no possibility of negotiation. Yet, presumably the whole thrust of the contemporary analysis of gender by feminist theorists has been to argue for a social constructionist view of gender acquisition and sexuality. This is not to say that we must understand 'construction' in the sense of a rational decision to put together some kind of appropriate gender identity for this or that child; rather, it is to point to the possibility that the parties to the construction are not simply representatives of forces over which they have no influence or control.

Put differently, when it is claimed that the traditional account of gender acquisition and identity is premised on the notion of 'stage irreversibility', what is meant is that children are not in a position to resist the imposition of social and cultural controls, that they accept their gender ascription in a totally passive way. This is true of the socialization

thesis, and it is partially true of masculine crisis theory in
that the acquisition of an insecure male gender identity is
attributed to key events in a man's childhood, which
continue to determine his behaviour. In both cases, it is
taken for granted that a child cannot influence the outcome
of his socialization, that he has not contributed to his own
identity construction.

It is this fatalism is challenged by writers like Kessler and
McKenna. Of course, gender attribution is not a haphazard
process in which there is a labelling 'free for all'. The
attribution process must not be confused with crude versions
of labelling theory in which the naming of people gives them
an identity. This is far too mechanistic – a label is only
experienced as an aspect of self-definition when it is accepted
as such by the object of the labelling attribution. In other
words, when one treats a male child as a boy, when one says
to him that little boys do not cry, or when one indicates to
him that his sexual organs are the sign of his difference from
females, this cannot be a one-way process in which parents
simply turn organic material into a gendered being. The
male child also makes his own attributions, he does his own
identity work – he is also a party to the negotiation and
construction.

In opposition to the accepted orthodoxy in the discussion of
gender identity, this position denies 'stage irreversibility'.
Gender is an accomplishment – moreover, it has to be
accomplished in every situation. Every encounter between
men and women, between straights and gays, is an occasion
for identity work. Note that it is not being claimed that each
episode evokes a potentially new gender identity – gender
identity is not something which can be discarded at will;
rather, it is seen as a set of reflexive strategies which are
brought into play whenever gender is put on the line. In
everyday life most heterosexuals do not have to do too much
identity work because they tend to function in contexts in
which heterosexuality is taken for granted. It is only when
they are confronted with the unexpected that they have to
put a lot of effort into their gender commitments. Furthermore, even when they do interact with people who have
different and alternative gender identities, they do not

usually suddenly accept the idea that gender is an accomplishment; they may feel uncomfortable or hostile, but they do not immediately change their sexual allegiances. The point is that their discomfort is a sign that identity work is going on, that they somehow have to defend their own position. To be sure, such a defence may only serve to confirm and reinforce their original self-attributions, but in so doing they also may have an intuition of the tentativeness of all gender identities.

Conclusions and Difficulties

In this chapter I have been concerned with the problem of gender identity. I have looked at three emphases in the contemporary debate about its relevance to the explanation of masculinity.

The first emphasis located the construction of male gender identity in the inexorable workings of the sex-role system. The prognosis for the future here is pessimistic because it assumes that socialization operates in such a way as to ensure complete gender and behavioural conformity.

The second emphasis derives from all those studies which see male gender identity as problematic. Coupled with this is the evidence deriving from those feminist writers who have used 'object-relations' theory to account for the dominance of the mother in identity acquisition. The hypothesis here is that until child-rearing practices are no longer the responsibility of women alone, there will be no dismantling of patriarchy. Patriarchy is made possible by the near universality of mother-dominated nurturing which continuously reproduces the sexual division of labour.

The third emphasis questions the validity of gender identity (and gender) as a real object of analysis. It states that gender is a construction, an accomplishment depending on the attributions of both children and parents who together construct gender by giving it a sense of reality. The important thing to note here is that it is both parties to the interaction who sustain the belief in the naturalness of gender. However, the difficulty arises, as in the case of transsexuals, where there is a discrepancy between self-attribution and the attribution of others. Yet even here, the original self-attribution is rooted in the intractability of the dichotomous gender system. Trans-sexuals usually define themselves as either male or female, not in terms of some third gender or transitional state. Gender constructions reflect the current generalized definitions of gender in the society of which one is a member. In modern Western society, the way that people accomplish gender is more or less guaranteed by the naturalization of heterosexuality, by the belief that biological differences are crucial in all matters relating to sexual and gender behaviour.

> The social construction of gender and the attribution process are a part of reality construction. No member is exempt, and this construction is the grounding for all scientific work on gender. The natural attitude toward gender and the every day process of gender attribution are constructions which scientists bring with them when they enter laboratories to 'discover' gender characteristics. Gender as we have described it, consists of members' methods for attributing and constructing gender. Our reality is constructed in such a way that biology is seen as the ultimate truth. This is, of course, not necessary. In other realities for example, deities replace biology as the ultimate source of final truth. What is difficult to see, however, is that biology is no closer to the truth, in any absolute sense, than a deity; nor is the reality which we have been presenting. What is different among different ways of seeing the world are the possibilities stemming from basic assumptions about the way the world works. What must be taken for granted (and what need not be) changes depending on the incorrigible propositions one holds. The questions that should be asked and how they can be answered also differ depending on the reality. (Kessler and McKenna, 1978, p. 162)

The observation that different cultural realities have separate ways of construing gender is not remarkable in itself. After all, this has been the claim made by social and cultural anthropologists ever since they started examining the sexual lives of pre-literate societies. It is the starting point of most 'relativist' dissections of human diversity. However, what is being claimed here is that scientific discussion of gender is mostly predicated on the 'natural attitude' of the practitioner. Now, while I find myself having some sympathy for this view, what I think is missing from such a perspective is any consideration of the political implications of gender attribution. Granted that our society makes dichotomous sex distinctions on the basis of biological criteria, and granted that other societies use religious and other criteria, this does not help us to understand why these distinctions are also critically important for patriarchy, for the prevalence of the masculine ideology. Why should a dichotomous construction of gender differences also be associated with gender inequality? Is gender inequality also an accomplishment? In one important sense it is, but it is not a neutral accomplishment; like all historical constructions, it is an expression of human interests and intentionalities. Gender inequality has its being in the historical construction of sexual differences. Why this should be so cannot be answered in terms of the attribution process alone. Why should most men start from the 'incorrigible proposition' that their biology gives them greater power than women? A very simple answer to this is that it is in men's interests to do so. Garfinkel's incorrigible propositions about reality and gender do not in themselves tell us why gender inequality and patriarchy exist.

Perhaps it would be appropriate to end this chapter by retreating from a too cavalier dismissal of an embodied gender hypothesis. Although I accept the notion that gender is an accomplishment, this does not mean that 'incorrigible propositions' do not have a deadly effect on human behaviour. The construction of male gender identity is enmeshed in a network of emotional and political processes. As such, it is experienced as real. It is this experience of its substantiality that gives various alternative accounts of gendered subjectivity their power, especially those which attempt to catch the real or imaginary potency of desire. It is in this respect that the next chapter deals with the problem of male sexuality, not simply as an accomplishment and a construction, but as lived experience. Whether or not psychoanalytic explanations of the origin of desire are rooted in the natural attitude is, of course, a relevant question, but it may be that we cannot deconstruct masculinity without examining the kind of evidence deriving from psychoanalytic sources. It

could well be that male sexuality (and sexuality in general)
is nothing more than a construction, but if this is the case
then it is a construction that has real consequences.
Although we may deplore the essentialistic tendencies in
psychoanalytic theorizing, this does not mean that we can
dismiss psychoanalysis as being irrelevant in any discussion
of gender and sexuality.

Accordingly, to assent to the notion that masculinity is an
accomplishment is to ignore the peculiar way in which this
accomplishment often saturates male existence with feelings
of anxiety and rage. The attribution process cannot explain
the 'depth' of a man's desires and feelings. It cannot, in other
words, tell us why it is that so many men feel themselves to
be the playthings of hidden forces which somehow make
them do things in the name of uncontrollable desire. Why
have men come to believe in the waywardness of their
sexuality? How is it that men 'objectify' women? I would
want to argue that the answers to these questions are not
simply to be found in the fact that gender is a construction or
an accomplishment, but also in the manner in which this
accomplishment is 'embodied' in men.

Reference was made earlier to Connell's point about the
way in which both psychologists and sociologists are 'blinded'
by their own professional commitments in their discussion of
socialization. Sociologists operate with a very bland and
uncomplicated view of gender acquisition, while psychologists
find it almost impossible to come to grips with 'social power'.
The notion that a man's gender identity is learned without
trauma is just as misconceived as seeing his aggressiveness
in terms of overwhelming 'drives'. The sociological view of
gender acquisition can be described as being too complacent,
too conflict-free. It assumes that individuals go through life
without ever facing difficulties and traumas. It assumes that,
in the final analysis, everybody will find his or her niche in
society. It assumes that men and women acquire gender in
more or less the same way that other roles are acquired. We
learn our gender identity in the same way that we learn to
play the piano or swim. In other words, it denies intentionality
to the person. So when I talk about the social being
'embodied' in men, what I am stressing is the political

construction of male gender identity. Thus, socialization is not simply about the acquisition of roles, but rather it is about the exercise of power by one group over another group.

Initially, it is parents who exercise power over children, especially over gender behaviour. Socialization can be seen, therefore, as the process whereby children acquire an ideology which naturalizes gender. It is also the process in which the 'body' becomes objectified in discourse, a discourse which takes for granted the 'reality' of sexual difference and inequality, and which assigns a particular kind of potency to the male body, and denies potency to the female body. This is the theme of the next chapter.

3

Male Sexualities

Masculinism in general tends to give a special status to male sexuality. It is often regarded as being some kind of primordial force which sweeps everything before it. It is sharply distinguished from feminine sexuality which, until very recently, was seen as being passive and male dependent. Male sexuality is construed as autonomous, adventurous and exploratory. Of course, the reality is far different from the image. Very few men are sexual athletes who can meet the Hollywood performance requirements popularized by Clint Eastwood and Burt Lancaster.

Somehow or other this view has become the dominant one in our culture, despite the fact that for most men there is a discrepancy between their actual behaviour and the demands of masculinism. Moreover, it has been supported and partly shaped by the popularization of certain versions of psycho-analytic theory, which attribute greater sexual potency to men. How is it that such a view has become so pervasive? How is it that the penis has come to be defined as the very basis of male power and dominance? Surely the penis itself is a pathetic instrument. It is only when it is sexually aroused that it assumes a kind of potency – otherwise it is a flabby and unaesthetic object.

Man is embarrassed by the vulnerability of his penis. He often finds it ridiculous in its normal state – the penis and testicles with their gentle swaying are more reminiscent of the udders of a half-starved goat than the instrument of power that he wants to have between his legs. Man neither accepts nor truly appreciates his penis unless it is in a state of erection. It then seems to him less fragile, and its movements more controllable:

it seems to harden like an ordinary biceps. And in this state it is ready to act as an instrument of appropriation: it becomes a necessary weapon to approach a woman. (Reynaud, 1983, pp. 36–7)

The Hydraulic Model

Here we have in a nutshell a constituting element of male sexual ideology. A man is only a man in so far as he is capable of using his penis as an instrument of power. It is a weapon by means of which he can subdue a woman. But, as we have already noted, this belief in the overwhelming drive of male sexuality is undermined by the reality of sexual experience. Nevertheless, we have to account for the generalization of this belief in our culture. How is it that the penis is regarded as the symbol of male power, as some kind of 'transcendental signifier'?

For Freud, the answer is given in the specific nature of the male resolution of the Oedipal complex, a resolution which leaves most men with some kind of internalized self-monitoring system which enables them to cope with their desires. When these internal defences break down, men are likely to be the plaything of an unbridled sexual energy which can, in some instances, lead to rape and other forms of sexual violence. In addition, the sexuality of so-called 'normal' men is always under the control of libidinal forces, even though they do not surface into consciousness in any direct way. Men's sexual fantasies may not necessarily be about rape, but they are suffused with images of their achievement as seducers and conquerors of women. In any event, for Freud, male sexuality is assertive, seeking immediate gratification.

It is, as many commentators have pointed out, comparable to the hydraulic mechanisms associated with flood control. In times of severe storms, the defences are overwhelmed, the dam bursts and the plains are flooded. Similarly with men, the failure of ego defences leads to the flooding of their consciousness with desires which are no longer constrained by ego defences. When this happens, the threat of castration is apparently no longer operative or, to put it differently, this threat was never really successfully internalized. The superego is weak and unable to handle the terrible demands of the id. Hence, sexual abnormality and violent male sexual behaviour are attributable to the failure of repression. And, because Freud seemed to imply that repression is never completely successful, it is not surprising that male libido is always straining to express itself in whatever way it can.

Recently, this hydraulic model of sexual repression has come under attack from Foucault among others (Foucault, 1981). He sees it as the supreme example of the new theorizing about sexuality which came into fashion in the nineteenth century. Sexuality was discovered to have some kind of essence, some kind of core energy constantly seeking instant release. Instead of the view that had defined it in terms of its reproductive function, it was now seen as the root of identity. Moreover, the retreat of the church from legislative control of sexuality and marriage was associated with the intrusion of the state into 'private' life. What was previously defined in moral and religious terms was now the domain of administrators who co-opted the expertise of the biological and psychological sciences (Weeks, 1981, 1985, 1986). Sexuality was constituted as an object of discourse.

Sexuality was considered to be both creative and dangerous. In its creative form, it was the driving force behind the emergence of civilization. This point of view was given impetus by various attempts to discover its 'natural' and 'uncontaminated' core. Rousseau's splendid savage was redefined to exemplify the repressed and hidden history of European men. If only the corrupt and stifling institutions of bourgeois society could be reconstituted, then this would enable people to live their lives as 'natural' beings. There are elements of this not only in versions of nineteenth-century romanticism, but also in Marx and Freud. However, for Freud 'instinctivity' was also dangerous. If left to itself, it would make social life impossible – it had to be tamed and repressed. Without repression, civilized life was not possible.

At the same time a whole tribe of sexologists were 'discovering' sexuality. Krafft-Ebbing and Havelock Ellis, to name but two, were among the first explorers of this new territory. Along with Freud, they brought sexuality into the realm of public discourse. In so doing, they also gave it the status of something that really existed. The implications of their work are still with us. We have only to look at the way in which Masters and Johnson attempted to measure and categorize the sexual response to realize that 'sexuality' is indeed available as a datum of inquiry. Such 'availability' presupposes that sexuality is just waiting to be discovered, that there is a whole sexual universe that will be revealed under the probing searchlight of research. Sex has been put on the scientific map.

The manner in which sex became a topic of inquiry is not fortuitous and contingent. The study and theorization of sexuality has largely been a male enterprise. Not only have men set the limits of the entire discussion, but they have also established the boundaries of sexual difference. Men were responsible for the construction of both female and male sexuality. Hence, the conventional definition of male sexuality as being assertive and explosive, as well as the definition of female sexuality as being passive and receptive, is duplicated in the texts and research of countless male experts. As Ehrenreich and English (1979) have so elegantly demonstrated, the history of child-bearing and rearing in the nineteenth century is a history of the way in which male experts defined, controlled and legislated these practices. Furthermore, as we have already noted, it is the male theoretician-cum-expert who split up the sexual world into male and female sexualities. Freud, for all his profound insight into the dynamics of personality acquisition, and even though he accepted that masculinity and femininity are often fragile and tentative (Freud, 1977, 1986), never abandoned his belief in the assertive power of the male libido. While he did not initially distinguish between the libidinal capacities of male and female children, the Oedipal resolution completely changed all this. Male sexuality was conceived of as the only relevant sexuality – females were confined to the role of passive child-minders and reproducers. All their energy dissipated in reproduction.

Sexuality as Discourse

Foucault takes a contrary position. He argues that the discovery of sexuality in the eighteenth and nineteenth centuries was not a discovery at all. It was simply an effect of discourse, where discourse is construed as the means whereby the sexual subject is constituted. Repression, from this point of view, only exists in discourse. Before this, the subject was constituted by other discourses, especially religious discourse. If one ventured into the subject's interior, one would find traces of God, or the Devil, or the voice of reason, but never something called sexual identity. Sexuality is not a global and universal force; rather it is a network of contradictory meanings and practices which cannot be studied outside discourse. By definition, what is constituted by discourse only exists as discourse.

So, repression, as understood by Freud, Reich, Marcuse and others, is an aspect of the discourse that constitutes sexuality. The whole project of sexual liberation is a chimera – sexuality is not there to be liberated (Foucault, 1981, pp. 105–6).

Now, while we may accept the argument advanced by Weeks that sexuality is historically constituted, that it cannot be regarded as something which exists independently of the meaning we give to it (Weeks, 1985, pp. 3–32), it is difficult fully to accept the implication of the stronger argument which sees sexual repression as being nothing but discourse. This would seem to deny the *experience* of repression and embodiment. As Seidler writes:

> If Foucault tempts us into agreeing with him that a proliferation of discourses relating to sexuality shows that we mistakenly think of the Victorian period as a time of sexual repression, he only begins to illuminate the difficulties in discourse analysis. Since he leaves us thinking that social practices are constituted through discrete discourses, we are left unable to illuminate a tension between the ways people talk about sex and the quality of their sexual experience. This is something individuals have to explore for themselves, albeit in a social context in which women have traditionally been forced to silence and repress their own sexualities. We certainly cannot assume that a proliferation of

discourses around sexuality is any evidence for a refutation of sexual repression. If we believe Freud we can suppose that people might well talk in order to escape making an emotional contact with the reality of their experience. This raises difficult questions about the relation of language to experience, questions which tend to be silenced with the declaration that since discourse is a material process, there is nothing beyond it to which we can appeal. (Seidler, 1987, pp. 106–7)

Here Seidler is illustrating a central difficulty of those approaches which relegate sexuality and the body exclusively to discourse and social construction. They make it almost impossible to account for the intense emotion associated with the experience of desire. Rape is not discourse, nor for that matter is male sexual fantasy. Also, they make it difficult to listen to those who claim they suffer sexual misery and pain. In reply, it could be argued that Foucault does not deny the reality of desire and suffering, but that he objects to the claim that they can be understood in terms of a general theory which tells us the 'truth' about the nature of desire and suffering – he objects to the delusion that such a theory can in any way 'liberate' us.

Perhaps one day people will wonder at this. They will not be able to understand how a civilization so intent on developing enormous instruments of production and destruction found the time and the infinite patience to inquire so anxiously concerning the actual state of sex; people will smile perhaps when they recall that here were *men* – meaning ourselves – who believed therein resided a truth every bit as precious as the one they had already demanded from the earth, the stars, and the pure form of their thought; people will be surprised at the eagerness with which we went about pretending to rouse from its slumber a sexuality which everything – our discourses, our customs, our institutions, our regulations, our knowledge – was busy producing in the light of day and broadcasting to noisy accompaniment. And people will ask themselves why we are so bent on ending the rule of silence regarding what was the noisiest of our preoccupations. In retrospect, this noise may appear to have been out of place, but how much stranger will seem our persistence in interpreting it as but the refusal to speak and the order to remain silent. (Foucault, 1981, pp. 157–8)

On the face of it, Foucault seems to be right. Never before has sexuality been so prominent in discourse and everyday life. Far from being repressed, it is flaunted on television. It is subject to continuous analysis and discussion by legions of experts. It provides the bread and butter for academics who theorize about 'sexuality as discourse'. But, as Seidler notes, this does not mean that 'the proliferation of discourse around sexuality' leads to the 'refutation of sexual repression'.

One of the problems here is that there is a great deal of confusion about how the concept 'repression' should be used. Sometimes repression seems to be conflated with oppression. This has been one of the ways in which Marcuse has been interpreted. His distinction between basic and surplus repression lends itself to this interpretation. Surplus repression is historically specific – it depends on the extant mode of domination. As such it will disappear when domination disappears. But this appears to be a tautology – it is like saying that domination will be overthrown when domination is overthrown. Marcuse, of course, does not say this. Surplus repression is not simply the imposition of the social on a bedrock of recalcitrant instincts; rather, it is intermingled with basic repression to produce an alienated and fragmented person who cannot cope with irrational demands from within, and political and social pressures from without (Marcuse, 1955).

The alternative view, that repression is missing in Western culture is forcefully put by a very despairing Phillip Rieff, in the third edition of his book on Freud:

> The absolute domination of desires, the mass production of endless needs as the object of late modern culture, is a prescription for filling our common lives with panic and emptiness. The end of this insane condition will now much resemble our present democratic child's play with toy authorities. After this preliminary child's play, there always occurs the main event, the great game of patricide in which every man is invited to play the next egalitarian despot. Our developing eroticracy trains every man to be his own despot, toward the achievement of a character so brazen that denials of the impressive imperative will be no longer necessary. The late modern Yea is designed to carry no prohibiting Amen. Made altogether human or abstracted

as 'society', the expressive imperative is to be censored as something limiting our expressive options. (Rieff, 1979, p. 371)

To be sure, this discussion echoes old controversies. When Freud entered the debate he seemed to suggest that the burial of the 'instinctual sexual underworld' under the weight of rationality and civilization was a cost that could never really be met by human beings. The price was too high; in his view, the emphasis on rationality in our society leads not to happiness and liberation, but to repression, to the proliferation of neurosis, anxiety and the prevalence of a vast reservoir of aggressive impulses finding an outlet only in cruelty, war and genocide. If civilization is only made possible through the instrumentality of repression, then the prognosis for the future must remain dark (Freud, 1975). But this presumes that repression is a necessary condition for civilization. Certainly, in the minds of male devotees of the counter-culture, repression was a dirty word – it represented a monumental 'cop-out', a flight from the reality of the body, and the urgency of 'feeling' and 'desire'. 'Repression' was not necessary, it only had meaning in a particular context. At most, a case could be made for some 'basic repression', but this was a minimal concession. Repression, sexual and social, is a travesty in a society in which ostensibly the problem of material production has been solved. In such a society, repression is a mechanism of social control, surplus to human needs, not something endemic to the human situation. Nevertheless, despite the arguments of the libertarian left in the sixties 'repression' remains very much on the agenda, especially for those commentators who believe that there is too little repression in Western societies.

So, in conceiving of repression as something that really happens, we are on very controversial grounds. Most non-Freudian psychologies find it perfectly possible to do without repression. Moreover, they do not find it necessary to posit an unconscious, or a splitting of rational and irrational processes. However, my intention here is not to get too involved in this debate. What I am concerned with is the argument that male sexuality is not simply a social

construction or an effect of discourse. While Freud's concep-
tual scheme may be problematic, and although his discussion
of sexuality is underpinned by patriarchal assumptions, he
seems to get much nearer the *feel* of male sexual experience
than almost any other practitioner.

The Privileging of Male Desire

To pull the various strands of this discussion together:

1 I have argued, along with Seidler and others, that we
   cannot simply regard male sexuality exclusively as
   discourse. At the same time, I do not accept the
   alternative claim that sexuality can be discovered beneath
   the skin in some measurable quantities. It seems to me
   that in order to understand how male sexuality is
   constructed, it is not enough to concentrate on the specific
   psychodynamics of this or that man. To say that men are
   capable of rape is not to give their sexuality some kind of
   essentialistic status; rather it is to point to the fact that
   the concept 'rape' has meaning in specific contexts.

2 While it may be true to say that sexuality is constituted
   by social practices, it is also true that such a constitution
   reflects real 'interests' in the sense that it is the male
   discourse about sexuality that is privileged. Such privileging is not an effect of discourse, rather it is the
   privileging that must be explained. I am inclined to agree
   with Foucault when he writes:

   > We must write a history of sexuality which is not guided by
   > the idea of repressive power, nor of censorial power, but by
   > the idea of an inciting power, of a knowing power, we must
   > strive to locate the regime of coercion, of pleasure and of
   > discourse which is not inhibitive but constitutive of the
   > complex domain of sexuality. (Foucault, 1981)

   I accept that there is no way in which we can successfully
   locate sexuality in this or that region of the body and the

mind, nor for that matter can we locate it in the dos and
don'ts of the superego, or any other mechanism of
repression. However, if we grant that male discourse is
privileged, in that it defines both male and female
sexuality, we cannot simply assume that this privileging
is itself an aspect of discourse. Furthermore, we also
cannot assume that the privileging is accidental or a
mere detail.

3   This means that the privileging of male discourse is
    embedded in gender relationships on the terrain of sexual
    differences and inequality. It is precisely on this terrain
    that Freud enters into the argument. Granted that the
    Freudian discussion of the Oedipal resolution appears to
    be both a justification and an analysis of male domination,
    it nevertheless gives us some purchase on the way in
    which male sexuality is reproduced. As noted, Foucault is
    not interested in the way in which sexuality is reproduced
    – he is far more concerned with the administration of
    sexuality, that is, in how sexuality came to be the
    discourse of social control. Psychoanalysis, from this
    perspective, is that body of knowledge which claims it
    knows what sexuality 'is'. As a discipline it defines
    sexuality and, by implication, has power over the sexual.
    So the claim that human happiness depends upon the
    liberation of desire from the grip of social regulation is,
    by this token, merely a claim to having special access to
    knowledge, that is, access to truth. To speak about ✓
    oppression or repression is to give credence to the idea
    that sexuality is an energizing force. Freud, in contrast,
    saw male sexuality having a 'real' history originating in
    the emotional quagmire of sexual differences in the
    family. Male sexuality becomes valorized in a context in
    which men are taught that possessing a penis is a sign of
    their difference and power.

4   The valorization of male sexuality, therefore, is an aspect
    of processes which validate male power. In this respect, it
    is feminist theorizing that has allowed us to see male
    sexuality in political terms.

> Sexuality, then, is a form of power. Gender, as socially
> constructed, embodies it, not the reverse. Women and men are
> divided by gender, made into sexes as we know them, by the
> social requirements of heterosexuality, which institution-
> alizes male sexual dominance and female sexual submission.
> If this is true, sexuality is the linchpin of gender inequality.
> (MacKinnon, 1982, p. 19)

If 'sexuality is the linchpin of gender inequality', then
male sexuality has 'historical roots in heterosexual
institutions' like the nuclear family. It is in the family
that men acquire their sense of power, their belief in the
ubiquity of their desires, and it is here that the penis
becomes valorized. To put it differently, it is in this
context that the penis is transformed into a phallus, into
a sign of difference and domination.

To be sure, the elevation of the penis as the sign of
sexual difference and power seems to be problematic. It
seems to be a very poor instrument of domination – it
does not seem to have the ideological weight we ascribe to
it. Surely male sexuality cannot be embodied in a flabby
piece of unaesthetic flesh. After all, the whole point of
Foucault's and Weeks's analysis of sexuality is that it
cannot be encapsulated in any one form or act. Diversity
is the rule of the game; no single organ or sexual act is
representative of sexuality. Why then should we talk of
the valorized penis as though it is the 'signifier of
signifiers'?

One answer is that the penis as phallus locates men in
the social relations of gender and, by extension, legitima-
tise their view of themselves as having authority over
women. Obviously, such a characterization of male
sexuality as being valorized in the penis does not entail
any prescriptive judgement; nor does it imply that
heterosexuality is inevitable.

5   In practice, it is evident that while some men may define
their sexuality in terms of sexual athleticism, the
majority finds it very difficult to live their lives as if they
were latter-day Don Juans and Casanovas. Furthermore,
there is a disjunction between the representations of male

sexuality and its actual expression. While we are constantly bombarded by images of unbridled male lust in literature and in the media, the reality is very different. The valorization of the penis is a requirement of various norms of masculinity, not of the penis. Hodson has written of the 'overburdened penis' (Hodson, 1984, pp. 70–91) and this is precisely the point. It cannot carry the load of cultural prescription, it cannot conquer the world under the aegis of natural desire because, in the final analysis, desire is itself a construction.

What this all means is that there is a myth of the valorized penis which enters into the practice of sexuality. It is received as fact, and is given respectability by legions of experts who believe that male sexuality is something that can be measured.

> Characteristic of this model is the assumption that there exists in every individual a given amount of sexual energy which builds up over time and sooner or later demands release. The amount varies according to the individual's biological constitution – some are more 'highly sexed' than others – and basically not under individual control. Men are generally regarded as having a greater 'sex drive' than women, though most modern sexologists now dispute this, and some claim the opposite is the case. The model thus reflects and reinforces the male supremacist notion that the (male) sexual urge is either uncontrollable or, if repressed, causes neurosis, or finds an outlet in sex crimes. (Jackson, 1984, p. 74)

Narratives and Scripts

But it is not only experts and sexologists who have constructed this view of an uncontrollable sexuality, it is also part and parcel of the mythology of everyday life. One can hear its main assumptions repeated in countless sites of male aggregation, such as pubs, rugby and football changing rooms, factory canteens, senior common rooms, working men's clubs, the House of Commons, board rooms, in fact everywhere men congregate away from women. Both experts and laymen participate in the elaboration and refinement of this myth, by the never ceasing narratives about male sexual prowess and adventure. In early adolescence boys learn the language of sexual objectification in the context of a climate of dirty jokes, and through stories of their peers' sexual exploits. Everywhere men are surrounded by images of male virility, everywhere sexual representations are suffused with the power of the phallus. Everywhere female sexuality is seen as being subservient and secondary.

It is no wonder then that the penis is overburdened by the demands put on it, and it is also no wonder that men are haunted by the spectre of impotence. In this respect, impotence is not simply their inability to achieve an orgasm through penetration, it is also a measure of their loss of confidence as men.

> That the failure of a man to penetrate a woman with his penis should be described in both scientific and everyday language as 'impotence' is perhaps not insignificant in terms of understanding heterosexuality and its relationship to male power. 'Impotent' means powerlessness and carries the implication that a man who is unable to penetrate a woman is also unable to exercise power over her; his penis is, or should be, a 'tool' of male power ('tool', being slang for his penis) and his failure to use it as such is, under male supremacy, a double disgrace, since he not only suffers a loss of status and power in relation to a particular woman, but also as it were, lets the side down. (Jackson, 1987, p. 74)

The impotent man, from this point of view, is the victim of a culture which constantly stresses the potency of male sexuality, with its preoccupation with penetration and orgasm. In actuality, very few men ever reach the orgiastic heights that Henry Miller writes about, nor do they ever achieve the sexual ecstacy of a D. H. Lawrence. But why is this belief so widely articulated in the media and in literature? If, as Weeks has so forcibly argued, 'sexuality' can never be encompassed in any single set of attributes (Weeks 1985, 1986), then how is it that the belief in the valorized penis appears to be such a dominant theme in our culture?

One answer, I suppose, is that male sexuality is not really like this at all, that the image of the penis as a tool and weapon is dependent on the prevalent social relations of gender. Since men control both the private and public spheres, it is their definition of the sexual which is sanctioned and practised. Or, to put it differently, the versions of sexuality which men write about, and which they represent in various discourses, are given the status of truth. Now while not all men are rapists, the discourses say that most men are potential rapists, that there is something dangerous about male sexuality. Indeed, the way in which male sexuality is portrayed in the media suggests that this view has some credibility.

For instance, as Richard Dyer (1985) has argued, male sexual narrative in films and television tends to take the stance of a voyeur who follows a female victim into the most compromising and dangerous situation. We are forced to see her fall down the stairs, we catch a glimpse of her thighs, and we are asked to participate vicariously in the act of rape and assault that is about to occur. Although the famous shower scene in *Psycho* has been endlessly analysed and dissected, it still remains a classic example of a male sexual narrative in which we are invited to indulge in a fantasy violation of a woman. Here the victim is not rescued, but in other versions the 'male hero' rescues the potential victim before the act of penetration.

Women are treated in two ways in this narrative structure. They are either sexually abused or they are rescued by a male hero at the last moment. In both cases, the narrative highlights the absolute dependence of women on men. Furthermore, there is often a merging of the rapist and rescuer in the narrative. After the rescue, the hero takes advantage of the situation by making sexual advances to the victim. He is rewarded for his bravery; his reward is seen as being both necessary and logical – after all, isn't this what the female victim really desires?

Dyer suggests that most narrative structures in the media seem to approximate to this notion of male sexuality in that their resolution is inevitably linked to some kind of climax. The achievement of penetration is equivalent to the resolution of the story, to its dramatic climax.

Even if the narrative appears to be about war, crime, business or
whatever, the drive to a climax is so bound up with the promise
of a woman at the end that all stories seem to be modelled on
male sexuality. It is no accident that the word climax applies to
orgasm and narrative. In both, the climax is at once what sex
and story aim at; the climax is the signal that the sex and story
are over. The placing of women and men in stories ensures that a
heterosexual model is reasserted, in which women represent
what male sexuality is ostensibly there for. Women are the goal
or reward, they are the occasion of male sexuality – and yet they
play no active part in it. The man drives himself, or his penis
drives him; it is he who 'reaches' the climax. (Dyer, 1985, p. 41)

To be sure, the narratives that Dyer discusses are highly
structured and formal. They typify the output of Hollywood
and Western cinema and television as a whole, but do they
typify the kind of narratives to be found in everyday life?
Surely this is not how men behave in the office and on the
factory floor? We do not normally expect to encounter a
Rambo figure in the board room or Dirty Harry at the
supermarket. A day spent at the office in London, New York
or Paris, does not necessarily emulate the narrative structure
of a soap opera. Everyday stories do not usually have a
resolution, they do not have a climax; they tend to be boring
and repetitive. True, at the end of the day, there is the pub,
the possibility of relief in alcohol, but there is no resolution
of the narrative.

Thus, while male sexual narrative is the rule of the game
in cultural representation, it is also the case that men come
to believe in the reality of their sexuality; they 'know' that
their desires are urgent and powerful, demanding instant
release and gratification. At least, this is what they think
they know. Although they might have experiences which
contradict the normality' of heterosexuality, it is almost
impossible to understand these experiences without reference
to prevailing definitions of what it is to be a man. These
definitions or 'scripts' are the means whereby men learn to
name their internal states, so that they come to believe that
the name is identical with the internal state (desire).

A sexual script may be conceived of as a set of meanings

ascribed to desires, arousal and performance (Gagnon and Simon, 1973, pp. 19–26). While male sexual narrative is the rule of the game in the media, it may be more appropriate to conceive of the way in which men accomplish their sexuality in everyday life as a sexual script. Of course, I am aware of the danger of representing human behaviour as over-theatrical. The sexual scripts that men adhere to must not be considered to be like master roles which predetermine the performance. The fact that the penis is valorized in Western culture does not mean all men attach the same meaning to sexuality. The script is not omnipotent; men are not aroused in the same way, nor are they likely to perform in a uniform manner. Scripts provide male actors with a number of possible guidelines and cues about the meaning of their sexual conduct. These guidelines can be interpreted in a variety of ways, but they powerfully influence the performance. For example, a gay person cannot easily transcend the parameters of the dichotomous model of sexuality. In his relationship with other gay men, he may find that he has to take either an active or passive role. The implication here being that even other sexualities are articulated in a system of meanings which are consensually validated as being natural. Our culture puts a great deal of emphasis on penetration, on orgiastic efficiency – it stresses the importance of genital sexuality, and positively values heterosexuality. In these circumstances, it is not surprising that men might find it an almost Herculean task completely to improvise their sexual scripts. Other sexualities tend to be scripted within the boundaries of the dominant masculine ideology.

But, as Weeks points out, the script metaphor implies that:

> there are a variety of possible sexual meanings coexisting at any one time. In the Christian West we have been subjected to a host of conflicting and often contradictory definitions. Medicine since the nineteenth century has worked hard to displace religion as the major force in the regulation of sexuality. Its language speaks less of morality and more of the 'natural' and 'unnatural', healthy and sick sexualities; its institutional focus is the clinic, hospital or psychiatrist's couch . . . We live in a world of rival and often contradictory descriptions and definitions. (Weeks, 1986, p. 58)

Accordingly, the claim that male sexuality is scripted in terms of the valorized penis must be tempered by the counter-claim that there are a multiplicity of sexual scripts which often appear to be mutually exclusive. If these scripts are contradictory, then does it make much sense to talk about the valorized penis as the *deus ex machina* of all male sexual activity? Certainly, it is true that there appears to be a wide range of possible sexual choices available to men. The point is, however, that this apparent plurality of sexual choices does not take place in a vacuum. By no stretch of the imagination is it possible to see a particular sexual script as being outside the social relations of gender. To be sure, men may believe that what they do in private is freely chosen, that the way in which they accomplish their sexuality is a very personal and individual thing, but this begs the question. If heterosexuality is the institutional context that defines and arbitrates all sexual relations, then male sexual scripts are always localized. Behind the pluralization and democratization of desire, there is the sanction of compulsory heterosexuality. I use this concept advisedly because the current emphasis on discourses, narratives and scripts tends to obscure the degree to which men are actually free to improvise their sexual conduct. Thus, the notion of sexual scripting seems to suggest that the script is invented by the male sexual actor in the course of actual sexual encounters, and this it seems is a far too optimistic and benign view of the independence of local practices.

Put differently, most male sexual scripts are still premised on the control and exploitation of women. They are based on the appropriation and objectification of female sexuality and labour power. Heterosexuality provides men with a set of already formulated scripts and norms about the 'rightness' of the act of penetration. The scripts may vary from class to class, culture to culture, but they all give the penis a special status. Most men learn that they are expected to be the sexual initiators, that their desires are explosive and powerful. This they glean from a variety of sources, including parents, siblings, peers, teachers and also from the stereotypical male sexual narratives that are the bread and butter of the media presentation of sexuality. Moreover, as we have noted, they also find confirmation in the sexological literature and in psychoanalytical accounts of genital sexuality. Hence, the use of the concept 'compulsory heterosexuality' is justified on the grounds that it highlights the pressures that are put on both men and women to conform to the dichotomous model of sex differences. Although the concept derives from a particular debate in feminist theory (Rich, 1980; Ferguson, et al. 1982) it is relevant to the present discussion.

I want now to go back to the earlier discussion of discourse. I argued that current emphasis on discourse does not allow us to understand why male sexuality is privileged. Now, it is certainly the case that the way in which sexuality has been constructed since the nineteenth century is largely due to the proliferation of medical and psychological models of normal and abnormal behaviour. This approach to human nature gives the 'expert' the aura of the 'knower' who has direct access to the 'secrets' of the body and the psyche.

Privileged male discourse is another way of talking about compulsory heterosexuality or, more simply, male domination.

> we observe first of all that those in the position to judge, compel, extract, question, punish, forgive, decipher, interpret, treat and cure have always been men; at the very least half, and in the last century the majority, of those judged, compelled, questioned, punished, forgiven, interpreted, and treated have been women. Certainly all priests and close to 100 per cent of physicians and psychiatrists have been men. If, then, the effect of these discourses has been control rather than liberation of the subject, we are looking at a mechanism of construction and control of women's sexuality that spans at least the last seven centuries. (Bleier, 1984, p. 179)

By implication, another effect of these discourses is to naturalize male control over sexuality. Those who have access to knowledge not only define the boundaries of that knowledge, but also assume that they have a *right* to that knowledge. Whether as priests, or psychiatrists and doctors, men have been in the position to propagandize their image of both their own and women's sexuality.

We see the same sort of thing happening in the current

reaction to AIDS. Although the media treatment has ostensibly been conducted as though it were a medical problem, it is nevertheless apparent that it has provided the occasion for the deployment of all sorts of moral and scientific discourses about the desirability and normality of heterosexuality. We are now being told that decades of sexual permissiveness and liberation have undermined the very fabric of personal and social well-being. Other sexualities are seen as the reason for moral and physiological decay and corruption. Men are cajoled into abandoning sexual adventures outside the family; women are encouraged to return to the home in order to reassert the primacy of their mothering and reproductive functions. Doctors, priests, psychiatrists and politicians have all joined in decrying the abandonment of the traditional heterosexual system which guaranteed marriage and emotional stability. Hence, the discourse of liberatory desire which has marked the past century is being challenged by a discourse which now says that sex is bad for you outside the family.

Whatever the long-term consequences of the AIDS outbreak are, there can be no doubt that we are witnessing the construction of a powerful moral discourse. Even before AIDS shot into public consciousness as public health enemy number one, a climate of opinion emerged in the United States and in Europe which opposed and rejected the liberatory model. This climate was, and is, fostered in the New Right's defence of the nuclear family, and its commitment to the maintenance of the sexual division of labour. Thus, in spite of the influence of generations of sexologists, psychoanalysts and the gurus of sexual liberation, the liberatory model is under severe attack. What has happened to the gay community, therefore, is seen as a terrible warning, a kind of portent of the end of male domination and legitimacy. And this is what is at issue. If men depart from heterosexual scripts, if they flee from family responsibilities, if they hand over power to women, then the whole moral basis of our society is at risk.

Now this is nothing new. To a certain extent the history of sexuality is the history of moral panics. But with AIDS the emphasis has shifted to the moral foundations of biology, that is, to the unnatural nature of homosexual desire. The implication is that men can only continue to rule the world, if they are prepared to live their lives in accordance with their real natures, their essential heterosexuality.

We have come full circle. Liberatory discourse is being pushed aside by the combined efforts of the New Right and a virulent virus. Sexual discourse is no longer based on the belief that repression is inimical; on the contrary, we are now being told that repression is desirable, that it is the only way to contain and maintain our society. The great secret of human nature, the hidden sexual self, that Freud and the sexologists supposedly discovered is now seen to be the most dangerous illusion, an illusion responsible for the breakdown of the patriarchal order. Repression is now the requirement of political and personal practice. Accordingly, the family is now given pride of place in the social policy of New Right theoreticians because it is only in the family that the natural desires of men and women can be carefully monitored and controlled. Homosexuality, lesbianism, all the varieties of sexual practice so typical of modernity, owe their genesis to the erosion of family life; hence, it is only by recovering what is lost that we can begin to cure society of evils. Of course, what is lost is the old dispensation in which men not only controlled the public, but the private sphere as well.

The irony of this return to 'repression' is that it is the experts who are now in the forefront of the movement. We have only to turn on our television sets any night of the week to see doctors and psychiatrists vying with each other to underwrite the need for sexual moderation. One-partner sex, preferably within marriage, is the slogan of the eighties. Male desire is still given privileged treatment, but men are now being asked to restrict their 'lusts' to the marriage-bed. In other words, the injunction now is, do what you want to do, provided you do it in the home.

This confrontation of liberatory and repressive discourse is played out on the terrain of sexual politics, that is, in the material world of gender inequality. Both discourses are located in the incorrigible propositions of heterosexuality. So, while we may go along with the notion that discourse to a large degree constitutes the ground on which sexual meaning and behaviour are possible and desirable, we also have to take cognizance of the fact that discourse itself is never neutral, that it is privileged. The privileging of male sexual discourse (for this is what it is) cannot be a simple effect of the discourse itself. This would be like saying that the discourse of racism constitutes racism.

What has to be explained, however, is how such a privileging of male sexual discourse enters into human experience, that is, how does it effect the way in which men live their sexuality? From a different perspective the question is, how is it that male sexuality comes to be identified with the valorization of the penis? How is it that such a belief has such a strong hold on the consciousness of so many men? How is it that the narrative structures of cultural representation take it for granted that men are the sexual protagonists? How is it that male sexual scripts and fantasies are premised on the degradation of women?

The Problem of Objectification

A conceivable answer is that male sexual discourse is the discourse of objectification. Although I do not for one moment want to suggest that the masculine ideology is simply the legitimating rationale of a ruling class of men, I do want to claim that sexual objectification is reminiscent of the relationship between the slave and the master. Perhaps this is nowhere better illustrated than in the manner in which contemporary pornography highlights the implicit violence of heterosexual (and homosexual) relationships. What we see here in its starkest form is the systematic degradation of women. As one commentator puts it:

> The logic of phallic desire is squarely grounded upon the subordination of women's sexual desire. Sexual intimacy, the expression of sexual pleasure, or fun and joy, is constrained by this order to the point where men have no language of sexual expression except that articulated by proxy through women. A woman's moans of pleasure in pornographic fiction articulate both the efficacy of the thrusting penis and the alienation of sexual enjoyment from phallic practice. The sexual oppression of

women organized and articulated within the pages of pornography represents in part the need men have to capture sexual pleasure in a woman's body, from which they are alienated. The siting of sexuality in a woman's body is thus a source of great yearning, and also a source of frustration and rage. Women keep the secret, the secret of bodily pleasure, to themselves, and from men, who strain long and hard for it, for this, women are envied and resented. This idea is implicit in the phallic myths sold by the tests and images of mainstream pornography. Explicit misogyny erupts in the sex and sales hype or in cartoons and jokes. Many of these target women as objects of contempt and ridicule – the dumb blond who's only good for one thing, or whose body is an incitement to penetration but who is romantic and sexually 'naive'; the woman who is unattractive, old or ugly, the feminist woman; the lesbian woman, and the pregnant woman. (Moye, 1985, p. 64)

Pornography, from this point of view, is not simply about distorted male sexuality, but about power and domination. It is reminiscent of what the slave owner does to the slave. Of course, it might be objected that there are all sorts of pornographic narratives and scripts which do not conform to the objectification thesis, that, for example, there is no real connection between 'hard porn' and popular literature. This is to ignore the fact that the consumers of both hard and soft porn tend to be men, that even though there may be a difference between the sado-masochistic scenarios of 'snuff' movies, and a film like *Once Upon a Time in America*, these differences are cancelled out by their common presentation of female sexuality, and their obsession with uncontrolled phallic prowess.

In this respect I go along with Kappeler's argument that pornography is not simply a matter of being an expression of a special kind of male sexuality – it is also a form of representation which exists independently of this or that man's desires (Kappeler, 1986). It is sedimented in everyday consciousness, in the images that flitter across our television screens, and in millions of best-selling novels. In whatever form pornography is represented, it always presumes a view of women as an object of male transcendence. Put another way, pornography is an articulation of privileged male discourse.

The argument throughout this section has been that the emphasis on the autonomy of male sexual desire is only understandable in what Weeks calls the web of sexuality (Weeks, 1985, p. 122). It is only in the context of a complex set of social relationships and meanings that the valorized penis becomes a critical component of male sexual discourse. Furthermore, as in the case of pornography, we are not talking about an inevitable and universal tendency. Yet, at the same time, we are faced with male behaviour. Pornography hurts and debases people. Rape, according to official statistics, is on the increase. Recently, there has been a veritable explosion of information about father–daughter rape. Accordingly, it is not only male sexual discourse that concerns us, it is also male sexual behaviour. Behaviour and discourse are not insulated from each other. Men rape in a climate which tolerates the objectification of women. But, at the same time, men are not simply passive embodiments of the masculine ideology. They rape with their bodies, they 'read' pornographic literature, they 'hire' pornographic videos. They 'do' all these things as active participants.

Obviously, not all men behave in this way; some men may consciously reject pornography, others fight against sexism, others may have never defined themselves in terms of the valorized penis. Yet, we cannot escape from the conclusion that in most contemporary industrial and industrializing societies, male sexuality is valorized, and that this valorization has disastrous consequences for both women and men. I say 'both' because the emphasis on virility has psychological implications for men.

These psychological implications, namely the peculiar divorce of reason and emotion in male conduct, are echoed in the split between masculinity and femininity. To say that men are split or alienated from themselves is not to say anything that has not been said before. In objectifying nature and women, men cut themselves off from a part of themselves, they deny their femininity. There is obviously a problem here. The belief that men have lost the capacity for emotional experience appears to be contradicted by the fact that frequently their passions break through the barriers imposed by the rational ego. This contradiction between their violent aggressiveness in particular contexts, and their supposed inability to express tenderness and intimate feeling needs some kind of explanation.

The danger is that we might be tempted to fall back on a last-ditch psychologism. We may find it easy enough to understand this conduct in terms of some kind of frustration/ aggression hypothesis, some vulgar version of the 'repression' concept. Very crudely, this explanation blames men's irrationality on the stifling reality of their everyday lives. It is capitalism, the mode of production, the increasing fragmentation of social and economic life that overwhelms the individual male. He has no recourse but to fall back on his own battered subjectivity, his pent-up sexuality and aggression.

This is a common enough theme in those critiques of industrial society that focus on the deadening effects of urban and factory life. The image of the alienated male worker has haunted radical social analysis for the past 150 years. But the emphasis now is on his alienation from his own body, from his sexuality, and from his subjectivity. All these elements were present in the original Marxist conception, but now they are seen as symptomatic of some deeply embedded malaise in the male psyche, a psyche which finds it impossible to balance reason and emotion. Something has happened to men; there is a crisis of masculinity which threatens to blow the world apart.

This is the view of repression that lends itself to oversimplification. It assumes something 'bad' (society) corrupts something 'innocent' (man). It implies that there is something typical and even universal about male (and female) sexuality.

The treatment of 'male sexuality' in much of the literature on violence against women is a case in point. So is the argument that explains pollution, indiscriminate exploitation of resources and the threat of nuclear war, by the personal aggressiveness and ruthlessness of the typical man.

The insight underlying this argument is certainly correct, power-hungry and emotionally blunted masculinity is part of the social machine that is wrecking the environment. But to theorize this as the direct outcome of masculinity is to miss the point of the social machinery that makes a given form of masculinity

environmentally destructive – it misses the social processes that
construct masculinity in the first place. (Connell 1987, pp. 57–8)

Concepts like 'emotionally blunted masculinity' and the
'valorized penis' are treated, as Connell points out, as if they
are 'trans-historical'. Although the thrust of psychoanalytical
thinking about male sexuality is focused on the supposed
interaction between desire and the social, it nevertheless
remains true that in the main it is desire which is privileged.
It is what happens to his desire which determines a man's
future. It is the repression of desire that produces the
potential rapist and child-molester. Repression, from this
point of view, is ubiquitous and universal. At least, this is
one way of looking at Freud. Other revisions and interpretations have emphasized the historical specificity of the
Oedipus complex and repression. I am not really concerned
with entering the debate about the validity of the Freudian
account of the unconscious and repression, except to reiterate
my belief that he somehow manages to get nearer the 'feel' of
male sexual experience than almost any other practitioner. I
say this advisedly, because I am aware that his account of
the dynamics of the male Oedipal resolution is severely
limited for historical and empirical reasons. Bearing this in
mind, it might be appropriate to end this chapter by looking
at three versions of repression and its relation to male
sexuality.

Repression and Embodiment

First, there is vulgar-repression which treats the unconscious
as being encapsulated by the social. Society is 'embedded' in
the unconscious. In many respects, this view is similar to the
'socialization case' discussed in chapter 2, except that the
latter does not pay much attention to the repression of
instincts. Embedding in the unconscious entails the policing
of desire by the internalized symbolic representatives of
society. In the case of men, this policing may have two
possible results; it leads either to an absolute control of

instincts so that they conform to authority or to an explosion of irrationality. It is this second possibility that is considered to be more likely the more civilized society becomes. Indeed, this is the most popular view of the consequences of repression for men. It seems to suggest that male sexuality will turn rancid if it is not cathected to a suitable object. The proliferation of male sexual problems, the increase of actual and reported incidents of rape, the obsession with pornography, are all supposedly symptoms of the failure of repression in contemporary societies.

Secondly, there is the version that goes much further than vulgar repression, in that it conceives of men (and women) being 'inserted' into predetermined sexualities. In the most sophisticated account of this process, Lacan (1977) maintains that it is only when a child takes up a subject position which has already been constituted in language, in the symbolic order, that he or she knows himself or herself as male or female. But, of course, the taking up of a subject position is not as simple as all this. The entry into the 'symbolic order' is dependent upon the child's 'recognition' of separation from his/her mother. Such a 'recognition' is simultaneously a repression, an abandonment of the sense of wholeness and integration which characterized the mother–child relationship. The child's insertion and induction into the symbolic order is accompanied by a feeling of loss. The male child can only define himself as male by what he lacks, and what he lacks he represses. In becoming a speaking subject, he loses part of himself, but not as much as the female child because the symbolic order is not neutral – it already is a patriarchal order in which the 'law of the father' is enshrined in discourse and practice. Repression, therefore, is almost a precondition of becoming a speaking subject. The moment the male child enters the symbolic order, he denies one half of himself (Lacan, 1977).

Any commentary on Lacan's account is obviously likely to be skewed. However, it does seem clear that there is not much leeway for resistance to gender ascription in his account. Resistance is the path to psychosis and chaos. The taking up of a subject position is equivalent to taking on a sexual identity. There are no positions and identities outside the (symbolic) cultural order. Nevertheless, the implication here is that existing gender identities can be subverted and deconstructed. This is certainly the view of some feminist writers who have appropriated Lacan. The problem is that, in this optimistic reading of Lacan, there is a tendency to ignore the totalitarian domination of the 'phallus'. Indeed, it is this domination that ensures an almost inevitable repression of desire.

Why the phallus should be privileged is, of course, an interesting question:

> Despite Lacan's own protestations to the contrary, Lacanian theory employs an anatomically grounded elision between the phallus and the penis which implies the necessary patriarchal organization of desire and sexuality. This organization is as fixed as the Oedipal structure itself. Men by virtue of their penis, can aspire to a position of power and control within the symbolic order. Women, on the other hand, have no position in the symbolic order, except, in relation to men, as mothers, and even the process of mothering is given patriarchal meanings, reduced, in Freud, to an effect of penis envy. (Weedon, 1987, pp. 54–5)

The privileging of the phallus, then, is not only something that occurs in the symbolic order – it is also privileged in Lacan's theory. This is not surprising because Lacan speaks as an 'authority' who understands the distinction between the phallus and the penis. It is he (and Freud) who speak of 'castration' and 'penis envy'. Concepts like these are produced in masculine discourse; they represent a highly attenuated and partial view of sexuality from the vantage point of 'authoritative' theory and clinical practice. What is lacking (repressed) in this discourse is the privileged status of male sexuality. In other words, both Lacan and Freud do not come to terms with institutional heterosexuality and its political articulation in contemporary society.î

There seems to be a contradiction here. On the one hand, they both emphasize the fragility and tentativeness of sexual identity. They systematically describe the splitting of desire and reason, and they demonstrate how our commitment to an autonomous ego is partly an illusion. On the other hand, they have a very undifferentiated view of the 'social'. When Lacan talks about the symbolic order, it is not his intention to provide us with a theory of society. Yet, we get the impression of human subjects being constituted the moment they acquire language. Indeed, the unconscious only comes into existence when desire is repressed, that is, when the 'social' says no. Hence, to be a subject is to be inserted into the symbolic order. But the symbolic order privileges the phallus.

It is the nature of this order that remains dark and unknown. We know it is patriarchal and powerful, but we do not know why it inevitably constructs male sexuality in one way, and female sexuality in another. Although Lacan argues that both men and women enter the symbolic through repression, he does not really tell us why it is the penis and not something else which is transformed into the phallus – the 'transcendental signifier'. To say it is chosen because of its visibility and tangibility in intercourse, or because of the image of its vitality, does not help us to come to grips with the conditions which make all this possible, nor does it allow us to understand why female sexuality is not privileged.

Although he rejects biological determinism, he favours a symbolic determinism in which the power of the phallus is almost total. This, it seems to me, is a form of fatalism, a belief in the inevitability of patriarchy, and also a belief in the impossibility of achieving subjectivity without repression. In a sense, this whole project could be seen as a very convoluted version of the 'embedding' version of repression discussed earlier.

Thirdly, repression can be seen as embodiment. In this version no distinction is made between the body and the social. The body is always social. From the moment a child is born her or his body is defined, dichotomized, sexualized, rewarded, punished and socialized by others. The body can never be outside the symbolic order. At the same time, the symbolic order can never be disembodied. The symbolic can only have meaning if there are human bodies to give it meaning. Certainly, from the perspective of a single body, of a person, the body appears as given – it is the ground on which the world is experienced and interpreted. It may be experienced as the fulcrum of existence, as the only thing that belongs to a person. In any event, its materiality is not usually questioned. A problem arises, however, when it is seen as the source of behaviour. When a man rapes, he often explains and justifies his conduct by reference to impulses which he cannot understand or explain. Indeed, this is the kind of justification generations of rapists have given for their behaviour. I would suspect that it is the most popular everyday theory for rape. Now, it is true, as we noted earlier, that men rape with their bodies, that they use their bodies as instruments of aggression, and that they treat other people's bodies as if they had no intentionality. But to say that men rape because of the kind of bodies they have is to say men rape because they are men.

Embodiment means that the way in which people experience and use their bodies will vary historically and culturally. For example, the emphasis on competitive sport in most industrial societies has resulted in the production of a particular way of expressing masculinity. As Connell argues:

> the concern with force and skill becomes a statement embedded in the body, embedded through years of participation in social practices like organized sport. And it is not a 'statement' that comes from the void. Its meaning condenses some crucial features of the social structures that environs, and participate in, those masculinizing processes ... The meanings in the bodily sense of masculinity concern above all else, the superiority of men to women, and the exaltation of hegemonic masculinity over other groups of men which is essential to the domination of women.
>
> The social definition of men as holders of power is translated not only into mental body images and fantasies, but into muscle tensions, posture, the feel and texture of the body. This is one of the main ways in which the power of men becomes 'naturalized'. . . It is very important in allowing belief in the superiority of men, and the oppressive practices that flow from it, to be sustained by men who in other respects have very little power. (Connell, 1987, p. 85)

In translating the 'social definition of men as holders of power' into 'the feel and texture of the body', there is more than a 'statement' involved. Embodiment is not simply about the embedding of social practices in the body – it is also about the *exclusion* and rejection of other practices. The emphasis on athletic achievement, on the development of skills and the appropriate muscle tone, is always at the expense of something else. In the case of athleticism this means that certain qualities and characteristics are excluded. A successful sportsman cannot afford to be 'soft' and 'passive'. Both in his muscular presentation and his behaviour he will embody an explicit aggressiveness.

This is true of other kinds of masculinity: the classic example being that of the soldier who is systematically trained to use his body as an instrument. Soldiers are taught to be aggressive, to kill their enemies efficiently. This is reflected in the way in which their bodies are expected to respond to particular cues in a disciplined manner. A soldier's body is a disciplined body. Discipline is embodied.

By participating in these 'masculinizing processes' men explicitly exclude 'feminizing processes'. They are encouraged to deny and repress any feelings and bodily experiences which run counter to the 'dominant' masculinity. Hence, the emphasis on valorized sexuality and its embodiment in the penis is built upon the exclusion of other forms of sexuality. The embodiment of a male sexuality depends upon historical and social processes. Perhaps this is too tame – it depends on the social practices that constitute 'hierarchic heterosexuality'. It follows that repression is not universal. It only makes sense to talk about repression when a specific form of embodiment is generalized in a given population. Some forms of embodiment are not repressive. Very simply, this means that the body is experienced differently in different contexts. In some contexts, it is experienced as an object; in others, it is experienced as autonomous. So when we talk about the penis as valorized, what we are in effect saying is that a specific form of sexuality is privileged. It is the privileging of this form that constitutes repression because, by definition, it excludes other options.

Obviously, it is often a major problem to identify what is excluded. Freud, the sexual radicals, Lacan, the object-relations theorists, all have versions of what is repressed. None of them has any clear idea of the conditions that make repression possible. Indeed, as Foucault claimed, they cannot theorize repression because repression has no existence outside the discourse in which it is located. What can be identified is a number of disciplinary practices which may have behavioural consequences for this or that population. However, what Foucault does not do is to tell us how these practices become embodied. He does not really allow us to understand how it is that so many men in Western societies (and others) appear to be so anti-homosexual. Nor does he explain the great amount of emotional investment involved in the defence of 'hierarchic heterosexuality'. While I go along with Foucault when he suggests that there is no hidden secret of human nature to be discovered by looking for the real human being in the recesses of a hidden and distorted unconscious, I think he underestimates the emotional power of these disciplinary practices when they become embodied.

4

Masculinity as Competitiveness

Perhaps the most popular image of masculinity in everyday consciousness is that of man the hero, the hunter, the competitor, the conqueror. Certainly it is the image celebrated in Western literature, art and in the media. But it is also given respectability by academic theorizing, by various attempts to examine gender biologically. Despite the reaction against biology in the social sciences, there can be no doubt that this view remains dominant in the Western world. Moreover, since the advent of sociobiology (see chapter 1), the belief in the genetic factor in human behaviour has acquired additional impetus. Be that as it may, what concerns me in this chapter is the way in which this image is accepted as the 'truth', not only by lay audiences, but also by a significant number of politicians, academics and intellectuals.

The Heroic Hunter as Bread-Winner

In a sense, the belief in man-the-hunter, or hero, would seem to have no foundation in the everyday world that most men inhabit. There are very few occasions available for men to be heroes, very few men hunt, except as a hobby or for sport. Man-the-hunter has been transformed into man-the-breadwinner. Opportunities for heroism only arise in the sporting field, not in the forest in hot pursuit of food for the tribe. Why then does this image still remain so firmly entrenched when the evidence points to a very different state of affairs, namely the hard slog of routinized work in a factory or an office? One answer is that the man-the-hunter thesis:

ties together a number of puzzling and disparate phenomena of modern social existence: women's economic dependence on men, the sexual division of labor, war, and male aggressivity. Yet therein lies its central flaw. In the effort to explain the *origins* of present-day gender-associated behaviours and social arrangements, popular theories of human evolution, such as Man-The-Hunter, start with implicit assumptions about the biological basis of such behaviours and characteristics and the existence of a woman's 'nature'. They then construct earliest evolutionary history according to an idealized image of modern industrial societies. Their central actor is the fearless, aggressive, creative, and dominant male, who generated civilization and, through his bonding and hunting with other men, fed and protected the passive, dependent, subordinate female, who generated babies. They postulate for their prehistoric model the very conditions that they are presumably attempting to understand and explain – the sexual division of labor with women as economic dependents and men as providers and doers. (Bleier, 1984, p. 135)

What the man-the-hunter thesis does is to explain present-day male domination in terms of a history which has its roots in the evolutionary imperatives of human behaviour. Although men are no longer hunters, their behaviour (it is argued) still exhibits the same competitiveness, except that it is now manifested differently. Instead of competing directly with each other for the best game and sexual prizes, men now compete in the political and economic arenas. Those who get to the top do so because of superior ability and talents; those who fail do so because of poor natural endowment. The winners take the prizes, the losers are left with the scraps and despair. Accordingly, the prevalence of competition and conflict in industrial society is not accidental, but is an essential requirement of evolutionary progress. The fact that men compete with each other at all sorts of levels is the means whereby a society guarantees that the successful occupy positions of power, the unsuccessful being left with the hard work. Hence, the division of society into classes and elites is a function of evolutionary necessity, not historical construction.

Now, this kind of crude Social Darwinism may no longer be fashionable, but its ideological resonance is still with us.

It appears with monotonous regularity in the literature of the extreme Right, and in the arguments of the anti-feminist backlash. Furthermore, it is given credibility in the pronouncements of politicians who see competition as being a law of nature underpinning economic life and social and individual well-being. Masculinity, from this point of view, is measured by a man's capacity to win. However, it is not only competition between individual men which is seen as being basic to societal survival, but the same arguments are advanced about the competition between groups. Those groups (tribes, races, nations) which win the fight for scarce resources and territory are judged by Social Darwinists to exemplify the cardinal principle of natural selection, namely the survival of the fittest. By definition, their place in the world is guaranteed by natural forces which are not subject to moral and rational control. Indeed, the Social Darwinist emphasis on the natural superiority of the white races was a central dimension of National Socialist ideology. While it may be correct to say that Social Darwinism was never a serious scientific theory, there can be no doubt that it was perceived as such by racists. In any event, these ideas remain dominant in racist discourse, although, to be sure, they are now reinforced by more sophisticated concepts deriving from the contemporary study of animal populations and behaviour.

The viewing of competition in biological terms is one aspect of its history. Long before Social Darwinism, political and social theory had looked at human behaviour and found it to be rooted in selfish needs. Hobbes's view of the intrinsic animality of human nature had a respectable pedigree well before evolutionary biology appeared on the scene. Man-the-beast had to be tamed by social convention and the threat of force. More significantly, economic theory from Adam Smith's time onwards has highlighted the necessity of competition for human welfare. Competition was discovered to be the fundamental law of economic life, a law founded on the notion that men always act to maximize their self-interests. If this is true for all men, as Smith argued, then the laws of the market must operate so as to benefit everybody, provided it is absolutely free and perfectly

competitive. The implication here is that the selfishness of
men operates for the common good if certain optimal
conditions are met. But behind this utopian view of the
market, the prior commitment is to a view of human nature
not much different from that of Hobbes.

In conjunction, economic and biological theories of competition had a very powerful influence on the development of
masculine ideology because they both presuppose that men
are intrinsically assertive and selfish. Both nineteenth-
century Social Darwinism and classic economic theory saw
women as passive and dependent. Or, to put it another way,
they did not question the primacy of men in political and
economic affairs. The main actors in history were men, they
were the conquerors, the explorers, the soldiers, the statesmen,
the inventors; it was they who risked their capital on the
market, and stoked up the engines of economic development.
The exclusion of women from government, and the controlling
heights of the economy, was therefore never really questioned.

Inevitably, the evidence for this was discovered in the
pages of history. The writing of history has been a privileged
male activity ever since the time of Thucydides. History was
written as though women did not exist. Until the nineteenth
century it was a chronicle of the decisions of 'great male
leaders'. It was largely about the wars they fought, the
territories they conquered, the laws they made. However, the
presentation of the past as the unfolding of male history
gave men a view of themselves which was often unflattering.
For example, a reading of Homer's epics pinpoints the sheer
irrationality and bloodthirstiness of the combatants. In
Homer's account, the Greeks act as armies of occupation do
in any war. They rape, pillage and enslave their victims.

A Bloody History

History, from this perspective, is the history of warfare. And
I suppose, to a large degree, this is a consequence of the way
in which men have been perceived to behave historically. If
we look at the history of genocide from the earliest times to
the present day, we could be forgiven for thinking that it is

nothing more than a chronicle of the slaughter of men, women and children by men. And this is the point. Men have not only written history, they have also appeared in it as the authors of atrocity and massacre. This is not to say that some historians were not disgusted by their material, by their 'facts', as they found them. Not all male historians gloried in slaughter. In the main, they detached themselves from their stories. This is how it happened they seem to say.

In a terrifying study of the number of 'man-made' deaths in this century, Gil Elliot (1972) estimates that they amount to at least one hundred million. This includes figures from both world wars, and other lesser conflicts. (The book was written before Kampuchea and the Gulf war.) Included are deaths in concentration camps, the Russian civil war, Hiroshima and Nagasaki. In other words, the scale of violence, as measured by statistics, is beyond any empathetic understanding. As statistics, they can be interpreted, glossed, reinterpreted, but we still find it impossible to comprehend their meaning. Certainly, to conceive of these events as having definite causal sequences in the manner of some social science discussions is to relegate our engagement with them to an attitude of cool detachment. Nevertheless, social scientists have attempted to do precisely this; they have suggested that we must see these events in the context of the structural stresses of industrial society. And, as events, they must be studied coolly and dispassionately, no matter how horrifying they may be. For example, when social scientists were confronted with the Holocaust and Hiroshima, they either tried to treat them as epiphenomena of underlying social processes or they somehow found their explanations in psychological and social psychological processes, which supposedly breed alienation and moral disintegration. In some cases, there was a temptation to see them as unfortunate episodes and momentary aberrations, or even as a tragic confirmation of the presence of the animal in man, or, alternatively, as being symptomatic of the crisis and contradictions of capitalism.

The contemporary analysis of war, therefore, tends to proceed on the basis that it can be understood in terms of general sociological, psychological or economic principles.

Men *per se* are usually left out of these explanations, whereas traditional accounts always spoke of men as being at the centre of the stage of war. Men fought for honour, for glory, for booty, for revenge, for women, for territory. Of course, there were stories about women warriors and Amazons, but these were never taken seriously by male historians. In short, men fought each other either because they enjoyed doing so or because they were exercising their natural self-interest. In any event, man-the-warrior was considered to be the ideal expression of masculinity. Of course, this is to presume that all men were warriors, that they all lusted after war, that they were obsessed with military glory. What this traditional story leaves out are the millions of men who worked the fields of their feudal masters, and who were often conscripted. This is not to say that other men rallied to the flag unwillingly. We have only to remember the enthusiasm of German, British and French men who flocked to the defence of the fatherland in August 1914 to realize that the idea of man-the-warrior is still with us. More recently, this was demonstrated by the enthusiasm for the Falklands War on the part of a large section of the British and Argentinian publics.

Notwithstanding, in both the traditional and contemporary discussions of war, the main actors are men. Whether we talk of wars being fought to secure markets, or for the sake of honour, we are referring to men. Why men should have this dubious distinction is the subject of a great deal of speculation and theorizing.

First, there is the argument we have already encountered about the innate aggressiveness of men. This argument states categorically that men are hunters and warriors out of evolutionary necessity. Because women bear children, men are programmed for the exigencies of the chase; they are also programmed to compete with other men for territory and women. When they are not engaged in open warfare, they channel their aggression into alternative competitive behaviour, such as sport. Even in so-called civilized societies, aggression is just below the surface, waiting for an appropriate outlet. One version of this argument claims that the ills of our society are occasioned by there not being sufficient outlets for male aggression. Too much civilization is inimical to the well-being of men, who need constant gratification for their aggressive drives. So, problems like rape, and other forms of sexual harassment, are largely a consequence of the frustration of aggression. The objections to this argument have been well documented (Bleier, 1984; Connell, 1987). For our purposes it is sufficient to state that there is no real evidence for it.

Yet a number of writers, while seemingly rejecting the essentialist implications of this viewpoint, have argued that men's power and domination derives from their ability to rape, to coerce women against their will. Thus, when men found they could rape, then they raped (Brownmiller, 1975). Male biology is used as an instrument of domination. This suggests that all men are potential rapists and, if given the opportunity, they will rape.

One related reading of history is that once men realized they could control women through the threat of rape and physical force, they could thereafter appropriate the female body as an object, as their property. From the subjection of women all other forms of subjection were made possible. What starts off as the colonization of women ends up with the colonization of the world. Men began to compete with each other because their competition for women provided them with an exemplar for all forms of subjection (Bunch, 1975).

Secondly, there is the counter-argument that posits learning as the critical dimension in the explanation of male aggression. Man-the-hunter, and man-the-warrior, are learned roles acquired in social contexts which positively evaluate aggression and competitiveness. Although there is a great deal of cultural variation in the expression of this aggression, the question remains, why is it that men are usually the soldiers and hunters? Why do men learn these roles and not women? One standard answer is that this is so because women bear children, and are dependent on men for the period of their pregnancies. The survival of the group therefore depended on men acquiring characteristics which enabled them to protect women during the time they were incapacitated by childbirth. In a hostile environment men had to become predators, they had to learn to fight other men for limited resources. Hence competitiveness and aggression are culturally sanctioned attributes which men acquired in a condition of scarcity.

The implication here is that given the right conditions men can be induced to abandon competitiveness. Of course, in putting it in such a bland way, male competitiveness is reduced to a matter of role acquisition. Men learn to be men by emulating their role models. If their models are hunters; then they will be hunters, if they are soldiers, then they will be soldiers. All that one has to do is to provide men with other viable options and then they will alter their behaviour. I suppose if it were simply a matter of men learning new role model behaviours, they could have been induced to give up their commitment to competitiveness long ago. But in our society competitiveness is so entrenched that it makes no sense to see it in terms of simple role socialization. One becomes a man not by emulating a role model, but by being exposed to a whole gamut of political, economic and social pressures. To be a man implies that one has to be a breadwinner (at least this was the case until unemployment became a fact of life). A successful man is measured by his ability to achieve at his job. Tolson puts this point clearly:

> In Western, industrialized, capitalist societies, definitions of masculinity are bound up with definitions of work. Whether it is in terms of physical strength or mechanical expertise, or in terms of ambition and competitiveness, the qualities needed by the successful worker are closely related to those of the successful man. As individuals, men are brought up to value work, as an end in itself, and to fix their personal identities around particular occupations. The roots of gender identity are interfused with expectations of achievement – 'becoming someone' through working, 'making something of yourself', to be breadwinner for the family, and which is threatened by lay-off or redundancy. There is in our society a collective masculine culture of work that makes firm distinctions between 'work' and 'non-work', 'work' and 'leisure', or 'career' and 'family'. It is a characteristic of such dichotomies that 'non-work' is not seen as a complement to 'work', but as its antithesis – as compensation for effort, or reward for success. (Tolson, 1977, p. 13)

The high valuation of men's work fits in neatly with the distinction between 'work' and 'labour'. In the formulation offered by Arendt (1958), work entails the transformation of the 'natural' world by the use of tools and technical knowledge. With the consolidation of capitalism as a mode of production, work becomes mediated, technical and artificial. 'Labour', on the other hand, is more basic. It is what food-gatherers do in order to subsist. In pre-industrial societies both men and women 'labour' to live. In this respect labour is similar to the food-seeking of other animal species. It is consumed at the site of its production. 'Work' is something more than this; it is embodied in products, in artifacts which assume some kind of objective status. In 'working', men transform the world, they dominate nature and they come to see themselves as above nature.

In a very general sense, women are seen as the quintessential labourers because they are more concerned with the basic necessities of life. Their preoccupation with reproduction, the nine months of *labour*, limits their contribution to production. The distinction between their labour and men's work became even more marked when pressures were put upon them to become domestic labourers in the nineteenth and twentieth centuries. This distinction between work and labour may be tendentious, but it informs, albeit implicitly, a great deal of contemporary discussion. It is premised on the dualism between nature and culture which relegates women to nature. The competitive model of masculinity assumes a natural sexual division of labour in which men's work is given a high status.

Thirdly, this emphasis on work as a defining characteristic of masculinity in Western societies leads us to the argument that sees competitiveness as an effect of scarcity. One version of this argument focuses on the way in which men become competitive when they secure control of property and agricultural surpluses. Once this happens, they have to 'protect' their property from the encroachment of other men. Thus, competitiveness is only entrenched in male consciousness after the mode of production changes from one in which there is no economic surplus, to one in which there is. Usually, this change is located in the transition from a hunting-gathering economy to a pastoral herding economy (Engels, 1972). With the advent of private property, men come into their own; they not only own property, but they also control the labour and reproductive capacities of their wives. The family becomes the site for the first class struggle in history, a struggle which leads to the 'world historical defeat of the female sex' (Engels, 1972). Accordingly, the emergence of private property has profound consequences for gender relations, establishing men as the owners and controllers of the means of production and reproduction. Moreover, it is also held responsible for the viewing of competition between men as normal.

One of the difficulties implicit in this version is that it is based on anthropological evidence which, to say the least, was not necessarily accurate. It assumes that women had no real economic significance before, and after, the development of private property. Furthermore, it takes for granted that men and women were on a more or less equal footing before the coming of class society

> All these questions tend to undermine Engel's claim that the women in pre-class societies were the social equals and even the social superiors of men . . . The current evidence is inconclusive. So far as it goes, however, it seems to indicate that women were not systematically exploited and degraded in pre-class societies, but that such systematic subjugation occurred with the introduction of class society; to this extent, Engel's account is vindicated. But evidence also exists that even in pre-class societies (and even with the importance of their contribution to food production) women were not entirely the social equals of men. It is interesting that Engels himself provides some of this evidence. For instance, in his discussion of pairing marriage which, he claims, occurred during a period when women were still equal or even superior to men, Engels remarks that the capture and purchase of women began at this time. He attributes this development to a shortage of women, although he never explains why women should become scarce with the advent of pairing marriage. Whatever the reasons for this shortage, it should be obvious immediately that persons who are being captured and purchased are not the equals of those who are doing the capturing and purchasing. If women were the superiors of men, as Engels suggests, it should have been they who were capturing and purchasing men. If they were even the equals of men, they

should have been selecting, accepting or rejecting husbands
according to preference, rather than being themselves captured
or sold. That Engels does not see that this method of betrothal is
incongruous with female supremacy and even with women's
equality is a glaring example of how certain aspects of women's
subordination may seem so natural that they are invisible, even
to those committed to women's emancipation. (Jaggar, 1983,
p. 73)

The Scarcity Thesis

If men were engaged in the 'capture and purchase of women'
before the advent of class society, then obviously competitiveness is not coterminous with class formation. Admittedly,
the reconstruction of gender history is often an exercise in
wishful thinking which glosses anomalous facts, but it seems
quite clear that some men competed for women long before
the establishment of class systems based upon private
property.

A second version of the argument from history explains
male competitiveness in terms of scarcity. In very simple
terms, where resources were scarce men competed with each
other because there was no perceivable alternative; moreover,
they also competed with each other for sexual access to
women who, for some reason, were supposed to be in short
supply. Levi-Strauss (1969) has argued that the basis of all
civilized life depends, in the first instance, on the avoidance
of sexual competition within the immediate domestic group.
In order to minimize competition within their group, men
exchange women with other groups. The basis of group
solidarity therefore depends on the establishment of links
between groups which exchange women. What is never fully
explained is why it is women who are exchanged and not
men? How do men become the arbitrators of women's sexual
and reproductive availability? Why is it that men are
presumed to be promiscuous prior to the 'contracts' made
with other groups for the exchange of women? For Marx and
Engels, women's oppression begins with private property; for
Levi-Strauss, it begins with the taming of the natural

brought about by the implementation of the incest taboo.
Although Levi-Strauss does not say this, it seems quite
certain that he assumes there can be no civilization, or
culture, without the oppression of women.

This reconstruction of the beginnings of human society is
very familiar. It assumes that there is a moment when the
'natural' is overcome by 'culture'. It assumes that men
suddenly come to realize that their promiscuity and competitiveness are dangerous. But this begs the question about the
status of the pre-civilized group. To talk about a state of
nature in which men behaved like brutes is to presume that
men no longer act like brutes. And yet, their supposed ascent
to civilization has not in any way diminished their competitiveness. Indeed, it could be argued that the advent of
civilized life has led to a greater brutalization of male
behaviour. One of the great themes in European thought
since the time of Rousseau has been the emphasis on the
corrupting influence of institutions and collectivities. The
myth of a golden age in which desire and feeling were
integrated into a harmonious relationship with nature, and
in which there was no sexual competitiveness, is still very
pervasive. Be that as it may, it would seem that most
attempts to write history on the basis of an imaginary
'natural' starting point are just as problematic as the search
for a real 'human nature'.

In any event, we are not concerned with the question of
the origins of the human species. What we are concerned
with is the history of hierarchy and oppression. Thus, while
there may be considerable difficulties in Engel's view of the
origin of class society and its relationship to patriarchy, at
least he locates his explanation in history, not outside it. The
problem with Levi-Strauss's reconstruction of the origins of
society and culture, as we have already noted, is that he sees
male competitiveness and promiscuity as the precondition
for the emergence of history.

Ultimately, both Marxist and exchange of women theories
are premised upon the concept of scarcity. What is meant by
scarcity is, of course, a moot point. Most discussions on
scarcity assume the niggardliness of nature. Human survival
depends, in this view, on the efficiency with which natural

resources can be exploited and controlled. Unfortunately, in the process of doing this, men find it necessary to exploit and dominate others. Scarcity can only be overcome by struggle, by challenging the access of other men to these resources. Writing about Marx's discussion of scarcity as the 'burden of nature', Bookchin suggests that:

> he placed considerable emphasis on human domination as an unavoidable feature of humanity's domination of the natural world. Until the development of modern industry (both Marx and Engels urged), the new surpluses produced by precapitalist technics may vary quantitatively, but rarely are they sufficient to provide abundance and leisure for more than a fortunate minority. Given the relatively low level of pre-industrial technics, enough surpluses can be produced to sustain a privileged class of rulers, perhaps even a substantial one under exceptionally favourable geographic and climatic conditions. But these surpluses are not sufficient to free society as a whole from the pressures of want, material insecurity, and toil.
>
> Hence emerges the other side of humanity's drama: the negative side of its development which conveys the real meaning of the 'social problem' as used by Marxian theorists. Technical progress exacts a penalty for the benefits it ultimately confers on humanity. To resolve the problem of natural scarcity, the development of technics entails the reduction of humanity to a technical force. People become instruments of production, just like the tools and machines they create. They, in turn, are subject to the same forms of coordination, rationalization, and control that society tries to impose on nature and inanimate technical instruments. (Bookchin, 1982, p. 65)

What Bookchin is doing here is to query the assumption that scarcity is the reason for oppression and domination. Or, to put it differently, he is questioning the legitimacy that scarcity gives to domination. To say that the beginnings of oppression are traceable to the stinginess of nature is to reify both nature and scarcity. It is to assume that if something is in short supply, then men will fight each other in order to secure that thing.

Why should we assume than men will compete for women? Why do we suppose that women were in short supply in hunting and gathering societies? Obviously a large number

of women died in childbirth, which may have led to an
imbalance in sex ratios, but this does not mean men
necessarily fought each other. Scarcity may have a different
outcome. Human beings may cooperate to lessen its effects.
The notion that all so-called pre-civilized communities were
engaged in a desperate sexual and territorial free for all in
which men behaved like brutes is not borne out by what we
know about contemporary communities. The struggle against
the elements, the hazards of the hunt, the danger of disease
and injury, are constants in communities without a sophisticated technological capacity, but this does not mean that
they always live their lives in abject misery. Nor does it
mean that the sexual division of labour is always hierarchical.
It is only when sexual difference comes to be defined in
terms of sexual stratification that we can talk about scarcity
and domination. It is only when men come to believe that
they are entitled to own and control economic surpluses, and
to own and control women's reproductivity, that we begin to
discern the beginnings of a view of the world in which
scarcity is defined as a law of nature.

Now this is not to suggest that scarcity is merely a figment
of the ideological imagination; rather, it is to emphasize the
use it is put to by this imagination. Why should one assume
that a low level of technology must of necessity entail a life
of abundance for only an elite few? Why could not the
economic surplus be distributed equally? Are we to assume
that once a community achieves some kind of surplus that
inevitably men appropriate that surplus? Are we also to
assume that if a significant number of women die in
childbirth, the men of the community automatically stake a
claim in the remaining women?

Certainly, we can always find evidence for the scarcity
thesis. We will always discover men fighting each other for
resources and 'conquering' nature. What we will not find so
often is a history written about human cooperation. Thus, for
Marxists, cooperation is something that happened before the
fall into class society. The rule of the game has been
competition and conflict. And, if one looks at the history of
capitalism, it is quite evident that competitiveness defines
the terms of existence. Indeed, it seems almost impossible to

envisage human relationships outside the cash nexus. Capitalist social relations are so saturated with the values of the market that we assume that this is the way the world is. Moreover, what Marx called the fetishization of commodities is replicated in the fetishization of human labour. Even when scarcity is overcome in some socialist future, the implication is that nature is there to be tamed and dominated. In the final analysis, it has to surrender its secrets, give up its bounty to the ever-increasing needs of a society geared to the 'rational' control of resources.

This vision of a rational future assumes that the control of resources entails the end of domination and hierarchy. But, the point that Bookchin makes is that hierarchy is not simply an effect of class relationships. Both hierarchy and domination existed before the emergence of class society. In what ways they existed is, of course, a controversial issue, not only for sociological and political theory, but for feminist theory as well. Elise Boulding (1976), for example, argues that in Neolithic societies the relationship between men and women was not always based on domination, but on a form of 'egalitarian complementarity' in which each sex developed different kinds of knowledge and techniques. Women were the custodians of the domestic fire, they invented pottery and basket-weaving, they understood the medicinal properties of various herbs and roots. Men, on the other hand, hunted, defended the campsite against the trepidations of wild beasts. The point is that, despite the ever-present possibility of disease and food shortages, social relationships were not necessarily competitive – the group's very survival depended on cooperation.

To be sure, there are other interpretations of Neolithic culture which picture it as brutish and uncivilized. Obviously, the Neolithic period was not some golden age in which men and women lived tranquil and secure lives. Nor was it a period absolutely dominated by scarcity and competition. It is easy enough to see the decline of this 'complementarity' in terms of the transition from one particular form of social formation to another. But we can be misled by the archaeological and historical records, especially when we are committed to a view of history which sees these transitions as if they had an inherent logic. For instance, the arguments that stress the introduction of animal husbandry as being a key determinant of the breakdown of 'egalitarian complementarity' in the Neolithic world do not necessarily always prove to be valid: an interesting case being the controversy provoked by the discussion of the Catal Huyuk. This was a society which should have exhibited the expected relationship between animal husbandry and male domination, namely that men controlled the distribution and accumulation of meat surpluses entailing their domination of all aspects of political and domestic life. Here the evidence can be interpreted to suggest that a degree of 'egalitarian complementarity' existed long after the transition from a hunter-gathering to an animal husbandry economy (Lerner, 1986, pp. 32–35).

Market Forces

Yet, we are still faced with the problem, posed by Bookchin and others, of the emergence of hierarchy and domination before the emergence of private property and class society. If we reject biological and simple learning and socialization models of male competitiveness, then we are obliged to look for our explanations in history. Hierarchy, domination and competitiveness are historical phenomena. I group them together because I do not believe that they can be separated. Competitiveness only becomes embedded in consciousness when hierarchy emerges. It is only when men begin to dominate nature and other human beings that it makes sense to talk about hierarchy.

We are still left with trying to understand how competitiveness is associated with masculinity and not femininity. If we look at the way in which capitalist social relations are now almost universal, then competition effects everybody, not only men. The argument here is that it is no use looking for the origins of competitiveness in some imaginary past; it is capitalism *per se* which gives competition such a powerful role in human affairs. Hence, competitiveness is a fact of everyday life in which men and women have to sell their labour power at the best possible rate. Of course, it is not as simple as all that. Those who control and own the means of production are in a much better position to impose their competitive power than those who only have their labour power to sell. Nevertheless, in the orthodox Marxist analysis, all relationships between capitalists and workers, men and women, are mediated by the market.

It is not only Marxists and mainstream sociologists who argue that something qualitatively new disturbed the slumber of the old traditional feudal world. For instance, Illich speaks of the old organic world in which relationships between men and women were defined by gender, not by sex. By this he means that gender relationships in traditional societies tended to be non-antagonistic and complementary, although not necessarily symmetrical; it is only when the new technology emerges to power the capitalist revolution that we can begin to see the consolidation of 'economic sex' which defines the relative power of men and women. For Illich, the abolition of gender means that women are now the victims of an unbridled sexism based upon discrimination against them in the market.

He argues that 'scarcity' is a modern phenomenon opposed to 'the reign of gender' (Illich, 1983 p. 3). Moreover, he also makes a distinction between gender and sex which, to say the least, is not orthodox.

> By 'sex' I mean the result of a polarization in those common characteristics that, starting with the late eighteenth century, are attributed to all human beings. Unlike vernacular gender, which always reflects an association between a dual, local, material culture and the men and women who live under its rule, *social sex* is 'catholic'; it polarizes the human labour force, libido, character, or intelligence, and is a result of a diagnosis (in Greek, 'discrimination') of deviations from the abstract genderless norm of the 'human'. Sex can be discussed in the unambiguous language of science. Gender bespeaks of complementarity that is enigmatic and asymmetrical. Only metaphor can reach for it. (Illich, 1983, p. 4)

This is not the place for an extensive critique of Illich's thesis, except to emphasize that he does not accept the claims made by those social theorists who see gender as the critical dividing point between men and women. Gender, or what he calls 'vernacular gender', is the idiom of the human species in some kind of balanced relationship with the world. 'Sex' belongs to a world in which human worth is defined in terms of scarcity and economic growth. Competition only has meaning in a context in which 'complementarity' has broken down, where men and women cannot define themselves organically.

> Under the reign of gender, men and women collectively depend on each other; their mutual dependence sets limits to struggle, exploitation, defeat. Vernacular culture is a truce between genders, and sometimes a cruel one. Where men mutilate women's bodies, the gynaeceum often knows excruciating ways to get back at men's feelings. In contrast to this truce, the regime of scarcity imposes continued war and ever new kinds of defeat in each woman. While under the reign of gender women might be subordinate, under *any* economic regime they are *only* second sex. (Illich, 1983, p. 178)

Thus, while he acknowledges that under the realm of gender men may oppress women, he seems to believe that this oppression is not absolute. It is only when gender loses out to economic sex that the exploitation of women becomes generalized. The entire labour market is arranged in such a way that women are rendered invisible; their work is undervalued and underpaid. The problem is not capitalism *per se*, but economic growth. Although Illich does not clearly state that the realm of 'vernacular gender' is intrinsically 'better' than the realm of 'economic sex', nevertheless this is the implication. If economic growth is the reason for the oppression of women then, presumably, we are to believe that the old traditional gender order was less hostile and dangerous for them.

The trouble with Illich's argument is that it tends to romanticize the past, a past in which the sexual division of labour was defined in terms of a cognitive consensus about what was 'natural'. Granted that the world has been transformed by capitalism, and granted that capitalist relations enter into sexual relations, this still does not mean that under the old dispensation patriarchy was some kind of agreement between men and women about who does what. In other words, what Illich appears to ignore in his discussion is the evidence that points to the 'nastiness' of gender and sexual relations in the past. This is not to say that the past was irretrievably nasty, but that patriarchy is a historical phenomenon in which genocide, rape and violence were not peripheral. The fact that there is an economic dimension to sexuality is not something new. The history of prostitution does not begin with capitalism, nor does sexual objectification. Despite the sophistication of much of Illich's analysis, it seems to me that he still ends up writing yet another androcentric account of history.

A related argument, albeit starting from different premises, has been advanced by Carolyn Merchant (1980). Although she does not make the distinction between gender and sex that Illich makes, she nevertheless also has a vision of the organic community disrupted by the shattering influence of critical economic, technological and scientific innovations in the sixteenth and seventeenth centuries. This organic community she identifies with female attributes, as an ecological system in which both men and women existed in relative harmony with both nature and themselves. The operative word here is 'relative' because she obviously does not suggest that this state of affairs was ideal. Merchant is one of a number of writers who have associated instrumental rationality with the consolidation of male power over women. The main thrust of her thesis is that gender relations in pre-scientific Europe were encapsulated in a cognitive and moral order which did not define nature as alien and hostile. Thus, following the logic of her argument, the real defeat of the female sex occurs much later than Engels supposed.

Between 1500 and 1700 an incredible transformation took place. A 'natural' point of view about the world in which bodies did not move unless activated, either by an inherent organic mover or a 'contrary to nature' superimposed 'force', was replaced by a non-natural non-experiential 'law' that bodies move uniformly unless

hindered. The 'natural' perception of a geocentric earth in a finite
cosmos was superceded by the 'non-natural' common sense 'fact'
of a heliocentric infinite universe. A subsistence economy in
which goods, money, or labour were exchanged for commodities
was replaced in many areas by the open-ended accumulation of
profits in an international market. Living animate nature died,
while dead inanimate money was endowed with life. Increasingly
capital and the market would assume the organic attributes of
growth, strength, activity, pregnancy, weakness, decay, and
collapse obscuring and mystifying the new underlying social
relations of production and reproduction that make economic
growth and progress possible. Nature, women, blacks, and wage
labourers were set on a path as 'natural' and human resources
for the modern world system. Perhaps the ultimate irony in
these transformations was the name given them: rationality.
(Merchant, 1982, p. 288)

Now, this emphasis on the sixteenth and seventeenth
centuries as the period in which capitalist instrumental
rationality conquers the world runs counter to those views
which focus on patriarchy as central to the understanding of
oppression and competitiveness. These views emphasize the
point that genocide, racism and sexism have a much longer
history than the transformations brought about by the
scientific and economic revolutions that Merchant writes
about. So, although racism in its systematized nineteenth-
century form appears to be different from the kinds of racism
prevalent in classical and feudal Europe, nevertheless, it
would be inaccurate to associate it only with the period of
European expansionism. Racism, genocide and competitiveness are not simply effects of the changes brought about by
the rise of capitalism. What does happen is that men begin to
oppress and kill each other more efficiently. War comes to be
experienced by entire populations culminating in the Holocaust of the twentieth century. It was no longer a local affair
between two tribes or feudal baronies. Genocide was not
confined to one's neighbours, it was exported to Africa and
the Americas. What is different is the sheer scale of these
processes. While the scale of rationalization does not explain
the sexual and racial objectification, it is easy to see why it
had such an important influence on sexual and gender
relationships and differences.

Instead of the religious justification of gender differences, in the sixteenth and seventeenth centuries these differences were beginning to be explained in another way. Previously, they had been codified in philosophical and political doctrines. They had a rationale legitimated by God, by reason and by the nascent political authority. But, from this time onward, differences were not decreed by the church, but by 'science' and its *spokesmen*, the 'discoverers' of the essential nature of men and women. Since all human beings are subject to the laws of nature, they could be 'worked on' and manipulated like other 'natural' objects. Where the church had demanded that women obey men because God willed it, the new science argued that women were inferior because they were made this way.

The broad sweep in which both Illich and Merchant cast their arguments has certain limitations. While it is true that the sixteenth and seventeenth centuries mark some kind of watershed for personal and social relationships, it is not necessarily the case that these relationships were completely transformed. Certainly, the 'radical' influence the economy had on the family and sexuality is not at question. But what is problematic is the tendency to see this influence in terms of some irreversible and logical progression. The transformation from gender to sex in Illich's discussion is far too simplistic. Sexuality, gender, masculinity, femininity become nothing more than epiphenomena dependent on the 'real' workings of the economic and technological systems.

Take a term like 'father'. Obviously, it does not have exactly the same meaning as it did in the sixteenth and seventeenth centuries. Yet, fatherhood has a continuity which can only be understood in historical terms. But, more than this, it must also be 'felt' in autobiographical terms.

Fatherhood, or whatever, has a history. This is not simply to say it has a past but that the assumptions and evaluations about fatherhood are part of the resources which are used by persons who occupy the status of father (and mother and child) and are shaped by the complex intersections between personal biographies, the overlapping of family careers over generations and wider patterns of socio-historical change ... in doing the work of fatherhood, I deploy understandings of what being a father means, not simply from my present generations but from the past, especially the past which is most available to me in terms of my own family of origin and the past that was interpreted and filtered through that source . . . The social construction of family identities therefore must be understood historically, not in terms of some kind of abstract history but of histories and biographies that are intimately connected and felt and understood. (Morgan, 1985, p. 181)

What is true for fatherhood is also true for concepts like masculinity. To be sure, masculinity was not a 'topic' in the seventeenth century, but this is equally true of homosexuality and heterosexuality. But this does not prevent us from discussing and imagining their historical presence. Admittedly, there is a danger of reading into the past versions of masculinity which are current today.

As men we have biographies. We have grown up in contexts which take masculinity and competitiveness for granted. A large number of us participate in competitive games, sports and occupations. Some of us will be successful, others will be failures. We are taught that competition is a moral 'good'. At least, this is what we are taught today. It is the bedrock of the theory and practice of the enterprise society, but at the same time it validates the virtues of a masculinity which men (you and me) supposedly have internalized. What this presupposes, therefore, is that the 'health' of a free-enterprise society depends upon the construction of a specific kind of male character structure which is receptive to the exigencies of competitive stress. Such a character structure is functional for the system. Presumably, other character structures are functional for feudalism and socialism.

The Rational Calculator

Everywhere we look we are confronted with the spectacle of winners and losers in the market, on the sportsfield and in interpersonal relationships. For some, this is normal, it is how the system works. In order for capitalism to work, you need men (and women) with the right motivation and commitment to competition. Men must compete with each other, as individuals or in groups, to maximize the common good. So when little Johnny wins the hundred metre's dash, we see this not only as arising out of 'natural' ability, but also as exemplifying the laws of competition. Both nature and the market are merged to give us a picture of the ideal character structure for capitalism.

For others, the raging assertive and competitive male character structure is simply a result of the internalization of the bourgeois ideology. Men become competitive in a mode of production which demands efficiency and achievement. Different modes of production emphasize different kinds of character structure. The implication of this is that masculinity in its competitive guise is powerful but tentative. In the past there were other masculinities – in the future, no doubt, there will be other versions.

It is true that at times patriarchy and capitalism appear to have had some kind of elective affinity, but this affinity is never straightforward. It is tempting to talk about 'capitalist patriarchy' (Eisensten, 1979). But, as Hartmann has argued, patriarchy and capitalism may at times co-exist in a relatively integrated fashion, while at other times they may be mutually contradictory (Hartmann, 1981, p. 1–33). (Whether patriarchal capitalism catches the relationship between the two any more successfully is another question.) Nevertheless, in this latter formulation the analytical and empirical independence of patriarchy and capitalism is stressed. In other words, capitalist relations may influence gender relations, but they do not constitute them. (This is something which is discussed in chapter 5.) One of the problems here is that it is difficult to reconstruct masculinity before the modern era. We can talk about the role of the father in peasant communities in Medieval Europe, but we find it difficult to dig out the subjective dimension of this role. We can theorize about man-the-warrior and hunter, but this is usually on the basis of evidence anthropologists have collected about contemporary small-scale societies; however, we do know that the history of rape and violence does not begin with the industrial revolution, just as genocide and warfare have had a much longer history than feudalism and capitalism.

As Morgan (1985) noted, we think we can understand fatherhood in the past. Because some of us are fathers, we may remember our own fathers and grandfathers; we have biographies which intersect with the biographies of parents and children. As men, we also may believe that there is some continuity between our experiences and those who lived before us. Although the large majority of men in industrial societies do not hunt and do not fight wars, they still find it conceivable that this is what they did in the past. The mercenaries who fight wars today do not find it difficult to understand the motives of some of the mercenaries who fought in the Crusades.

In other words, we see the past as some kind of validation of who and what we are now. The image of economic man, the rational calculator, who takes a risk in order to maximize his profits and advantages, is so much taken for granted that it is not surprising we tend to read all history in these terms.

Today, this thesis remains a very persistent dimension of everyday and academic discourse. Although the social sciences have supposedly demystified some of the cruder aspects of essentialist thinking, they nevertheless keep on reappearing in various guises especially in psychology and economics. One of the recurring claims made by free-market economists is that market forces are determined by the competitive choices of rational decision-makers.

> It is a guiding assumption of economics that economic rationality is a characteristic of human nature. Rational economic agents are born not made. Human motivation to engage in cost–benefit calculation in the service of maximising preferences is an unalterable part of us, as much a part of what it means to be human as the fact that people speak, have opposable thumbs, and walk on two legs. The pursuit of self-interest requires no more justification than the fact that the planets revolve around the sun. (Schwartz, 1986, p. 80)

In the best of all possible worlds this would entail that everybody would get his/her just deserts. We would all maximize self-interest. But, this is not the best of worlds.

Some people get more than others. And others never get the opportunity to act in their best interests. What we can see very clearly is that some people have more power, advantages, influence and prestige than others. This is fine, say the self-interest theorists. In terms of a straightforward model of self-interest, those who get to the top must be more rational than those who do not. Those who do not have lost out because of some lack in their rational capacities. In the heyday of *laissez-faire* economics and Social Darwinism, it was self-evident to politicians and scientists that competition differentiated between the strong and the weak, between the rational and the non-rational. Those individuals who controlled society, who commanded the economy, and who were successful in science, war and art, did not achieve this by chance. It was competition that was the driving force behind their achievement.

The emphasis here is on the individual and *his* motives. Capitalism, therefore, was the most appropriate framework in which men could express their *specific* interests. The theory behind all this is that each competitor should be free to be himself, that is, to act without the interference of the state or any other collectivity. This freedom had been severely curtailed in classical and feudal times, but with the coming of a market economy individuals could fully realize themselves. They were free to express themselves as 'preference maximizers'. The market was the arena in which individual autonomy was tested. Success, or failure, represented a validation of the laws of competition. Before the advent of the market these laws had been distorted. There was no way in which the natural proclivities of men could find an outlet in circumstances governed by tradition or custom. It was only with the unshackling of feudal restrictions that the individual came into his own. In these terms, classes, groups and societies can have no real existence, except as conglomerations of individuals who perceive they have similar interests.

Since it was obvious that a large proportion of the world's population was not in a position to reach the standards of the European bourgeoisie, nothing was easier than to draw the conclusion that the differences between people and classes

were intrinsic. This conclusion, in various forms, remains a
dominant theme in twentieth-century political and social
ideology and practice. The sneering condescension with
which African poverty is handled in the media, the
concentration on violence in working-class contexts, the
constant emphasis on gender differences, and the moralizing
reaction to homosexuality certainly had their counterparts
in the nineteenth century. What has changed are the
specifics, but not the substance of theorizing about group
differences. The irony of this is that the social sciences
cannot contain the flood of pseudo-theories about group
differences. It is only economists who have some influence on
government policy and they do not find it difficult to see
group differences in terms of market forces. While govern-
ments pay lip service to the primacy of the individual, they
base their policies on the assumed distinctions between
groups. Despite the welfare state and the counter-theories of
the left, the prevailing orthodoxy about individual and group
differences is rooted in an essentialist bedrock.

I began this chapter by examining and rejecting both the
man-the-warrior and man-the-provider images of male competitiveness. I did so not because men were not hunters,
warriors and providers, but because these images encapsulate
historical processes in a strait-jacket which excludes a whole
wealth of counter-examples. One asserts categorically that
men are not by nature hunters or rapists, not because they
do not hunt and rape, but that when they do, they do so in a
context in which both hunting and rape have meaning. Rape
has significance only when it is seen as a political act and
not simply an expression of lust. Before men rape, women
must be defined as appropriate targets. In a sense, therefore,
rape is a paradigmatic form of human domination. Because
it is political it is already implicit in male discourse. The
claim that the exchange of women was the ground on which
civilization was built is only true if we accept the argument
that men 'knew' that incest was dangerous. But if they
already 'knew' this, then this must mean that in the so-
called pre-civilized state they had a definite conception of the
relative power and value of men and women. Such 'knowledge'
was culturally mediated. It was rooted in the historical

construction of gender differences, in the matrix of social relations. Distinctions and evaluations are social phenomena which are meaningless to other animal species. Men and women make distinctions between culture and nature, animals do not.

In any event nature is identified with women, culture with men. Men reach out for culture because of their responsibility for the well-being of the group. They have to defend *their* women and children from the ravages of nature, from the attacks of wild animals and other men. It is this 'transcendental' activity which defines masculinity, according to theorists like Simone de Beauvoir. From the moment men construct themselves as over and above nature, they begin to oppress and objectify both women and the natural world. Yet, contemporary anthropological evidence questions this peculiar assertion of male responsibility for culture. The truth of the matter is that women were co-partners in the construction of culture and modes of production (Lerner, 1986, p. 36). Indeed, it is quite clear that women were largely responsible for the invention of fire and for the development of agriculture. The trouble is (as noted earlier) that men have been largely involved in the writing of history, and this has led to a view that identifies history with the heroism and activities of men who transform the world in their image.

It might be objected that what men wrote is perfectly consistent with what they did. It was they who fought wars and raped, it was they who destroyed the delicate balance between the human species and nature. Consequently, written history is nothing more than a reflection of the reality of male behaviour. This is merely to gloss the counter-history of half the human species. Just as slaves, serfs, peasants and workers were left out of history, so were women. This is hardly news. The problem is that until recently this male version was not only taken for granted, but it also coerced our sense of reality. So, the idea that men were naturally competitive was never really questioned, for the simple reason that this is how generations of male scholars saw men. And, when in the nineteenth century, the biological sciences seemed to confirm that there were natural hierarchies in both animal and in the human species, it became very easy to use this kind of 'evidence' to justify race, class and gender inequalities.

However, the other histories which locate male competitiveness in specific economic contexts also have their difficulties. The problem is that most accounts look for the origin of hierarchy and competitiveness in the dynamics of this or that economic or social process. For instance, Engels's account of the emergence of the patriarchal family was correlated with the consolidation of private property in the hands of men who appropriated agricultural and economic surpluses. But, as has been pointed out by various feminist and radical writers, the evidence is that hierarchy and domination have a much longer history than class domination. On the other hand, some writers have argued that the real defeat of women only takes place when men have completely broken away from their compact with nature. Merchant, Illich and others insist that it is only when the traditional world of gender breaks down that we can speak of objectification or economic sex. They argue that it was the collapse of the old affinity with nature that was undermined by the technological economic and scientific revolutions of early modernity. This affinity lasted as long as human beings were tied to local communities, to the particularity of geographical and temporal horizons. Although patriarchy was the traditional form in which gender relationships were cast, it was, nevertheless, much more in tune with the needs of both men and women whose mutual dependence was self-evident. This assumes, therefore, that a qualitative change in the kinds of domination and oppression occurred after the triumph of capitalist instrumental rationality.

Put differently, domination in the pre-modern era was personal and direct. In very general terms, it was based upon the rule of the father who actually existed in the family, the kinship group, or even perhaps, more remotely, in the manor house or chieftain's hut. In the modern era (using this term in a very broad sense) the immediacy of personal domination was replaced by objective and abstract criteria. Patriarchy was no longer local and family based. It now became a principle of social organization in which the power of the father was replaced by the power of the state and the economy. What was previously justified by reference to tradition was now justified in the name of science and economic progress.

There is a problem implicit in this last point. It seems to suggest that there are various versions and forms of patriarchy. First, there is the version that locates patriarchy in agrarian societies:

> A patriarchal society is one in which power is held by male heads of households. There is also clear separation between the 'public' and the 'private' spheres of life. In the private sphere of the household, the patriarch enjoys arbitrary power over all junior males, all females and all children. In the 'public' sphere power is shared between male patriarchs . . . No female holds any formal public position of economic, ideological, military or political power. Indeed females are not allowed into the 'public' realm of power. Whereas many, perhaps most, men expect to be patriarchs at some point in their life cycles, no women hold formal power. (Mann, 1986, p. 41)

This version, according to Mann, (although an ideal type) was broadly typical of most societies until the eighteenth century. Although power at both the domestic and public levels is vested in men (as patriarchs), women were not completely defenceless and powerless. Their position, to a large extent, was guaranteed by custom and law (Mann, 1986, p. 42). What is certainly true is that women in patriarchal societies do not wield 'official' public power. This argument corresponds roughly to that of Illich and Merchant, despite their different theoretical presuppositions. What matters, however, is that they all seem to believe that patriarchy should not be applied to gender inequality in the contemporary rational capitalist world.

Secondly, there is a version of patriarchy which does not limit itself to the pre-industrial and capitalist world. Most feminist discussions, for example, while conceding that there is a difference between the forms of male domination and oppression associated with traditional agrarian societies, and those associated with capitalist societies, do not limit the concept patriarchy to a specific mode of production or historical epoch. Accordingly, even though patriarchy may be strictly defined as 'the rule of the fathers', this does not entitle us to describe male domination in capitalist societies as being non-patriarchal. What has changed is not the *fact* of male supremacy, but its expression. Instead of being vested in the authority of the *pater famialis*, it is now vested in the authority of the state. Furthermore, the fact that women are no longer confined to the bounds of a domestic mode of production, but have considerable access to the public economic sphere, means that they are now doubly oppressed, in the home and in the workplace. We can still, therefore, speak of male domination in terms of patriarchy. While we might want to argue that this state of affairs is not equivalent to the traditional version (and of course it is not) we could, nevertheless, posit that the position of women relative to men has not changed significantly, that conceivably it has worsened. Accordingly, whether or not we want to label this contemporary form of male domination as patriarchy or not, does not make one iota of difference to its reality.

Since I have already argued that hierarchy, domination and competitiveness are related to each other, and that male supremacy can only be understood as arising out of a set of circumstances in which men begin to dominate nature, women and other men then, obviously, we have to look for the source of this domination in the past. Although there is a difference between the forms in which male domination are articulated, we cannot simply dismiss the period before the advent of capitalism as being relatively benign. Very generally, ever since Neolithic times, history has been punctuated with atrocities, genocides, conquests and rapes. This is not to say that this is what history is about, but it is to say that human beings have done terrible things to each other for a very long time. Thus, it might well be that the history of domination begins with the history of patriarchy, with the first self-image that men have of themselves as being the 'tamers' of nature. But, it is only with the emergence of a worldview based upon the tenets of techno-logical and instrumental rationality that this self-image is translated into a rationale for the *systematic* appropriation of nature. More accurately, it is only when certain groups of men in Western Europe begin to define the world in this way that we can fully begin to see the competitive edge of the masculine ideology at work.

5

Men as a Collectivity?

The object of this chapter is to ask whether it is possible to see men as a collectivity with a collective set of interests. Should men be regarded as a ruling class? Put this way, there appears to be no possibility of discovering a collective entity with a collective interest. Indeed, it is doubtful if such an entity exists. What we may discover are specific groups of men who have definite relations with women, and other groups of men. For example, in South Africa some men (white) stand in a particular relationship to white women, as well as to black women and men. In these circumstances is it possible to maintain that black and white men have the same interests or that they have a common ideology?

Men as a Class?

The question we really have to answer, therefore, is this. When we talk about men having a collective interest in maintaining gender inequality, do we mean all men or do we mean a specific group of men? If the answer is the latter, then we have to identify this group. And therein lies the difficulty. Who are the ruling group of men who define the masculine ideology, and dominate all other men and women? One partial answer is that they are white and middle class. But this presumes that other white men who are not middle class do not oppress women and non-white groups. Furthermore, it also seems to imply that gender inequality in non-Western societies is not important.

Clearly this is problematic. Alternatively, if we assume that *all* men constitute a class, then we have to spell out the criteria which allow us to assent to this. I take it that, very minimally, a class must have some image of itself as having some kind of collective identity, and that at the empirical level its members should have similar access to the means of production. Now, it is the case that specific groups of men do indeed appear to have some kind of consciousness of their community of interest in relation to their location in the occupational structure. Coal miners, for example, have long been regarded as typifying a particular kind of class consciousness. In addition, it might well be that not only coal miners, but large sections of the working class may at time exhibit a radicalized consciousness, especially in times of economic recession. In other words, it is theoretically possible that the British male working class as a whole may act in a cohesive way in protecting and consolidating its interests. In exactly the same way, it is theoretically possible that the controllers or owners of the means of production may act collectively. Be that as it may, by no stretch of the imagination could it be said that the interests of workers and managers coincide.

Accordingly, at this level of analysis at least, men do not share the same class position. Moreover, if you ask what community of economic interest there can be between a black mine worker in South Africa and a white managing director, then it is clear that the fact that they are both men is irrelevant. The answer may be that class theory is not an appropriate vehicle to understand gender inequality. If gender inequality is a fact of life in most industrial societies, then one presumes that we are not referring to employment and economic factors alone. Gender is a pervasive factor in the positioning of men and women in respect to access to power, status, privilege and scarce resources in general. Membership of the category 'man' or 'woman' is not simply a convenient way of classifying people – it is rather a major form of inequality. The category 'man' is not neutral – it implies power and domination. Consequently, the argument here is that, no matter the site – whether it is in a factory, a school, the House of Commons, the sportsfield, the university, the family – men are the dominant group or category. So, although the word class in its strictest sense may not be applicable to gender relationships, nevertheless, men and women stand in a political relationship to each other. If this can be demonstrated to be generalized in industrial and non-industrial contexts, then could it not be that whether or not we call men and women classes is irrelevant, because male power is not simply associated with the economy and the policy, but is sedimented in most of the sites in which the two genders confront each other?

Of course, there is a considerable difficulty with this last point. If gender inequality is generalized and sedimented in our society, then does this mean that it is universal? Obviously, to assent to this would entail a view of gender which would put it outside history. The entire thrust of our argument is that male domination is not universal, just as class is not universal. There are anomalies in social and historical contexts which suggest that the relationship between men and women is not always asymmetrical (Lerner, 1986, pp. 36–53). To be sure, when we examine the position of women today in both the industrial world and the Third World, gender inequality is the rule of the game. This must be qualified. For example, in South Africa, America before the Civil War, historic slave societies and in societies with a clearly demarcated and visible class system (Britain in the nineteenth century?) a large number of men were subordinate to some categories of women. In South Africa, the dominance and power of the white minority guarantees the power of most white women over *both* black men and women. It might be objected that these examples are highly untypical. But this is precisely the point, namely that we cannot speak of the category 'men' who always dominate the category 'women'. Who dominates who will depend upon the context. The apparent triteness of this observation is undermined when we realize that all other options inevitably push us back into essentialism.

While we might agree that men do not constitute a class, this is not to say that particular groups of men do not sometimes *act* like a class. Take employment, although women constitute nearly half the working force in most advanced Western societies, this is not reflected in their earnings and job opportunities. Without exception, except in some professional enclaves, the structure of rewards and responsibilities is heavily skewed in favour of men. Why this should be so has concerned countless volumes of analysis. The question we have to ask here is, how is it that long after women entered the labour market in large numbers, they have not achieved equal status with men? Engels had expected that the problem of women's inequality would be solved by their entry into the labour force, but this has not happened. Why this should be so is, of course, the million dollar question. Other practitioners see gender as being irrelevant to any analysis of the stratification system of advanced industrial societies. They claim that gender may be a complicating influence on social stratification, but that, in the final analysis, it is subordinate to market and production forces. Thus Lockwood writes:

> To a large extent then, discussion of women's place(s) in the class structure has been dominated by conceptual debates whose energy derives more from their political significance for the protagonists than from the explanatory power of the vying arguments. Certainly the sociological value of such work has to be shown. Mere observers of such debates are unlikely to be excited by such belated recent discoveries, as that the whole domestic labour debate throws no light on the fact that it is usually women who do housework, or that the 'reserve army of labour' thesis appears to be vitiated by the fact of sexually-segregated job markets. Nor will they be impressed with the explanatory power of a theory whose main counter-factual appears to be that the withdrawal of women from housework would mean the collapse of capitalism. (Lockwood, 1986, p. 17)

Lockwood is here casting doubt upon those Marxist–feminist approaches which attempt to incorporate gender relations into class relations. At the same time, he takes issue with those theories which focus on patriarchy as being the cardinal dimension of social stratification. What Lockwood appears to be objecting to is the tendency to subsume stratification under the aegis of concepts derived from the analysis of the family and kinship. Society is not an extension of the family. It is not the family that constitutes the social order – on the contrary, it is the social order that constitutes the family. In the final analysis, it is the structures of domination and stratification in the public sphere that determine the kinds of interaction and inequality in the family, not the other way around.

Now this argument of Lockwood's is not new. To a certain extent it has been the prevailing sociological orthodoxy. This orthodoxy suggests that stratification operates in a sex-blind way. Men and women are allocated to classes or strata on the basis of a variety of objective indicators such as income, education, inheritance, etc. Nevertheless, despite this commitment to sex-blindness, it is still the case that the class position of the male breadwinner is seen as being the prime determinant of a woman's class position – at least in the case of married women (Goldthorpe, 1984). From this viewpoint, men and women cannot have different class interests because, by definition, they belong to the same class.

The counter-argument, deriving from Delphy and her supporters, is that the entire discussion of class and gender has depended far too much on Marxist and sociological concepts which disguise the real foundations of men's material exploitation of women. This is not the place to get involved in a detailed discussion of this controversy. Delphy makes a very strong case for considering the family as the critical site in which the material exploitation of women occurs. Delphy's earlier discussion of this issue (Delphy, 1977) focused on the two modes of production that co-exist in contemporary capitalist societies, the industrial and the domestic. Although women are exploited in the industrial mode, their primary oppression occurs in the domestic mode. This oppression, while having similarities to the exploitation of the working class by capitalists, cannot be theorized in the same way. For one thing, in the domestic mode of production, it is always men who derive advantages and benefits from the services of women – whereas in the industrial mode, it does not necessarily follow that men occupy all key ruling class positions. For another, it is the nature of the services provided by women in the domestic mode that distinguishes it from the industrial mode. The point here is that men expropriate women's labour and sexual services in a hierarchical family structure, a structure which is no less exploitative than the class system.

> If we were to use the same formal terms to analyse the family as have been developed for class analysis, namely, to see it as 'a structure of positions associated with a specific historical form of the social division of labour' we think it would be recognized that the family is a social system in which subordinates work unpaid for a head (generally a husband/father) and are in turn maintained by him (or provided with a contribution to their maintenance when they are in employment and earn some of their own keep). Dependents are also usually entitled to an inheritance on the death of their family head. The number and nature of family dependents is regulated by kinship and marriage (i.e. this is the idiom in which these work relationships are located). Dependents today are recruited mainly by marriage (they are mostly wives), the possibilities for family production having been much reduced. (Delphy and Leonard, 1986, p. 62)

The family, therefore, is the site in which men benefit materially from the services provided by women. Furthermore, the implication is that this benefit is not confined to a single stratum of men. Married men of all classes stand in an exploitative relation to their wives. Thus, although men may not constitute a class in the sense that they collectively identify with each other, nevertheless married men appear to have a collective interest in the maintenance of the marital status quo.

The Privileged Breadwinner

Perhaps the entire debate about the relationship between class and gender can be understood in the context of the assumed authority and power of the breadwinner. In simple terms, the person who brings a wage into the household is presumed to have some kind of privileged status in regard to other household or family members. In principle, one would expect that any household member who does so should be afforded status and some kind of authority. So, in a family in which both the husband and wife go out to work, there should be no real difference in their status. But the evidence is that even in those households in which the wife's wage corresponds to that of the husband, there is a peculiar imbalance in the household division of labour. In general, the role of breadwinner is considered a male prerogative, so even when a woman's wage is brought into the home, the male wage is privileged. This privileging is reflected in the allocation of household tasks. To be sure, if one looks at the recent explosion of literature and research on the father's role in the family, in relation to household tasks and child caring, we find that a rather optimistic picture has been painted by recent commentators. Fathers are variously reported as contributing to the routine jobs like house cleaning, washing up and child-minding to a greater extent than they ever did in the pre-war period. Some practitioners have even gone so far as to talk about the new democratic family in which the division of labour is not determined by the husband's role as breadwinner, but by the mutual negotiating strategies of each partner – who does what and when being decided by some democratic consensus. So, when the man is the breadwinner, this is due to a rational decision about his value on the labour market, and not to a belief in his innate superiority as a breadwinner.

This optimism about the family and the role of the father has been tempered by evidence which questions the notion that there has been a shifting in male attitudes and behaviour. We are bombarded with images of fathers cooking the evening meal and changing the baby's nappy, but these images often relate to the marketing of consumer products rather than to a real change in the sexual division of labour in the household (Lewis and O'Brien, 1987, p. 34). Why the male breadwinner should be so privileged is not simply answerable in terms of his superior earning power. In certain middle-class families women earn more than their husbands. This has still not subverted the sexual division of labour in these households, even when 'domestic help' is used. The fact is that this domestic help is inevitably female.

It is as though there is some over-arching meta-theory which legitimates the appropriate division of tasks in the household along gender lines. In actuality this division of labour:

> is not . . . one of a rigid division of tasks; it is not a question of women cooking and cleaning and caring for children and men never doing these things. Such tasks are 'women's work', are not valued highly, and are often invisible; but men sometimes do them. Rather, domestic work is women's work in the sense that the status, the conditions of doing it, the relations of production of this work are now nearly specific to wives. What makes it wives' work is not the tasks or even the sum total of tasks, but their particular organization. There is not a division of tasks, but a division of labour – tasks *plus* their conditions of performance and remuneration and status. (Delphy and Leonard, 1986, pp. 62–3)

It is the privileged position of the male breadwinner that determines the way in which the household structures its tasks. Although this position will vary, depending upon the historical specificity of the household, it is nevertheless the case that men are usually household heads. Such a state of affairs is obviously not accidental. It puts men in a real position of power. Now whether or not this position is to be defined as a class position will depend on the kind of version of class one is operating with. Certainly, married men cannot constitute a class in the Marxist sense because the Marxist analysis refers to the economy of which the household is a constituent part. But, if there is a division of labour in the household in which men appear to derive material advantage, then why should we not see this advantage as being collectively determined? It is not *one* man who is so privileged – it is the majority. Even though there are great differences between men, between workers and capitalists, they nevertheless all stand in a similar relation to housewives, namely one of dominance. Delphy's argument implies that, in the last instance, the structure of gender inequality is rooted in the domestic mode of production. It is not the class system which is the main determinant of gender inequality, rather it is the domestic mode which shapes the relationship of men and women in the industrial mode of production. More accurately, the domestic mode of production permeates the industrial mode. (The attribution of primary causal efficacy to any one domain or mode tends to obscure analysis.) Although we may shy away from claiming causal priority to the domestic mode, there is no doubt that, to a large degree, the domination of men in the domestic mode is echoed in the industrial mode.

What is at stake here is the problem of patriarchy. If men dominate both the industrial and domestic modes of production, if the male breadwinner role is privileged in the home and is given more status in the public sphere, should we not abandon any attempt to define this domination and privilege in terms of class? Should we not define this domination as patriarchy? In general, patriarchy has a particular connotation:

> Patriarchy, strictly speaking, refers to a particular form of the family, kin, household, lineage. It was this form which was found extensively in Europe before the modern period. Mann has reminded us, at that time the patriarchs constituted the society and what there was of the state. Such a society could reasonably be called 'patriarchal'. What we now have is what I prefer to call a 'male dominated gender order', what Cockburn refers to as the 'sex-gender system' extending beyond the relations of production. Mann uses the term 'neo-patriarchy'. (Stacey, 1986, pp. 220–1)

The question this all boils down to is whether or not the privileging of male power in the public and private spheres is to be conceived of as being qualitatively different from the privileging of the bourgeoisie's power over the working class. When Stacey (1986) refers to a 'male dominated gender order' does this mean that we can spell out the basis of this dominance in the same way as we can spell out the basis of the bourgeoisie's control of the means of production? If gender inequality is rooted in men's material control over women's labour and sexuality, then surely we are entitled to see this control as exemplifying a general relationship, provided we acknowledge that we are not talking about class in the standard Marxist sense? While the term patriarchy is problematic, it nevertheless points to the fact that there is a power imbalance in gender relations. Furthermore, it also suggests that this imbalance is generalized throughout society.

The problem, then, is to tease out what we mean exactly by patriarchy or a male-dominated gender order? I take it that one way of understanding male dominance is by looking at the manner in which men control women's labour power and sexuality. By control, I mean that men are in a position to allocate job and domestic responsibilities without reference to the wishes and needs of women. Can such control be absolute? There are certainly contexts in which men appear to have an absolute right over the labour and bodies of women. This was true of slave societies, and also was true of various kinds of family relationship in the past. However, in contemporary industrial societies, the presumption is that men no longer have this right. Now, while it may be the case that the public sphere is no longer the exclusive fief of men, in that women appear to have greater access to occupations and professions which were always regarded as being the province of men, it nevertheless remains true that this access is policed by men. Men are the 'gatekeepers' who decide and limit entry into professions, bureaucracies, union membership etc.

Accordingly, while millions of women have entered the labour force, this has not been associated with a corresponding increase in their power and influence. At the risk of repeating the obvious, men still fill the top positions in industry and politics. Even though we have seen women like Margaret Thatcher, Indira Gandhi and Golda Meier reach the pinnacle of political power, this does not represent a significant undermining of male dominance. Not only do women not earn as much as men, but they discover that the jobs they do are regarded as being inferior to men's jobs. In theory this should not be the case because capitalism as a mode of production is supposed to be gender-blind. In the Marxist sense, it is labour which defines what a human being is – it is production that gives men and women their social and cultural identities. In other words, if what a person does as a productive worker determines who he or she is, there can be no personhood outside production. Who you are will depend on your concrete relationship to the productive process. This meant, until recently, that it was only men who were treated as contributing to production.

Women were conceived of as being non-productive – they only entered history when they entered the labour force. What work they did in the household, in the family, was never really considered to be part of production, except in so far as it was seen to be functional for the reproduction and nurturing of future generations of workers.

Reproduction and Production

Recently, Hearn has persuasively argued that the reason for the confusion about the relationship between class and gender is that we have tended to subsume reproduction under production. Certainly, some practitioners seem to understand reproduction as being the reproduction of labour power (Hearn, 1987, pp. 33–58). Reproduction, from this point of view, is not about the actual material processes involved in the relationships between men and women, but is about the need of capital to ensure a ready source of labour. Hearn writes:

> Marxism is a materialist theory and a materialist practice. But it is essentially a materialism of production, subsistence and survival. Whereas in production, people produce things which indirectly provide the conditions for and constraints on their future, with reproduction people both produce people and are produced by others; reproduction directly and literally provides the possibility of existence in the first place. It is this – that is usually forgotten, or thought to be unimportant . . . Reproduction is both a form of relations between people, particularly between men and women, and also a form of reproduction of other new people. (Hearn, 1987, pp. 60–1)

Although reproduction is about the replacement of labour power, it is also a complex of relationships in which men secure the sexual, child-rearing and labour services of women. Reproduction is not neutral, it is not simply the means of replacing the human species. It can be best represented as being a series of 'moments' in which men exercise control over women. From the act of penetration, to marriage, to childbirth, to child caring, to the assumption of the breadwinner's role etc., men dominate reproduction.

This control will depend on the historical specificity of reproduction, that is, what rights men believe they are entitled to with regard to women's bodies and children. In the contemporary Western world, we assume that these rights have been modified by legislation, and the emergence of a morality which asserts the right of every individual to her or his body. The body is not supposed to belong to anybody else but yourself. It is presumed that it is only in slave and totalitarian societies that the body is at the disposal of others. One of the central tenets of humanistic liberalism is that the body is inviolable, that it is the base upon which the individual claims autonomy. In principle, therefore, men have no rights over women's bodies because women are supposed to be autonomous. Hence, to suggest that men dominate women and control reproduction is to go against the axioms of humanistic liberalism. It is also to go against those arguments which assert that one loses control of one's body by selling it as labour power to the owners of the means of production, the implication of this being that after the worker has sold his or her labour power to a capitalist she or he is left with an eviscerated and alienated body suitable only for basic biological functions. Indeed, certain versions of this argument go on to say that capitalism as a mode of production turns all bodies into commodities whose only value lies in their market price. But, again, this is to give 'production' a privileged status – it completely ignores reproduction.

Reproduction then is the site in which male domination is secured. Inevitably, such a statement lays itself open to the charge of universalism. It has to be stressed that we are talking about the historical construction of reproduction. Reproduction was not always controlled by men. Some theorists, like O'Brien (1981), argue that the historical origins of men's control of reproduction, was associated with their consciousness of their alienation from the birth process. As long as men did not understand the relationship between intercourse and conception, their control over reproduction and women was tenuous. It was only when they discovered the real facts about their role in conception that they constructed institutions to compensate for their estrangement from the production of children. In other words, it was their 'consciousness' of paternity which generated the whole structure of patriarchy. At the same time, the knowledge that they contributed their 'seed' to conception added an element of uncertainty about claims to the child. O'Brien suggests that it is this more than anything else that provided the initial impetus for the institutionalization of fatherhood, and men's insistence on women's monogamy and marriage. It was only through the rigid policing of sexual access to a particular woman that a man could be sure of his claims to his children. Marriage is, therefore, a kind of collective bargain among men that legitimates their control over a specific woman's sexuality and children.

The inference to be drawn from this is that men construct institutional frameworks to compensate for their reproductive inadequacy. Or, to put it another way, women's oppression becomes systematic only when men become conscious of the real facts of sexual reproduction. Accordingly, it is not the biology of reproduction that determines the sexual division of labour and gender inequality – rather, it is the consciousness of these facts which pushes men and women into imbalance. It is men's interpretation of biology which provides them with a rationale for domination.

In a sense, the discovery of fatherhood was critical because it enabled men to discover a common interest in establishing the means to overcome their felt reproductive inadequacy. It is central to the historical separation between the public and the private. As Hearn writes:

O'Brien's exposition of the link between the patriarchal control of production and the creation of the public–private divide is *based* in the process of biological reproduction, including the care of dependent children. Although there are difficulties of detail in her definition of reproduction – the case is made that men's exclusion from biological production, both from our semen and any 'subsequent' children under the dominant mode of reproduction is all-important. It is this that creates the material possibility for the discovery of paternity, the creation of the institution of fatherhood, and the division of the private world of individual fathers and the public world of 'men', that 'underwrites' *a mutual contract between men* in 'fraternity' to sanction private inhibitions in law and public political life. This is not 'some notion of psychic need or existential yearning for fatherhood' . . . but a material and political struggle. (Hearn, 1987, pp. 85–6)

The institution of fatherhood, the formalization of marriage rules and the objectification of women's sexuality, are historical and social processes. There is nothing about the concept of a mode of reproduction which necessitates the appropriation of children and women's bodies by men. Such an appropriation is a political act – it represents a means of redressing the perceived biological power of women to produce children. Now, whether or not we can go so far as to say that the entire infrastructure of male domination is rooted in the discovery of paternity is, to be sure, dubious. However, this is not the point. What O'Brien and Hearn (in a different way) are arguing for is a view of reproduction as a material sphere in which the main protagonists, men and women, may or may not stand in an antagonistic relationship to each other. In a *non-antagonistic* mode of reproduction, the central importance of women as both child-bearers and rearers was emphasized. Their role as nurturer was not necessarily forced upon them, but may have been a rational response to the exigencies of the struggle to cope with a harsh environment.

We know from the study of past and present primitive societies that groups find various ways of structuring the division of labour for child-rearing so as to free mothers for a great variety of economic activities. Some mothers take their children with them over long distance; in other cases older children and old people act as child-tenders. Clearly the link between child-bearing and child-rearing for women is culturally determined and subject to societal manipulation. My point is to stress that the earliest sexual division of labour by which women chose occupations compatible with their mothering and child-raising activities were functional, hence acceptable to men and women alike. (Lerner, 1986, p. 42)

Such a mode of reproduction, therefore, was not dominated by men. In contrast to the *antagonistic mode,* it was men *and* women who made the appropriate decisions about the allocation of labour between mothering and economic activity. A key question, therefore, is when did men begin to dominate the mode of reproduction? For Lerner this domination was achieved over a period of nearly 2,500 years, from the ending of the Neolithic age to the emergence of the state in a rudimentary and archaic form. It is in this long period that there appears to be a shift away from some kind of 'complimentary egalitarianism'. It is also within this time-scale that men learned about their role in biological reproduction. Now, whether or not this discovery led to the construction of the public sphere of men, and the confinement of women in the private sphere, remains controversial. Certainly, by the time the archaic state came into being, both heterosexuality and fatherhood appear to be taken for granted. Lerner argues that even before the development of a central political apparatus the mode of reproduction was controlled by men or, more accurately, 'The sexuality of women, consisting of their sexual and reproductive capacities, was commodified even prior to the creation of Western civilization' (Lerner, 1986, p. 212).

In other words, women were objectified before the advent of the state. The centralization of political activities in the archaic state provided a model for the future development of patriarchy, in that it defined the arena in which men could collectively enforce their control of reproduction, but even before this:

> Men-as-a-group had rights in women which women-as-a-group did not have in men. Women themselves became a resource acquired by men much as the land was acquired by men. Women were exchanged or bought in marriages for the benefit of their families; later they were conquered or bought in slavery, *where their sexual services were part of their labour* and where their children were the property of their masters. In every known society it was women of conquered tribes who were first enslaved, whereas men were killed. It was only after men had learned how to enslave the women of groups who could be defined as strangers, that they learned how to enslave men of these groups

and, later, subordinates within their own societies.

Thus, the enslavement of women, combining both racism and sexism, preceded both the formation of classes and class oppression. Class differences were, at their very beginnings, expressed and constituted in terms of patriarchal relations. Class is not a separate construct from gender; rather, class is expressed in generic terms. (Lerner, 1986, pp. 212–13, emphasis added)

Patriarchy and the Gendering of the Body

Here, in a condensed form, we have the critical elements of the emergence and construction of patriarchy. What is very clear is that this construction is about the way in which men appropriated the mode of reproduction. The fact that it was women who were exchanged, enslaved and used as sexual and labour resources and not men, suggests that men already acted as if they had rights over women and children before the emergence of class. The emphasis on production and the primacy of class, in Marxist and radical social theory, has glossed the lived relations of reproduction in both the private and public spheres. In this respect, it seems to me that Hearn is right when he argues that what is missing from standard discussions of reproduction is any sense of the sheer physical immediacy of the reproductive process.

In a sense, reproduction is about the way in which human bodies experience pleasure, pain and alienation. It is also about the way in which they have been systematically differentiated into genders. The 'gendering' of the body is a political act in which one person lays claim to another person's body and 'products', i.e. 'children'. The oppression of women is, accordingly, not only about the fact that they are unpaid houseworkers or domestic labourers – rather, it is about the extraction of what Hearn calls 'human value' (Hearn, 1987, p. 68). As I understand it, 'human value' is what human beings consider to be the intrinsic worth of other human beings. Such a 'value' will vary historically, but what is important about the concept, is that it can be used as a basis of exploitation and appropriation. 'Under the present form of patriarchy, it is that which is appropriated, dominantly by men from women and children, and ranges from the energy and creativity of particular people in particular situations to the whole person, their very existence' (Hearn, 1987, p. 68).

The paradigmatic example of such an appropriation of human value is the housewife who provides her husband with sexual services, goes through all the traumas of childbirth, nurtures and socializes children, does all the housework and is expected to accept this without resistance. The point about this is that even though this example may no longer be typical of the manner in which particular men appropriate human value from women, it nevertheless still provides us with a model of how society at large controls women's reproductive labour power. Even when fathers are absent, either through divorce or desertion, the fact remains that women put more labour into reproduction than men do. Moreover, by implication, they are also expected to do this without adequate compensation. Thus, instead of particular men who enjoy the particular services of particular women, we now have a situation in which the state extracts human value from women. What men extract from women is their reproductive labour power, their value as human beings. The state does the same in a more remote and abstract fashion.

This is not to say that we can really specify what the concept 'human' means, only that the assumption made by those theorists who stress the primacy of production tends to ignore a whole range of activities which make up the 'materiality' of existence. Reproduction involves labour – it involves a great deal of work on the part of women. Even in a *non-antagonistic* mode of reproduction, the burden falls on women, except that this work is not devalued. The devaluation of women's reproductive labour constitutes one of the pivots of patriarchy and the masculine ideology. It is the appropriation of this labour, or 'human value', that enables men to continue to dominate women, and by extension, to dominate each other.

The emergence of patriarchy (and the male appropriation of reproduction) did not happen overnight, nor for that matter did it always follow the same course. It might well be that in a variety of contexts, there were different reasons for its emergence. Whatever the specifics and reasons for the creation of patriarchy, it is clear that we are talking about a mode of domination which cannot be reduced to class domination. Although, from one perspective, history may be the history of class conflict, this perspective takes for granted the sexual division of labour, that is, to revert back to an earlier discussion, it accepts without question the 'incorrigible propositions' of gender. Balbus puts it this way:

> Although the capitalist mode of production generates its own reproduction requirements, in and of itself it does not determine the sexual identity of the individuals who are obliged to fulfil these requirements. That capitalism requires a reserve army of labour, private producers of labour-power, authoritarian social-izers, and 'expressive' nurturers, does not mean that capitalism requires that women monopolize these tasks. That they become the preserve of women is a function not of the capitalist mode of production but rather of the way in which this mode of production is obliged to adapt to a preexisting and persisting sexual division of labour in which men dominate women. It is patriarchy, not capitalism that determines the sexual identity of those who perform the various functions that capitalism demands, and, for this reason, it is precisely patriarchy that remains completely unexplained after an analysis of capitalist functions has been completed. (Balbus, 1982, p. 80)

When we talk about the sexual division of labour, we are already presupposing some kind of inequality and hierarchy. We are assuming that sexual differences logically entail male power. The argument advanced here, and it is certainly not original, is that sexual differences only become important after the establishment of male domination, that is, after men appropriate women's sexuality and reproductive labour power. Indeed, one of the basic commitments of any ideology naturalizing inequality of any sort is to insist on the importance of differences. This is true not only of masculinism and sexism, but of racism and classism as well (Mackinnon, 1987, pp. 1–77). In the case of racism, the naturalization of differences still underpins political and mundane discourse. Although various commentators emphasize culture rather than biology, nevertheless, it is the 'fact' of difference which provides the cornerstone of explanation for racist oppression. Be that as it may, what is important is that differences only assume significance as a rationale for inequality.

It would be useful at this stage to list the key issues involved in this discussion.

1　To claim that men do not constitute a class, in the sense that the bourgeoisie or the working class constitutes a class, is only true if we limit the discussion of class to production. We know that Marx and Engels discussed social reproduction as being intrinsic to production, but, as noted by a number of commentators, reproduction is never fully explicated or theorized in its own right. For instance, Hearn observes that in chapter XXIII of *Capital* vol. 1, there are at least six different versions of reproduction (Hearn, 1987, p. 46). Men are not dominant only because they control and own the means of production, but because they dominate the mode of reproduction.

2　If this is the case, then the implication is that the mode of reproduction is decisive in determining the structure of gender domination in most extant societies.

3　However, there is a problem here. When we talk about men controlling the mode of reproduction, do we mean all men? What about those men who do not marry, are not fathers and who appear to have opted out of marriage and family relationships? We could argue that those men who consciously decide to opt out of reproduction, or who join men's groups, have abandoned patriarchy, and joined the ranks of the oppressed. How then can we talk of men as though they are a homogeneous group with a monolithic ideology? Moreover, what about the instances of oppression of men by women?

4　Obviously, there are contradictions and disjunctions in the male domination of the mode of reproduction, and in the mode of production. For example, to take a well-documented case, in feudal society, this domination was flexible enough, to allow women to inherit and control property and fiefdoms. If there was no male heir, land and status would pass on to the eldest daughter (Shahar, 1983). The point about this is that even when women were in a position to exercise power because their fathers and husbands were either dead or were busy playing 'knighthood games' and journeying to the Crusades, patriarchy was not challenged. Women exercised power as 'stand-in' men. In the final reckoning, control of property always reverted back to the male line. What is important is that women derived their authority from their participation in a structure of relationships which sanctioned male domination. They could not assume authority in their own right.

Another example makes this point clearer. Even though the past few decades have seen the growth of other masculinities, notably powerful gay communities in certain parts of the United States and Europe, this has not meant that mainstream heterosexuality is on the retreat. Despite the oppositional stance of some of these masculinities, it remains true that they all operate within an over-arching frame of reference which legitimates heterosexuality as 'incorrigible'.

The Heterosexual State

It would therefore seem to be apparent that the term heterosexuality is crucial to any discussion of men as a collectivity or a class. At a superficial level, heterosexuality is often regarded as a descriptive term for the dichotomous model of gender; it is the way in which nature has programmed sexual relations in the human species. To suggest that heterosexuality is institutionalized goes against traditional commonsense understandings of gender and sexuality. So, when Rich (1980) talks about 'compulsory heterosexuality', Hearn (1987) 'hierarchic heterosexuality' and Carrigan et al. (1985) 'hegemonic masculinity', this undermines the whole basis of the world of gender relationships that is taken for granted. To use words like 'compulsory', 'hierarchic' and 'hegemonic' to describe men's domination of women is to transform biology into politics. Whatever term is used, the implication is that men benefit from the subordination of women.

What constitutes a dominant form of masculinity in any context has to be imposed, negotiated and legitimated. This means that there is opposition to the dominant mode. Today, this opposition is largely articulated in feminist theory and practice, and also in gay politics. Their opposition is not simply directed against individual men, but against the institutions that reproduce and legitimate hegemonic masculinity. More than any other institution, it is the state that guarantees and expresses the dominant form of heterosexuality.

the negotiation and enforcement of hegemony involves the state. The criminalization of male homosexuality as such was a key move in the construction of the modern form of hegemonic masculinity. Attempts to reassert it after the struggles of the last twenty years, for instance by fundamentalist right-wing groups in the United States, are very much addressed to the state – attempting to get homosexual people dismissed as public-school teachers, for instance, or erode court protection for civil liberties. Much more subtly, the existence of a skein of welfare rules, tax concessions, and so on which advantage people living in conventional conjugal households and disadvantage others, creates economic incentives to conform to the hegemonic pattern. (Carrigan, et al. 1985)

The state legislates for and enforces heterosexuality. This it does, not by directly saying to men and women that there is only one way to behave in bed, and one way to bring up your children. It rather uses the persuasive apparatus of the mass media, the school and the inducement of family benefit. The state has taken over responsibility for the mode of reproduction. But the state is not some amorphous abstraction. It intervenes in peoples' lives by laying down procedures and requirements for appropriate sexual and domestic behaviour. Its commitment to heterosexuality does not allow much leeway for negotiation. This is nowhere more apparent than in its attitude to gay men and women. This attitude is never neutral – it is saturated with negative feeling and rhetoric. Although recent government pronouncements on the gay community and AIDS have been toned down and even appear to be 'objective' in that medical and health problems are stressed, the hidden agenda is easily recoverable. In a sense, the state embodies heterosexualism, so that any transgression and opposition is treated as if it is a form of betrayal. And, indeed, betrayal is a central aspect of the discourse employed by the state when it attempts to contain opposition. For instance, the fact that Philby, McClean, Burgess and Blunt were Russian agents was compounded by their homosexual preferences. Their homosexuality was seen as being the ground on which their political activity was built.

The state punishes gender transgression in an uncompromising manner, not necessarily by making it a crime, but by turning it into a medical problem. It employs a whole army of professional experts and consultants to reinforce and define the boundaries of 'proper' sexual and gender behaviour. The state buttresses hegemonic masculinity by appropriating the discourses of biology, medicine, psychiatry and social science. It polices 'reproduction' by laying down guidelines and norms about the desirability of certain behaviour. In the case of homosexuality this is well documented in the work of Weeks (1977). Weeks argues that homosexuality only became recognized as a specific form of sexual identity in the nineteenth century. Before this, homosexuality was, in the main, a form of behaviour open to all men. Homosexual acts were considered to be immoral, against the will of God, but they did not constitute the basis for a homosexual identity. Initially this identity was constructed in response to, and in defiance of, attempts to make specific forms of sexual behaviour criminal and subject to medical treatment.

What is crucial here is the way in which the state took the lead in deciding what was normal. And we come to the heart of the matter. State-enacted legislation on prostitution, on child labour, on divorce, on abortion, legitimated a particular version of the family in which the father was both breadwinner and the upholder of heterosexual values. What had previously been a fusion between church and state was

now an alliance between the state and the medical and
biological sciences, of which psychiatry and sexology were
constituent parts. While the state was enmeshed in capitalist
social relations, it not only reflected the interests of the
bourgeoisie, but also the interests of 'men'.

One of the peculiar things about most discussions of the
state is that the obviousness of this last point is obscured by
reams of sophisticated theoretical analysis. From Aristotle to
the intricacies of contemporary Marxist accounts of the
nature and function of the state, the fact that it is men who
occupy the key positions in government has never been
problematic. During the nineteenth century, when legislation
about the family and prostitution was passed in the
legislatures of Western 'liberal' states, it was inevitably men
who were responsible for the drafting of the appropriate
laws; it was men who offered their professional advice about
childbirth and women's education. It was men who established
the criteria of normality in sexual conduct.

In other words, the administration of reproduction and
sexuality was securely entrenched in the hands of particular
coteries or networks of men who accepted without question
the 'scientific' discourse of experts. This last statement must
be qualified. It is not that male politicians suddenly found
that they had the support of the experts; rather it was that
their discourses were discovered to be more relevant to the
exercise of power than others. The state has always been
dominated by men, but what nineteenth-century biology,
economics and psychology did was to transform this domination into a law of nature. Both the social and biological
sciences provided administrators and politicians with discur-
sive resources to establish a natural foundation for gender
differences and inequality.

But, as Foucault has argued, the consolidation of any
discourse is never absolute, for the simple reason that it is
challenged by counter- or reverse-discourses. The state is not
a monolithic institution – it is composed of a variety of
institutional frameworks in education, law, medicine, defence,
education etc. All these institutions have particular ways of
defining the truth about the human body. At the same time
they are opposed by oppositional groups which contest the

official doctrine. For example, the discourse that enshrines the family as being the proper place for women to fulfil their essential biological role as mothers was challenged by nineteenth-century feminism, just as the turning of homosexuality into a medical problem led to resistance by homosexuals. Despite this, heterosexualism remains almost uncontestable at the level of government and administration. We only have to look at the way in which the full force of the law is brought into play to ensure sexual and gender conformity to realize that official discourse is male discourse. Nowhere is the law more direct and moralistic than in defending and propagandizing the sexual division of labour and heterosexuality.

> The state . . . upholds the sexual hierarchy through bureaucratic regulation. Immigration policy still prohibits the admission of homosexuals (and other sexual 'deviates') into the United States. Military regulations bar homosexuals from serving in the armed forces. The fact that gay people cannot legally marry means that they cannot enjoy the same legal rights as heterosexuals in many matters, including inheritance, taxation, protection from testimony in court, and the acquisition of citizenship for foreign partners. These are but a few of the ways that the state reflects and maintains the social relations of sexuality. The law buttresses structures of power, codes of behaviour, and forms of prejudice. At their worst, sex law and sex regulation are simply sexual apartheid. (Rubin, 1984, pp. 291–2)

Rubin goes on to write: 'in its most serious manifestations, the sexual system is a Kafkaesque nightmare in which unlucky victims become herds of human cattle whose identification, surveillance, apprehension, treatment, incarceration, and punishment produces jobs and self-satisfaction for thousands of vice police, prison officials, psychiatrists, and social workers' (Rubin, 1984, p. 293).

The state, then, represents the most abstract and the most violent aspect of patriarchy and heterosexualism. In its 'abstract' aspect, it disguises its patriarchal commitments by presenting a picture of rationality, objectivity, impartiality and 'sexlessness'. The 'liberal' view of the state is one in which it adjudicates between competing interests. In theory, the state is not supposed to express the interests of any one group. The liberal vision is one in which both men and women have equal access to key positions in government and the civil service. The reality is different. We only have to look at the way in which women are excluded from key areas of state activity to realize that the claim of equal participation is mythical. For instance, in areas such as 'defence' and 'law and order', the exclusion of women from positions of authority is obvious. Certainly women join the police force and army. One of the features of the past few decades is the degree to which various states have used women in defence and law and order contexts. But nowhere have they achieved equality in these areas.

The truth of the matter is that when we talk of the state as if it were some kind of abstraction, we tend to lose sight of its violence. Thus, in its 'violent' aspect the state is clearly male dominated. And what is also clear is that this violence is expressed in terms of a rigid and intolerant heterosexualism. The state is at its most vicious when the gender order is questioned. In the case of homosexuality, it reacts by treating gays as criminals, deviants or as abnormal. In the case of women who oppose the official line on the family, mothering, sexuality and the sexual division of labour, the state musters all its ideological and physical means of persuasion. A relevant instance is the recent history of the Greenham Common women. What outraged government spokesmen, the media and millions of other men was the fact that it was women who were cutting perimeter fences, lying down in front of cruise-missile carriers. This sense of outrage was not merely a typical reaction by state authority to transgression. In its virulence and nastiness it resembled the kind of response of whites to black opposition in societies like South Africa and the American South before the civil war. It dramatically highlights its coercive nature.

In seeing the state as an abstraction, we have tended to give it an almost neutral and benevolent aura. True, Marxist accounts of the state have stressed its link with class domination and exploitation, but what they have not done is to spell out the way in which it articulates the interests of men.

The Public and the Private

This discussion about the state must out of necessity involve us in the debate about the relationship between the private and the public. Mary O'Brien's assertion that the public sphere is constructed by men to compensate for their reproductive inadequacy is one of a number of positions taken in this debate. One influential position emphasizes the separation of the family from the economy and the polity brought about by industrialization. It is a point taken up again and again by mainstream sociology. The central argument here is that the world in the late eighteenth century was still dominated by a rural and agrarian ethos, in which there was no real distinction between the private and the public. It was only in urban contexts like London, Paris, Venice and Florence that it makes any sense to speak about this division into two spheres.

With industrialization all this changed. No longer was the household the unit of economic self-sufficiency. The family was now enmeshed in market relationships, which meant that men sold their labour power in factories and mines, while women were 'theoretically' supposed to remain at home and mind their children. I say 'theoretically' because the thrust of so much recent feminist scholarship has been to dispute this emphasis on men being the sole or even the main breadwinners for their families (Boxer and Quataert, 1987).

In any event, by the end of the nineteenth century the separation of the private and public spheres was supposedly complete. The implication of this argument is that both the private and public spheres are dependent upon structural and historical determinants which ineluctably encapsulate women in the home, and men in the factory or office.

The *pessimistic* version of this position is that the two spheres are subject to continuous fragmentation and atomization. At the same time the question of power is emphasized. The separation of spheres entails the subjection of the private to the public. Thus, the family does not exist in some isolated limbo divorced from the decisions of policy-makers and bureaucrats – it is policed and monitored continuously by state functionaries who set the limits of appropriate gender and socialization practice. In short, the public sphere is controlled by men who simultaneously control and dominate the private sphere. The separation of spheres, therefore, ensures the privatization of women and the ascendancy of men.

The *optimistic* version welcomes the separation of private and public life. It is founded on the belief that the family is a kind of emotional servicing station in which both men and women find some kind of relief from the harsh realities of the public domain. Various writers have suggested that the contemporary family, whether middle class or working class, is becoming increasingly compassionate and democratic (Shorter, 1975). Furthermore, they argue that the family is not only a refuge or haven, but is the site in which men, women and children affirm and negotiate identities which enable them to cope with the outside world. What are glossed in this version are the brute facts of power and manipulation. The image of the family as the supreme venue for the validation of identity and the consolidation of self-esteem presupposes a completely symmetrical relationship between husbands and wives, and parents and children. It is based upon the presumption that women are free to control their reproductive labour in the home, as well as being free to enter the public sphere.

Both the pessimistic and optimistic versions take it for granted that the private/public dichotomy is a fact of contemporary life in industrial societies. They also take it for granted that this dichotomy is expressed in gender terms. So we get a situation in which the public and private spheres tend to be given the status of fundamental principles of social organization with the family operating as the training ground for the public sphere. Indeed, if we examine the literature on the family produced by writers like Adorno, Horkheimer, Marcuse and, in other contexts, Reich and Fromm, we find it described as the main instrument of oppression in modern times; it is the instrument whereby the dominant patriarchal authority is filtered into the psychic system of 'masses' of passive children who internalize the 'need' for authority at the cost of individuality and spontaneity.

In Europe, it is the petty bourgeois family whom these theorists single out as the carrier of the authoritarian syndrome, a syndrome that had sinister consequences for the recruitment of an entire generation of young people into the ranks of totalitarian and fascist organizations.

What Horkheimer and others attacked most trenchantly was the prevalence of patriarchal authority in the bourgeois family. Generations of the father's dominance in the home was one of the main reasons that the bourgeois family reproduced the ideological structures of bourgeois society. Yet, there is a strange ambivalence to Horkeimer's analysis. While castigating patriarchal authority, he simultaneously argues that it is collapsing in the modern bourgeois family.

Writing in 1941, Horkheimer appears to say that the decline of the father's authority is a precondition of fascism:

> During the heyday of the family the father represented the authority of society to the child, and puberty was the inevitable conflict between these two. Today, however, the child stands face to face with society at once, and the conflict is decided even before it arises. The world is so possessed by the power of what is and the efforts of adjustment to it, that the adolescent's rebellion, which once fought the father because his practices contradicted his own ideology, can no longer crop up. The process which hardens men by breaking down their individuality – a process consciously and planfully undertaken in the various camps of fascism – takes place tacitly and mechanically – everywhere under mass culture, and at such an early age that when children come to consciousness everything is settled. Since Freud, the relation between father and son has been reversed. Now, the rapidly changing society which passes its judgement upon the old is represented not by the father but by the child. The child, not the father, stands for reality. The awe which the Hitler youth enjoys from his parents is but the pointed political expression of a universal state of affairs. This new relationship affects even the very first years of life during which the father image and superego are supposed to arise. Psychologically the father is represented not by another individual but replaced by the world of things and by the crowd to which the *boy* is tied. (Horkheimer, 1941, pp. 41–2, emphasis added)

The breaking of the traditional superego ties with the father is, in Horkheimer's view, tantamount to the surrender

of the individual (the boy, the man) to the state. The state
becomes the arbitrator of socialization and education practices – the family being nothing more than an assembly
plant turning out new generations of recruits for its service.
Thus, the discontents of life in 'mass' society are blamed on
the decline of the father's authority. Ironically, because the
patriarchal family has been the site of the oppression of
women and children during the past few centuries, one
would have expected its demise to be greeted with loud
Hosannas, but no – instead, it is mourned as the last bastion
of a sense of moral authority or, more accurately, the last
stronghold of individuality. The argument seems to be that,
once you dethrone the father, and demystify the superego,
this allows Hitler in by the back door. Recently, this
argument has been supplemented by formulations which
pinpoint the decline of the family as being the main reason
for the paucity of political and personal life in the late
twentieth century (Barrett and McIntosh, 1982, pp. 105–25).

Now, whether we see the family as being the last refuge of
individual autonomy, or as a privatized hell, or believe it to
be the breeding ground for a new kind of narcissistic
character structure, or as the mediating mechanism between
the state and the individual, it is entrenched as the core
institution of a separate private sphere. But it only achieves
this separate status with the advent of capitalism (as least
this is what the fragmentation thesis presupposes).

There is an alternative position which does not blame
capitalism for the split between private and public life. This
position focuses on the historicity of the distinction between
the two spheres, a distinction which is given an almost
universal status. The classic formulation of this view is to be
found in the work of those writers who superimpose the
distinction between nature and culture on the distinction
between the private and the public. In very general terms,
this line of reasoning is that women are nearer to nature
than men because of their involvement in childbirth and
child care. Men, on the other hand, have no such ties. They
transcend the limits of nature by directly confronting and
appropriating it. So, from the very beginning, they are the
creators of culture and the public sphere. Put differently, the

argument here is that the private/public distinction is rooted in the sexual division of labour, a division of labour which is as old as social organization. Hence later developments in capitalist societies, in which the public/private distinction is given recognition by political and social analysis, are merely moments in a long history.

Whether or not the public/private split is intrinsic to the sexual division of labour depends on whether or not we accept the proposition that the sexual division of labour is intrinsic. In this respect it is essential to grasp the point that the distinction between the natural and the cultural, and the public and the private, is made within discourse itself – it is a constructed distinction, a system of oppositions which has no real existence outside culture. To be sure, there is some kind of heuristic advantage in highlighting the difference between them, but these differences cannot be used as explanations. Nor, for that matter, can we leave the public and the private exclusively in the hands of men and women respectively. If we are to use the public and private as concepts, then we have to take account of what actually happens in the real world.

Both spheres interpenetrate. They are not encapsulated. Men, women and children exist in both. The family is locked into the economy and the polity. Although we might argue that the family constitutes a distinct 'domestic mode of production' in Delphy's sense, this mode interacts with the mode of production. Similarly, 'the mode of reproduction' is not insulated from the 'mode of production', just as the state and the economy are not the exclusive domain of men. At the risk of stating the obvious, women work, they also go into politics and government. The question is, therefore, why is it that even when interpenetration is taken into account we come across the bedrock of male domination? Why is it that gender relationships in the factory and the home privilege men and not women? It does not take much theoretical and historical sophistication to discover what we already know, namely that however you categorize the relationship between men and women we are talking about inequality. This inequality cannot be explained under the rubric of the public/private dichotomy. When we use concepts like 'Public

Man' and 'Private Woman', we must be very careful not to fall into the trap of reification. These concepts are largely aspects of male discourse. They represent a theme in social theory which takes the sexual division of labour for granted, and finds it almost impossible to operate outside a dichotomous model of gender.

This is nicely illustrated in Sydie's recent discussion of the relationship between gender and sociological theory. What is clear from her work is that mainstream sociological theory, and Marxism, have been put in a strait-jacket by biological and essentialist commitments to the dichotomous model (Sydie, 1987).

> Sociology inherited a sex-dichotomized scientific approach as well as the nineteenth-century cultural ideal of the dichotomized relationship between the sexes as appropriate to their 'natural' talents. The sociological concern with uncovering the laws of society and improving it was therefore coloured by this inheritance. In general, the resulting focus was on men in the public world and, when women entered the sociological picture, on the family and socialization tasks of women. This dichotomy was often accompanied, in the nineteenth century, by the idea of the moral superiority of the female because of her exclusion from the public sphere and her closer connection to nature. This doctrine of 'separate spheres', however, reinforced the seventeenth century masculinization of thought that had excluded 'feminine modes of knowing, not from culture in general, but from the scientific and philosophical arenas, whose objectivity and purity needed to be guaranteed'. The result was that woman was regarded as the mediating form between nature and culture. (Sydie, 1987, p. 206)

This bifurcation of modes of knowing and feeling in gender terms was, until very recently, the official orthodoxy in sociology and other social sciences. In the 1950s and 1960s it achieved some kind of sacrosanct status in American sociology under the aegis of Parsons and his followers (Parsons and Bales, 1955). This is not to say that Parsons believed that his distinction between instrumental and expressive roles was necessarily universal and inevitable – but, nevertheless, this distinction remains a very powerful and influential legitimation of gender differences.

The Danger of Categorization

In using such concepts as the public and private, the danger is that we tend to lose sight of the dynamics at work. We oppose the category man to the category women, and then completely abandon any notion of historical and cultural specifity. Similarly, in using concepts like the family and the state, we fail to unpack the multiplicity of contradictions in these terms. Accordingly, when we argue that men dominate the public sphere, we have to be very careful about spelling out what we mean by 'men'.

It is clear that the category men needs to be unpacked. In doing so we come up with concepts like compulsory heterosexuality, hierarchic heterosexuality and hegemonic masculinity or heterosexualism. Even these terms cannot be used in an all embracing manner. Not all men are heterosexuals, and not all male heterosexuals are dominant. To speak of 'hierarchic heterosexuality' is to presume that some men are more powerful than others. Although a large number of men may benefit from patriarchy and heterosexualism, this does not mean that they all benefit equally; similarly, not all women are equally oppressed. This is not special pleading; rather, it is to re-emphasize the points made in the introductory chapter about the multiplicity of masculinities which may co-exist with a dominant and powerful masculinity. So, while we recognize the pervasiveness of heterosexualism in the state and the family, we can also point to real divisions among men, to competing and other sexualities, to those men who identify with feminism, to the millions of men who do not rule *per se*.

An analogy may be relevant at this juncture, albeit not a perfect one. The coming to power of the National Socialists in Germany in 1933 was not supported by the absolute majority of Germans. Moreover, the Nazis themselves were not a homogeneous group (although the petit-bourgeois nature of their membership has been continuously stressed by commentators). By 1938, Nazi paramountcy was almost complete, but this is not to say that every German was now a Nazi. The image of the Nazi State as completely Nazified and totalitarian was never accurate. Millions of Germans never accepted Nazism, thousands opposed it, and ended up in concentration camps. To reiterate, not all Germans were Nazis. But it is the case that over a period of time enough Germans were convinced and converted to Nazism to make it seem as if it was generalized in German society.

As in the case of Nazism, heterosexualism is not total. Although the modern state underwrites gender divisions, supports the nuclear family, makes a distinction between a man's and a woman's labour power, it cannot manage the consent of everybody. There are counter-ideologies and practices in gender relations which continuously challenge the prevailing orthodoxy. And, like the Nazi state, the heterosexual scaffolding of the contemporary state sometimes assumes a terrifying aspect, especially when it encounters resistance, as in the case of the Greenham Common women and the gay movement.

In his analysis of 'hegemonic masculinity', Connell writes:

> There is an ordering of versions of femininity and masculinity at the level of the whole society, in some ways analogous to the patterns of face-to-face relationships within institutions. The possibilities of variation, of course, are vastly greater. The sheer complexity of relationships involving millions of people guarantees that ethnic differences and generational differences as well as class patterns come into play. But in key respects the organization of gender on the very large scale must be more skeletal and simplified than the human relationships in face-to-face milieux. The forms of femininity and masculinity constituted at this level are stylized and impoverished. Their interrelation is centred on a single structural fact, the global domination of men over women.
> (Connell, 1987, p. 183)

As Connell points out, 'hegemony' in this respect does not simply entail the imposition of an ideology through force, although this is a distinct possibility. Rather, it entails a continuous negotiation and management of discourse and practice by dominant heterosexual men. Hegemony can never be absolute – it is always challenged by other men and women. Hegemonic masculinity is built upon heterosexualism. And heterosexualism constitutes the 'single structural fact' that guarantees 'the global domination of men over women'.

Particular men and particular women may confront each other in a variety of ways. In *this* marriage, we may have evidence that a woman is dominant – in *that* marriage the reverse is true. In this factory *some* women may have authority over men. *Some* women occupy very powerful positions. So do homosexuals and lesbians. Yet, despite the variety of relationships, they all exist on the terrain of heterosexualism.

Even though it is both crude and misleading to speak of a homogeneous category of men ranged against a homogeneous category of women, we cannot deny the reality of gender inequality. The fact that men are divided among themselves along class and ethnic lines, and that competing versions of masculinity may be present in the same class or ethnic group makes the task of analysis difficult and confusing. But, if we accept some of the implications of Hearn's and O'Brien's discussion about reproduction, then it becomes easier to understand how men collectively appropriate women's reproductive labour in the family and in the public domain.

6

True Male Discourse

Recently, Robert Solomon has argued that Western humanism, and western culture as a whole, are marked by an invidious attempt to universalize a particular kind of human nature, a human nature embedded in the illusions of the bourgeoisie. Roughly, his argument goes like this. With the advent of industrial society and the decline of the old, closed, feudal society, the emerging bourgeoisie, through their spokes*men*, the philosophers of the enlightenment, defined their interests and ideology as if they were the common property of all humanity. Beliefs in the power of reason, a common human nature and individual moral autonomy were all aspects of what Solomon calls the 'transcendental pretence'. He writes: 'We – the white, middle-classes of European descent – were the representatives of all humanity, and as human nature is one, so its history must be one as well. This transcendental pretence was and still is, the premise of our thinking about history, "humanity", and human nature' (Solomon, 1980, p. xii).

Autonomous Man

Solomon goes on to argue that the two abstractions of an autonomous individual and a universal human nature constitute the fundamental premises upon which Western liberalism and humanism are based. All humanists accordingly pay some kind of lip-service to the individual and the 'democratic' universality of human nature but, despite these *universalistic* commitments, humanism was initially a *particular* ideology of a class in opposition to the dominant feudal and aristocratic order. The victory of the bourgeoisie, therefore, entrenched an ideology which made universalistic claims about human nature, but they were claims that were ethnocentric, and resonant of the European middle class, not humanity at large.

For Solomon, the entire fabric of Western bourgeois culture and society is based upon the 'transcendental pretence'. At the same time, he is particularly concerned to demonstrate how the 'transcendental pretence' is used by the bourgeoisie's severest critic, Marx, to serve as a new kind of universalism, namely the universalism of class. The humanism that Marx was committed to, or perhaps the early Marx, was by this token a radical inversion of the bourgeois ideology. In this view, the proletariat is the class of humanity or, more accurately, it is the class which will realize human universality and *brotherhood*. Nevertheless, the implications are almost identical. While capitalism spawns the most alienated kind of human existence by 'dehumanizing' workers, bourgeoisie, men, women, children, it also contains within its present contradictions the possibility of a future universality. So, instead of the universal bourgeoisie standing for all humanity, we have the universal proletariat. In overthrowing the bourgeois world, the proletariat, for the first time in human history, allows us to discover our essential humanity. It is this continued attachment to universality that Solomon believes to be a measure of Marx's involvement with the 'transcendental pretence'. The thrust of his polemic is, therefore, directed against the way in which local European views about human nature have been used to colonize the cultures and philosophies of other societies. In fact, what Solomon is in effect doing is re-emphasizing traditional arguments about the arrogance and exploitative nature of the Western ideological onslaught on non-European societies:

At best, talk of the 'human' is crude polemical generalization, an uncritical gloss of a million unknown cases based on a few casual experiences away from home. Talk about the 'human' is like talk about 'Orientals' or 'Americans' or 'Texans' or 'New Yorkers' –

indispensable for tourists and historicists but never to be taken
literally. If it is true that all generalisations are dangerous, then
talk of the 'human' is worse than dangerous. It is a pretentious
fraud, a glib generalization parading as an essence. And if we
still find it difficult to avoid the word, it must be 'under erasure',
as Jacques Derrida says, to be used as a tool of reference which
probably has minimal meaning. It is what seems beyond
question that needs questioning. (Solomon, 1980, pp. 358–9)

But if the 'human' is 'under erasure', then it follows that
other terms are equally problematic. Is dehumanization
'under erasure'? And what about the term 'man'? Surely if
any concept is problematic, it is 'man' or 'mankind'. The
trouble is that all these terms have become so entrenched in
everyday discourse that it is almost impossible to question
them without violating commonsense. At a very simplistic
level they include both men and women. But, as we have
already noted in chapter 3, the history of 'mankind' is the
history of male accounts and interpretations of that history.
Moreover, the history of gender, the family, sexuality, was
largely (until the twentieth century) the province of male
experts and theoreticians. In a way, therefore, the 'transcendental pretence' is not only about the universalization of
bourgeois human nature, it is also about the universalization
of male human nature. In most historical contexts, it is men
who define the 'incorrigible propositions' of gender. It is, in
Mackinnon's memorable phrase (MacKinnon, 1982), the
'male epistemological stance' that underpins theorizing and
discourse about human nature and society. Indeed, the 'male
epistemological stance' predates the emergence of the European
bourgeoisie and its humanist ideology. But, what is interesting
here is that humanism itself is saturated with notions of the
global and autonomous self – a self which is assertive,
rational and masculine.

Commenting on this, Toril Moi argues that:

traditional humanism . . . is in effect part of patriarchal ideology.
At its centre is the seamlessly unified self – either individual or
collective – which is commonly called 'Man' . . . this integrated
self is in fact a phallic self, constructed on the model of the self-

contained, powerful phallus. Gloriously autonomous, it banishes from itself all conflict, contradiction and ambiguity. In this humanist ideology the self is the *sole author* of history and of the literary text: the humanist creator is potent, phallic and male – God in relation to his world, the author in relation to his text. History or the text becomes nothing but the 'expression' of this unique individual: all art becomes autobiography, a mere window on to the self and the world, with no reality of its own. The text is reduced to a passive, 'feminine' reflection of an unproblematically 'given', 'masculine' world or self. (Moi, 1985, p. 8)

The question remains, of course, why does this kind of discourse about the 'seamless self' become such a dominant theme of academic and lay thought. It could be that it is associated with the emergence of bourgeois society and the ideology of bourgeois individualism, but this is to conceive of masculine discourse as an effect of class discourse.

In a relevant debate between Chomsky and Foucault in 1974, Foucault makes a number of points about the emergence of human nature and autonomous creativity in standard humanist discussions of the history of knowledge in Western society. This standard history makes two claims. First is the 'claim of attribution' which particularizes the context of discovery as well as naming and specifying the 'discoverer'. Everything new, therefore, must have an 'inventor' or a 'creator' (usually male). In other words, we have a view of the 'subject' of history (the individual, man, human nature) pitted against the 'collectivity' (the 'general', 'society' etc). The individual discoverer is positively valued in usual accounts of Western thought, while the collective is often defined as an obstacle or limiting condition (Chomsky and Foucault, 1974, pp. 148–50).

Secondly, there is the claim of 'truth'. Here the truth is primary, not the subject. The truth is not 'created' by humans but waits to be unveiled and expressed in history. When the barriers to 'truth' are overcome, then we may, if we wish, talk about discovery, provided we realize that, by discovery, we mean making known what already was or is 'there'. Foucault argues that both these two claims have been conflated:

the phenomena of 'collective order', the 'common thought', the 'prejudices' or the 'myths' of a period, constituted the obstacles which the subject of knowledge had to surmount or to outlive in order to have access finally to the truth; *he* had to be in an 'eccentric' position in order to 'discover'. At one level this seems to be invoking a certain 'romanticism' about the history of science: the solitude of the man of truth, the originality which reopened itself on to the original through history and despite it. I think, that, more fundamentally, it is a matter of superimposing the theory of knowledge and the subject of knowledge on the history of knowledge. (Chomsky and Foucault, 1974, p. 149, emphasis added)

Foucault questions the validity of this conflation. He objects to the assumption that the 'subject' is instrumental in discovery. Furthermore, the entire relationship of the 'subject' to truth is an 'effect of knowledge'. In his examples from the history of medicine, he argues that the 'claim of attribution' and the 'claim of truth' are not the critical considerations in attempting to characterize and describe the transformations of medical practice between 1780 and 1830. What happened in this period cannot be construed as the progressive application of subjective human powers to the world. What changed was the fabric of beliefs, attitudes and theories, constituting medical explanation and understanding. This change cannot be traced to the intentionalities of individual actors or subjects; it cannot be the result of conscious reason or the free play of the ego. Rather, it is indicative of a transformation of discourse in which new rules and logics arbitrate and legislate nature and human nature. In other words, there is a discontinuity between one period and another, a discontinuity which is not an effect of individual consciousness and agency, but which must be examined in its own right as an effect of discourse.

Now when it comes to nineteenth-century and contemporary humanist accounts of human nature, we are merely using a special kind of discourse and analysis. It is the analysis which constitutes the human. The mistake that humanists make is to equate the analysis with reality. The analysis may serve as an appropriate means to 'discover' the 'object', but the analysis is *not* the object. What we call human nature, the person, the self is a token of discourse, not reality. But while the idea of human nature once had a specific location in analysis, it has now outlived its usefulness as a site for further scientific and epistemological advance. The thrust of Foucault's argument is difficult and open to misinterpretation, but his critique of the 'transcendental pretence' has forced us to re-examine the foundations upon which our conceptions of social science are built.

Perhaps, what is missing in Foucault's position is any real consideration of the way in which the discourse of humanism and human nature was also implicated in heterosexualism and patriarchal discourse. Indeed, one of the problems of a great deal of structuralist and post-structuralist theorizing has been its apparent blindness to gender and gender inequality. It was left to feminist theorists to appropriate aspects of this kind of theory, while at the same time demonstrating its ambiguities and male bias.

'True' Male Discourse

It may be that what remains relevant in this theorizing is its insistence that the human subject is not some kind of 'seamless unity' or transcendental ego. So discourse which constantly pays attention to the autonomy of the subject, to the meaning of individual existence, is by this token not merely an epistemological mistake made by bourgeois philosophers and social scientists – it is, rather, a sediment, a relic, an archeological remain which operates in the contemporary world as a powerful impediment to newer forms of knowledge. Indeed, knowledge in this sense, is power. Social scientists who seek to understand 'human nature', who 'study' human behaviour, and who offer solutions and prescriptions for the treatment and amelioration of social and individual problems, are guilty (if that is the word) of fostering the illusion that they have privileged insight and knowledge about human beings, and that this entitles them to some kind of consideration and deference. The power that the psychiatrist has over the patient, the social worker over the client, the politician over the constituent, is a measure of the extent to which the 'transcendental pretence' is accepted at its face value both by experts, and their patients and clients. The belief, for example, that psychiatrists can 'tell' us something about human nature, that they can make real distinctions between the normal and the abnormal, and that they can, therefore, help us to understand and know ourselves as 'subjects', is not only arrogance, it is a claim to knowledge as power. More generally, the claim to knowledge is the claim of male authorities to power – it is this aspect of the 'transcendental pretence' that fuses truth with the 'male epistemological stance'.

One of the peculiar ironies of the decentring of the subject in both structuralist and post-structuralist thinking has been the 'authoritative voice' in which this decentring has been uttered. Foucault, Althusser, Lacan, Barthes, Derrida are not hidden from their discourse. We recognize their style, their argument, their presence. Just as behind Goethe there is Goethe, behind Kafka, there is Kafka, and behind Lawrence, the real Lawrence is indubitably present, so the texts attributed to structuralists and post-structuralists *and* to Marx, Freud, Kant, Weber, Hegel and Nietzsche are the products of particular subjectivities. Indeed, it was, and is, such a deeply ingrained dimension of humanist scholarship to search out the intentional presence of an author, that it is not surprising that even anti-humanist texts are read in this way. For instance, a consideration of Lacan's ferocious attack on the emphasis put on the ego in contemporary psychoanalysis is undermined by the peculiar way in which he defended his position and his intolerance of criticism (Turkle, 1978). What is very clear in any reading of Lacan is the authoritative voice in which he speaks, a voice which is firmly in the tradition of the male intellectual hero, from Socrates to Freud. It is not only the fact that Lacan is given the status of intellectual hero that is at issue here – it is also that his arguments are couched in the language of one 'who knows', that is, as a purveyor of discourse about the illusion of selfhood and the autonomous ego.

Nevertheless, despite the obvious masculinism built into the post-structuralist and deconstructive enterprise, it is the case that this enterprise has close affinities with the critical stance of various feminist approaches to the reading of texts, and their critique of patriarchy. As one commentator puts it:

> It is no coincidence that these theorists are all men: this is a consequence of the gender relations which have structured women's absence from the active production of most theory within a whole range of discourses over the last 300 years. It is also a mark of the particular conditions under which prestigious and powerful bodies of knowledge were and are produced. This is manifest in the professional institutions of science, social science, medicine and the humanities which exclude alternative forms of knowledge, in particular those produced by women under different social conditions of knowledge production. Examples include the medical knowledge produced by wise women and midwives in the past and self-help groups now. The fact that most theory has been produced, until recently, by men has not been without its effects on the theoretical writings among feminists. It has helped fire the move to reject theory as inherently patriarchal. This tendency has been given impetus by the impenetrability of many important texts for women without privileged access to higher education and by the fact that most of the theorists who have produced post-structuralist texts are themselves unsympathetic to feminism. However, it is important to distinguish between the political potential and usefulness of a theory and the particular affiliations of its author. If Foucault's theory of discourse and power can produce in feminist hands an analysis of patriarchal power relations which enables the development of active strategies for change, then it is of little importance whether his own historical analyses fall short of this. (Weedon, 1987, p. 13)

What is important in this respect is the manner in which a theorist like Foucault forces us to re-examine some of the ways in which various discourses become enshrined in practices. Thus the declaration of the human sciences that human nature was knowable implied that it is subject to some kind of ameliorative therapy. The neurotic, the sick, the mentally disturbed, the unhappy, the alienated, the sexually repressed, the deprived and the exploited can be nursed back to normal by the judicious application of the methods and theories of the social sciences, methods and theories which are 'authoritative' and 'rational'. In talking about damaged personalities, negative gender identities, impotence or about deviance and so forth, the social scientist displays his/her (usually his) 'knowledge' about the hidden meaning of the client's world. The client or patient comes to believe that the therapist or social scientist has at his/her disposal the means to unravel the presence behind the word, the real behind the symptom, the self behind the mask. In offering to decipher the 'significance' of symptoms, the therapist assumes the role of an expert who can cure and treat the root cause of the symptom. But this offer may turn out to be bogus because the client has taken at face value the therapist's claim to knowledge and authority: whereas, in reality, what has happened is that the discourse of therapy has become part and parcel of the discourse of the client.

Put differently, both practitioners and clients are participants in a discourse, in which both parties believe there is some kind of 'presence' to which reference can be made when certain terms are used. Moreover, as Foucault has forcefully argued, the discourse of the human and social sciences does not merely constitute this presence – it simultaneously constitutes its opposite, what he sees as some shadowy double or 'unthought':

It seems obvious enough that, from when man constituted himself as a positive figure in the field of knowledge, the old privilege of reflexive knowledge, of thought thinking itself, could not but disappear; but that it became possible, by this very fact, for an objective form of thought to investigate man in his entirety – at the risk of discovering what could never be reached by his reflection or even his consciousness: dim mechanisms, faceless determinations, a whole landscape of shadow that has been termed, directly or indirectly, the unconscious. For is not the unconscious what necessarily yields itself up to the scientific thought man applies to himself when he ceases to conceive of himself in the form of reflection? . . . The unthought (whatever name we give it) is not lodged in man like a shrivelled-up nature or a stratified history; it is in relation to man, the Other: the Other that is not only a brother but a twin, born, not of man, nor in man, but beside him at the same time, in an identical newness, in an unavoidable dualism. (Foucault, 1970, p. 326)

The attempt to express human nature in terms of some universal formula inevitably produces a frightening negative, a 'shadowy double' by means of which the true essence of the human is revealed. Nineteenth-century human and social science 'discovered' a 'natural' human nature but, simultaneously, discovered the fragile grounds upon which it is constructed. For example, in demonstrating that human nature is a bourgeois abstraction, Marxism points to commodity fetishism and alienation as constituting the 'Other'. Similarly, in arguing for the reality of the unconscious, Freud stretches the definition of knowable human nature to its limit – the 'Other' as the unconscious is always with us in a form that questions the very foundations of self-knowledge.

Hence, in centring upon the human, upon the 'transcendental pretence', the social sciences can only know what is human by what it is not. There is, in other words, no way of explicating human nature except in terms of negative definition. So, the social scientist as humanist can only express his/her image of 'positive' or 'normal' or 'healthy' human nature by the construction of negative counter-images. We can only get at the human if we know what the inhuman is. It is precisely this claim, that we can know and control the inhuman by the methods of science, and by the use of the appropriate kind of ameliorative therapy, that leads to the elevation of various experts (psychiatrists, sexologists, doctors, sociologists, economists, the various helping professions etc.) into positions in which they alone have access to specialized knowledge, and which enables them to exercise this knowledge in the name of humanity, mental health or a better future. Such a claim, if validated and legitimated, gives power to those who make it because clients, patients and constituents, find it difficult to construct counter-discourses which would allow them to challenge the voice of authority. Both experts and clients assent to the reality of neurosis, mental pathology, deviance, alienation and gender identity, but it is the experts who are in a position of power, not their clients.

In summary, the implication of all this is that the humanistic intent of social science and therapy is subverted by its practice, not simply because it is misguided, but because it is unable to appreciate that the object of its discourse, 'human nature', is a creation of this discourse. The belief in the authority of human and social scientists has led to the position in which their 'knowledge' is used to police human beings in the name of truth or health. Our prisons, mental hospitals, clinics and schools are not to be conceived of as educative and custodial institutions designed for the benefit of inmates and clients; they are policing institutions in which the object of practice becomes the adjustment of the individual to the requirements of the state, class or gender. In ministering to the problems of the 'maladjusted', the expert sets *him*/herself up as the arbitrator of the abnormal and undesirable.

Admittedly, this formulation seems to be overstated. It seems to presume that experts are always in a position to make arbitrary decisions about their clients. It also assumes that it is the discourse that determines these decisions. In attacking the 'transcendental pretence' and the doctrine of the autonomous ego, it seems to deny the very possibility of human agency. The trouble is, however, that human agency is often defined in terms of human dignity. And it is precisely human dignity that the 'oppressed' experience as missing in their everyday lives. In a very broad sense, it is the denial of dignity that informs feminism as a counter-discourse to masculinism.

The Problem of Dignity

But what do we actually mean by dignity, and how do we know it is missing? One contemporary answer is that dignity is lost when we can observe the consequences for individuals of the dehumanizing influences of technology and industrial society. This presumes that the concept dignity is equivalent to the concept human. Strip a person of dignity and you strip her/him of humanity. Obviously, this is tautological. Also, we are not sure what is meant by human and, by extension, we cannot be certain that we know what dehumanization entails. It may be suggested that we can only know what human dignity is by negative instancing but, as Passmore points out, such negative instancing can be very ambiguous:

One ought certainly to regard with an initial suspicion such
expressions as 'truly human' and 'dehumanizing'. The accusation
that the technological perfect society is dehumanizing is often
levelled, but seldom made sufficiently precise. Often enough,
such phrases as 'truly human' are used quite illicitly, as
polemical devices, to suggest that certain particular forms of
human activity, those of which the writer approves, are somehow
more 'in accordance with man's nature' – whereas other forms of
human activity are in some obscure way, not really human at all,
for all that they are undoubtedly characteristic of many human
beings ... The same criticism can be applied more generally.
Cruelty and envy are peculiarly human forms of behaviour; to
assert of someone who is cruel or envious that he is not 'truly
human' is undeservedly to complement the human species. It
takes a human being to be a Marquis de Sade, to construct the
concentration camps at Auschwitz, to wage war, to lie, to betray,
to hate. Man is never less an animal than in the depths of his
depravity. To describe a state of society as 'dehumanising' merely
because it encourages men to deceive, to lie, to be cruel is, on the
face of it, arbitrarily to admit as human only what is 'good'.
(Passmore, 1970, pp. 279–80)

This argument certainly seems to leave 'human dignity'
without any substance. Taken to its logical conclusion, it
would mean that any critique of sexual objectification and
pornography is simply grounded in some kind of moral
relativism; and I am sure this is not the point Passmore
wants to make.

It has already been admitted that, as a concept, human
dignity is both vague and rhetorical, especially when it is
tied into the associated rhetoric of the 'transcendental
pretence'. Manfred Stanley has proposed that dignity can be
rescued, provided we strip it of its 'soft' associations. He
suggests that there are three ways of talking about dignity –
namely the phenomenological, the constitutive and the
definitional (Stanley, 1978, p. 208).

1 By the phenomenological approach, Stanley appears to
   mean those events and actions that are immediately
   recognized as constituting indignities. In other words,
   this is similar to the notion of 'negative' instancing
   discussed above. We can only come to grips with dignity
   if we observe its violation in a concrete situation. We can

see that this particular woman has been battered and assaulted by her husband, and it does not take much theoretical sophistication to see this as being morally unacceptable to observers who might witness the assault. However, although we could multiply these instances, it is often difficult to verbalize the dignity that is being violated. In a sense, therefore, it is far easier to talk about injustice than about justice, just as it appears easier to talk about the abnormal rather than the normal. The problem is that, until recently, wife battering was not even regarded as being a suitable topic for moral discourse because it was not publicly visible. Indeed, violence against women was sanctioned by the notion that men owned or possessed women in marriage. In other words, men monopolized the discourse of dignity, and it was their perceptions that were 'recognized as constituting indignities'.

2   In contrast, the constitutive approach is premised upon the decoding of assumptions and presuppositions that make 'dignity talk' intelligible in our society. It is not merely concerned with 'negative instancing'. Thus, such 'dignity talk' is constitutive of practice, just as practice is constitutive of 'dignity talk'. If, for example, we assert that rape is a violation of human dignity, that it constitutes a gross act of violence by one person against another, then the talk itself only becomes intelligible if we grant that the act is reprehensible to a large number of people (women and some men) who have been subjected to rape, or who have some kind of link with those who have. The fact that they may, or may not, be able to articulate the rationale for their feelings of abhorrence is irrelevant. In general, constitutive rules are not formulated at the everyday level by people, except under pressure when they are called upon to justify their actions to themselves and others: 'the primary social significance of such rules is not their cognitive status in the minds of individuals, but their latent status as presuppositions of practice. They take on intellectual form only when people consciously seek the deeper

intelligibilities of their actions, which does not happen often' (Stanley, 1978, p. 219).

In the case of men, it is not often that they question the presuppositions of their gender and their masculinity, except when they are directly confronted with resistance and counter-discourse. Men do not become reflexive about heterosexuality until they are challenged by feminists and oppositional sexualities. It does not usually occur to them that when they pay lip-service to human dignity they exclude half the human race. The constitutive rules of 'dignity talk' in our society have limited applicability.

3 If the phenomenological and constitutive approaches to dignity are not satisfactory, then the definitional approach is also beset by difficulties, not least of which are the shaky grounds upon which a minimal definition of dignity can be defended and affirmed as being both plausible and existentially satisfying. We may point to indignities, and we also may try to tease out the constitutive rules whereby dignity is supposedly embedded in everyday practice, but we still may not be able to define dignity adequately.

Stanley rejects both motivational and instrumental definitions. In the first case, he argues that it subsumes dignity under the rubric of a concept of 'needs' which reduces dignity to the status of an organismic variable, and in the second case, he claims that an instrumental definition demotes dignity to being a servant of other ideals and ends. For example, the appeals that politicians make to their audiences are often couched in the rhetoric of human dignity as a means to an end. In other words, Stanley wants to suggest that there is more to dignity than sheer expediency.

What the 'more' is, of course, is the heart of the matter. The danger is that in looking for some defining characteristic of dignity, we might start floundering around in some essentialist morass that is no different from the 'transcendental pretence'. To search for the essential nature of dignity is as misguided as looking for 'human nature'. Also it might be that dignity is a local European concept, in the same way as humanism may be a Western ideology. But Stanley is a bit more daring. He believes that there is no society that trivializes the status of being human. Hence, if we look at the entire range of past and extant societies, there is not one of them that denies the status-worthiness of its citizens. Even Nazi Germany did not trivialize its chosen citizens. To be a German was not a superficial thing – it implied a whole complex of characteristics which were deemed to be worthy of self-respect. Of course, tragically, the same status-worthiness was not accorded to those who did not qualify as Germans or Aryans.

Minimally, therefore, despite cultural and historical variation, dignity depends upon the near universality of the non-trivialization imperative, an imperative we tend to take for granted at some pre-theoretical and ontological level. Conversely, we could assume that there will be no dignity when human beings are denied the opportunity for status-worthiness. Obviously, we can think of a host of examples in which human beings are trivialized (objectified?), the most horrific being exemplified by concentration camps, prisons and, at the everyday level, the way in which people trivialize each other in their interpersonal relationships. However, the non-trivialization imperative is not enough for a positive definition of human dignity. This, Stanley finds in what he calls the awesome potency of human intentionality:

> The dignity of the human status, then, resides in the extraordinary human capacity for intentional creativity (and, of course, destruction) humankind participates in that potency capable of world creation and destruction. Therein lies its mystery, its dignity, its awesomeness. This power if it is assumed to exist, transcends utilitarian definitions of personal interests. Respect for it rests not just on how it is used, nor even its recognition of one individual person. Human dignity as respect-worthiness rests in the sheer factuality of human potency and in the assumption that to be human is somehow to share in this power for agency, regardless of one's personal desires or merits. To no other creature of (profane) nature is imputed such potency for creative and destructive agency. The eclipse of honour is a crisis of one or another society; the possible eclipse of dignity would be an ontological crisis of the human status itself. Without dignity,

man would be *man* (as a biological object). *He* would no longer be human. (Stanley, 1978, p. 220, emphasis added)

So, dignity is implicit in the power of human intentionality. Take away this power and we are no longer dealing with human beings, but with animals or automatons. In its strongest sense, human dignity is: 'The respect worthiness imputed to humankind by reason of its privileged ontological status as creator, maintainer, and destroyer of worlds' (Stanley, 1978, p. 223).

Such a privileged status suggests that we have to accept that, under some conditions, 'dignity talk' makes little sense. Certainly, we have all heard stories about the absolute degradation of prisoners and inmates of custodial institutions who no longer have any control over their lives and who, according to various versions of social and political theory, are merely 'objects', trivial things. We can only believe in the status-worthiness of the human if we are prepared to grant that it is constantly under threat of trivialization, a threat which is a common enough condition in a world in which 'horror' has become such a dominant dimension of social life.

It may be that trivialization can be equated to dehumanization in a very special sense. If to be human means asserting human potency in a world of objects, then the absence of such potency implies that humans are themselves objects. To talk of dignity under these circumstances seems to be a nonsense. But, as Stanley maintains, it might well be that human potency is not trivialized – rather it is engaged in a self-destructive exercise. The gloomiest dystopian images of our time are not about completely conformist societies; they are rather about the consequences of excessive human potency, of too much rationality, and the fear of ecological and nuclear disaster as a direct result of the application of human powers to the world. The implication here is that human power is not simply awesome, but perverted, irrational and destructive. Instead of dignity, the human condition today is described in demonic terms.

Yet, as Passmore (1970) noted in the quotation above, there is a tendency to define 'human' in terms of 'good'. Why

should the behaviour of concentration camp functionaries be
any less human than the victims they are brutalizing? Why
should the rapist be any less human than *his* victim? Why
should the 'human' be defined in terms of rationality, rather
than irrationality, or excessive potency? We might answer
these questions by coming back to Stanley's argument that
there are phenomenological and constitutive grounds for'
dignity talk' in our society. The question is whether or not
we can go further and assent to his further claim that there
can be a minimal definition of human dignity which makes
sense in a world where belief in such dignity is subject to
trenchant criticism. Can we, in other words, talk about
dignity without being guilty of allegiance to the 'transcendental pretence'?

The 'transcendental pretence', as I understand it, refers to
the universalization of human nature – it does not refer to
human potency. To be sure, there may be difficulty in
specifying exactly what is meant by human potency. There is
also the danger that talk of human potency could lead to the
establishment of an untenable dualism in which potency is
seen as pitted against the intractability of nature. And there
can be no doubt that certain versions of 'hierarchic heterosexuality' and masculinism elevate the potency of 'man' in
the struggle against nature and women. Nevertheless, if we
do not accept some kind of formulation like Stanley's then
we may be faced with the problem of a debilitating nihilism
in which political practice is simply a form of expediency,
and oppression means absolutely nothing.

It might well be that nihilism is only a problem for middle-
class male intellectuals who have seen their cherished
values eroded by the force of circumstances in advanced
capitalist societies. If life is meaningless, if all action is
equally valid, if human dignity is merely a pathetic illusion,
then one can see the reason for the prevalence of pessimism
among male cultural elites who believe there can be no
justification for supporting any kind of political and moral
commitment. Why should one commit oneself to socialism,
when the evidence is that socialism betrays itself when it
comes to power? Why take any notice of feminist theory,
when inevitably feminism is yet another illusion of liberation?

If moral commitments and ideals have no substance when they are faced with political realities, then how can one defend such a nebulous concept like dignity?

The problem of nihilism is made more acute when we confront critical areas of collective activity which demand some kind of moral choice. Why, for instance, more than 40 years after the Holocaust, do Marxists, liberals and humanists in general believe that the fight against fascism was justified? Or, more appositely, why do the same collection of people still believe that fascism must be opposed now? A thoroughly consistent nihilist could not for one moment uphold any such belief. Our view of fascism is not neutral. For both liberal humanists and Marxists, fascism cannot be tolerated. Yet at the same time, it would seem that, despite their consensus about the need to oppose fascism (and sexism), they find it difficult to define what it is they think worth defending. Perhaps it would not be too far off the mark to claim that they are defending a version of human dignity, which they see as being negated by fascism's suppression of the human potency of so many of its victims.

'Going Beyond'

Ultimately, therefore, it is the intuition that fascism represents the final assault upon human dignity that makes it possible to state that we need to go beyond phenomenological and constitutive accounts of 'dignity talk'. 'Going beyond' does not mean that we cannot ground our defence of dignity on anything more than a vague feeling that human potency is at risk. Moreover, it does not entail positing a universal human essence – all it does is to point to the fact that humans tend to resent being treated as objects or, more accurately, they resent being made to *feel* powerless. Of course, it may be asked, whose dignity are we talking about? The loss of human dignity may simply be nothing more than the view of an observer who projects horror into the world. The 'critical theorists' who were so shattered by fascism in the 1930s did not reflect the views of millions of Germans who saw in Nazism the solution to all their problems, and who believed that the 'new order' gave their lives some meaning. In a way, it could be said that those who talk about the loss of dignity are very often *not* the same people who supposedly have been turned into Objects. The attribution of loss of dignity often comes from the perspective of outside observers (intellectuals, artists, writers, academics, etc.); this perspective may refer to *their* consciousness and situation, and *not* the consciousness and situation of the victim as object.

This objection is naive. If millions of people were herded into concentration camps and gassed, and if millions of others were busy destroying each other, then surely we are not talking about the perspective of horrified intellectuals. It must be that we are also talking about the reality of experiences which negate the foundations of a possible civilized life, and which mark the strongest attack on human dignity. The claim that intellectuals distance themselves from the pain and suffering of the world they observe is also not true. Enough intellectuals died in Nazi and Soviet concentration camps to make this claim ridiculous.

It could be said, however, that the problem of dignity is not solved by simply seeing it in terms of some 'intuited' notion of human potency. Furthermore, dignity is not necessarily understood in the same way by different classes, cultures and genders. Indeed, there are structures of inequality and domination which inhibit any belief in its universality. Thus, in some parts of the world 'dignity talk' is reduced to 'survival talk'. Famine, disease, the cycles of monsoon and drought, urban and rural squalor, and persecution are not conducive to theoretical discussion about the nature of human dignity. To speak of dignity in these circumstances can be the grossest self-indulgence. Yet, in the last instance, what other grounds are there for attempting to mount a critique of a particular form of social organization that makes these 'miseries' possible. What is the purpose of a 'critical' social theory if it cannot provide humans with a cogent analysis of their life, society and the prospect of a better future?

At one point in their debate, Chomsky challenges Foucault to defend and justify his position with regard to the possibility of the working class ever acting as revolutionary standard bearers for humanity. Chomsky believes and argues that the working class should only act in the name of social justice, that they should not forcibly overthrow the bourgeois state, unless they can do so in such a way that the end result approximates to a state of affairs in which the ends of justice can be met. Socialism must have a human face – it must allow for the development of human powers and potentialities. He says to Foucault: 'Give an argument that the social revolution that you're trying to achieve is in the ends of justice, is in the ends of realising fundamental human needs, not merely in the ends of putting some other group into power, because they want it' (Chomsky and Foucault, 1974, p. 186).

Chomsky's challenge is a statement of his belief in some kind of moral justification for political action. It reflects his commitment to an image of human dignity which is realizable in the context of a just society, although he is not so naive as to suppose that a just society must, of necessity, be a perfect society. Foucault will have none of this. He replies:

And contrary to what you think, you can't prevent me from believing that these notions of human nature, of justice, of the realization of the essence of human beings are all notions and concepts which have been formed within our civilization, within our type of knowledge and our form of philosophy, and that, as a result from part of our class system; and one can't, however regrettable it may be, put forward these notions to describe or justify a fight which should – and shall in principle – overthrow the very fundaments of our society. This is an extrapolation for which I can find no historical justification. That's the point . . . (Chomsky and Foucault, 1974, p. 187)

The point that Foucault is making here, and in other texts, is that when political action is justified in the name of individual freedom and justice, this justification is rooted in a certain kind of discourse appropriate to a certain kind of class and power arrangement. It is a discourse made universal by the bourgeoisie, so that bourgeois human nature served as a model for proletarian human nature. It is the bourgeois model that was taken over by Marxists and socialists, despite their claim that socialist humanism is completely different from the bourgeois version.

Foucault seems to rule out of court any notion of a politics which is centred on human liberation, or which speaks in the name of human dignity. As long as critical consciousness is concerned with the search for human dignity and the good society, it will end up finding the self-image of the bourgeoisie. More appositely, we could say that the search for dignity is really a quest for the essence of manhood, for the heartland of an ideal masculinity. In a sense, the definition of dignity in terms of 'the extraordinary capacity for intentional creativity – and destruction' is a version of the masculine ideology. It assumes that nature is there to be dominated and challenged, but not only nature – other men and women are also subject to the intentionality of those men who 'make' history. In standard versions of European history, we have been presented with an image of men as explorers, as conquerors, as frontiersmen, as lonely intellectual heroes who battle to push back the limits imposed by the ignorance of the masses. The picture of history as the history of great men is obviously no longer fashionable, but it still remains embedded in aspects of contemporary consciousness. Take, for example, the controversy about the influence of Hitler on National Socialism. In some histories, Hitler is given prime responsibility for the ideology and practice of Nazism. But it is not only Hitler, the same claims have been made about Stalin and Napoleon.

To be sure, different epochs and cultures have different models of heroism. Today, the great man is not a politician or a military man. Heroes are media constructions like Clint Eastwood and Sylvester Stallone, or they are great sportsmen. This is not to say that contemporary heroes are simply eviscerated media abstractions – rather, it is to emphasize the relative constancy of the male appropriation of heroism. Although greater coverage is now given to women in sport, especially in athletics and tennis, this coverage remains condescending and limited. Indeed, it can be argued that the near male monopoly over sport is a central mechanism in maintaining gender division in most industrial societies. An interesting instance of this is the way in which girls have been excluded from participating in school league football in England. Football is supposedly a man's and boy's game which is not 'suitable' for women and girls. This has led to school football being divided into two leagues along gender lines.

> As in other sports, historically, sealing off women in separate organizations is a device which, while conceding male monopoly over the whole sport, also seals off the established game as a male preserve. It is particularly important, from the point of view of maintaining the status quo, to prevent interruption of the established processes of male identity formation and socialization in the schools; for to be effective, socialization with respect to this process has to take place at a relatively early age. De-differentiation at the school level in physical activity poses a threat to one of the main bases of gender divisions. (Hargreaves, 1986, p. 177)

The exclusion of women from direct participation with men in sport echoes other exclusions. Exclusion from power is in reality a denial of dignity to the excluded. It is a way of saying that the excluded group has no 'respect-worthiness', that whatever potency and power they may possess is irrelevant and trivial. In the case of the millions of black South Africans who are denied participation in the political process, this is equivalent to ignoring their lived experience as intentional human beings. In general, the excluded group may be stigmatized as deserving of trivialization, either because of some intrinsic defect or because of moral depravity which disqualifies them from being treated as respect-worthy. If we look at the way in which gay men and lesbians are defined as being both naturally and morally defective, we can readily see how it is their 'respect-worthiness' which is being attacked.

Trivialization and Objectification

This leads to a central question. How is it that those in power tend to trivialize those they oppress or dominate? A simple answer is that they fear the oppressed group, that they are frightened by their implicit 'human potency'. Thus, men oppress women because they have an intuition of their potency, their potential and actual power. This implies that oppression can never be total because, if this were the case, the term itself would be meaningless. It would be absurd to maintain that we can oppress a stone or any other inanimate object. The paradigmatic case of the master–slave relationship illustrates this. The fact that the slave had no recourse to law, that as a person she or he was completely at the mercy of the slave owner, does not entitle us to draw the conclusion that the slave was devoid of respect-worthiness and potency. Granted that slaves were trivialized and objectified, yet this did not entail their absolute degradation (Genovese, 1975). In the long run, slaves, and other stigmatized and oppressed groups, resist and find the means of proclaiming their dignity, albeit not in terms of a ready-made theory of respect-worthiness. This is not to say that an oppressed group will always manage to assert its dignity in a contest in which it attempts to secure its autonomy and freedom. The present struggle in South Africa between the white supremacists and the black majority has no necessary quick and optimistic resolution.

A relevant concern here is focused on the manner in which this objectification is expressed and represented in pornography, rape and anti-gay practice. It is not my purpose to replicate in detail the arguments of Dworkin and others about the extreme objectification of women, except in reiterating their point that pornography and sexual violence are so sedimented and entrenched in our culture that we almost take them for granted. It is my argument, however, that most men do not find this state of affairs objectionable precisely because they implicitly deny women both respect-worthiness and potency. This denial is so fundamental that it is not surprising, when somebody like Andrea Dworkin exposes the degree to which women are subjected to sexual terror and violence at both the individual and collective level, that she is attacked by a veritable host of indignant commentators who accuse her of exaggeration and bias. What is denied, ignored and ridiculed is the testimony of those women, gays and others who have been subjected to the most horrific kinds of degradation by men in both official and unofficial capacities. As Dworkin writes:

> The accounts of rape, wife beating, forced childbearing, medical butchering, sex-motivated murder, forced prostitution, physical mutilation, sadistic psychological abuse, and the other common-places of female experience that are excavated from the past or given by contemporary survivors should leave the heart seared, the mind in anguish, the conscience in upheaval. But they do not. No matter how often these stories are told, with whatever clarity or eloquence, bitterness or sorrow, they might as well as have been whispered in sand: they disappear, as if they were nothing. The tellers and the stories are ignored or ridiculed, threatened back into silence or destroyed, and the experience of female suffering is buried in cultural invisibility and contempt. Because women's testimony is not and cannot be validated by the witness of men who have experienced the same events and given them the same value, the very reality of abuse sustained by women, despite its overwhelming pervasiveness and constancy, is negated. It is negated in the transactions of everyday life, and it is negated in the history books, left out, and it is negated by those who claim to care about suffering but who are blind to this suffering.
>
> The problem simply stated, is that one must believe in the existence of the person in order to recognize the authenticity of her suffering. (Dworkin, 1983, pp. 20–1)

We must believe in the dignity of those who report their suffering. But this is ruled out of court by the presumption that a theory of suffering is 'subjective' and 'experiential'. It is simply a counter-discourse whose status is of no more significance than the discourse which legitimizes the practice. The point is that we have become so obsessed with deconstructing 'true' discourse that we find it almost impossible to give credence to those who testify from the front-line of suffering. When I say 'we', I mean 'we' as men. Suffering does not go away when it is exposed to the full blast of analytical social science. It does not go away because 'men-as-theorists' ignore the evidence of women who tell of their husband's brutality.

Reference must be made again to the notion of potency. If human beings lose this potency as a result of the action of other humans, or if they surrender their belief in their own potency when faced with horrific circumstances, are we not entitled to see this as a very definite 'loss'? What is lost is not some kind of essence, but the freedom to act. We are horrified by concentration camps not simply because of our moral sensibility, but because they represent, in some ultimate way, the complete denial of intentionality and potency. The loss of potency is real, it is not something dreamed up by sentimental liberal commentators. And yet, when 'men-as-theorists' are confronted with the testimony of women about their experience of rape in marriage, they are not taken seriously because somehow or other this testimony is regarded as fictional and ideologically suspect. 'Men-as-theorists' and moral commentators, especially if they have access to analytical and critical discourse, find it very difficult to come to terms with loss of dignity and oppression. To be sure, before the emergence of the anti-humanist turn in social and cultural theory, men as critical theorists were committed to the proposition that loss of dignity could be explained politically, and restored through the appropriate emancipatory action. But, of course, this is to suggest that critical theorists knew what dignity is and, as we have observed, the attempt to define dignity is beset by all sorts of difficulty, particularly when it is defined in essentialist terms. However, if we argue that dignity and intentionality are coterminous, as Stanley does, then indignity can be seen as the denial of intentionality or potency by forces external to a person.

It is easy enough, from this point of view, to discover indignity in empirical terms. We look at the Soviet Union and we talk about the absence of human rights and freedoms; we examine the South African situation and find it is impossible not to be overwhelmed by the evidence of mass indignity; we are shocked by unemployment statistics that reveal the extent to which millions of people are subject to the whims of government policy and the operation of market forces; we attribute all these indignities to the coercive power of economic and political institutions. So, accordingly, the implication is that dignity is problematic in a society whose rationale is premised upon impersonal market forces and/or instrumental rationality.

This is as far as 'critical theory' goes. With the possible exception of Marcuse, the problem of gender inequality and male power has not been central to its view of human oppression. They did not come to grips with the kind of 'indignities' that Dworkin writes about. Rape and pornography, if considered at all, were described as being effects of mass society and the market.

Heterosexualism and the Denial of Intersubjectivity

Perhaps this the place to take stock of my argument in order to make exactly clear what is at stake.

1 My concern has been to take issue with the kind of theorizing that purports to speak authoritatively for humanity. Solomon calls this the 'transcendental pretence'. Ever since the bourgeoisie emerged as the dominant class in European society, it has equated its self-image with the self-image of humanity. In a disguised form this self-image has also filtered into the Marxist account of the universal nature of class.

2 An additional and, perhaps, more fundamental concern is the way in which the 'transcendental pretence' remains an untheorized dimension of the 'male epistemological stance'. The attack on bourgeois thought and ideology mounted by Marx, and the critique of rationality deriving from psychoanalysis, were only partly successful in exposing the flimsy foundations of those discourses which purported to reveal the 'truth' about human nature. Both Marxism and psychoanalysis themselves assume the status of 'true discourses'. Moreover, they never face up to their implicit 'masculinism'. They do not acknowledge their commitment to the 'incorrigible propositions of gender' (although, in the case of Freud, it is true that he

was more explicit about his acceptance of the necessity of heterosexuality). I suppose it is Foucault more than anybody else who challenged the illusory basis of the 'transcendental pretence'. His analysis and critique of the claims of the human and social sciences has made it possible for us to understand the powerful grip that various discourses of the 'true' have on our consciousness. Also, he points to the emergence of 'reverse' or 'counter'-discourses which allow the subject of discourse to speak. Thus, in *The History of Sexuality*, the category of the homosexual moves away from the margins of history and assumes the status of a speaking subject who demands legitimacy in terms of the criteria used by institutionalized medical and judicial discourses (Foucault, 1981). It is worth quoting Foucault at this point:

> There is no question that the appearance in the nineteenth century psychiatry, jurisprudence, and literature of a whole series of discourses on the species and subspecies of homo-sexuality, inversion, pederasty, and 'psychic hermaphrodism' made possible a strong advance of social controls into this area of 'perversity'; but it also made possible the formation of a 'reverse' discourse: homosexuality began to speak in its own behalf, to demand that its legitimacy or 'naturality' be acknowledged, often in the same vocabulary, using the same categories by which it was medically disqualified. (Foucault, 1981, p. 101)

However, the fact that homosexuality begins 'to speak in its own behalf' does not mean that it necessarily challenges the discourse of 'perversity' which gives it its vocabulary. The fact is that this discourse is the discourse of 'hegemonic masculinity' or 'hierarchic heterosexuality'. It is a privileged discourse which glosses and distorts the interests of powerful groups of men. To be sure, these interests cannot be described simply in the language of traditional political and social theory. Yet, if we ask what interest does 'hierarchic heterosexuality' have in continu-ously denying 'homosexuality' any access to institutional influence and authority, then it is easy enough to discover the empirical and material grounding of this interest.

3   In excluding and denying gays political and cultural influence, privileged male discourse explicitly differentiates between the status-worthiness of different categories of human. It denies them the privilege of dignity and intentionality. This, it seems to me, is the truth about privileged male discourse and 'hierarchic heterosexuality'. It cannot comprehend that 'others' have intentionalities – it cannot comprehend the 'dignity' it excludes.

4   This is what is really meant by objectification. It is a belief that only some people deserve the status of persons. This may sound simplistic and naive, but we only have to look at pornography to see how this is exemplified. But there is something more at stake here. Pornography not only trivializes women, it also portrays them as willingly accepting objectification. In other words, pornography is not merely a question of 'representation' – it is also about the producers and consumers of pornography – it is about the subjectivity of men who make and view 'snuff' movies and write and read the countless millions of pornographic publications.

> The objectification of women means the simultaneous subjectification of men. The relationship is usually put the other way around, as Simon de Beauvoir notes: 'He is the Subject, he is the Absolute – she is the Other . . . The discussion of the objectification of women in our culture concerns the *gender* of women . . . the objectifier, the surveyor of women is the male gender . . . .
> The objectification of women is a result of the subjectification of man. He is a pure subject in relation to an object, which means that he is not engaging in exchange or communication with that objectified person who, by definition, cannot take the role of the subject . . . Social relationships are relationships between subjects: if there is exchange or communication, each partner is and remains a subject and agent of action, or a subject of speech and communication. The roles are reciprocal, the situation is one of intersubjectivity. (Kappeler, 1986, pp. 49–51)

Objectification implies a denial of intersubjectivity. There can be no real communication between the subject and the object because, by definition, the object is not a person, is devoid of status-worthiness. In Hegel's discussion of the master–slave relationship, the master attempts to dominate the slave by treating him or her as a thing without feeling and intentionality. But, in so doing, he can no longer communicate with the slave. For all practical purposes intersubjectivity is dead. The master as subject receives no 'recognition' from the objectified slave. Ironically, therein lies the possibility of the slave's freedom. The slave begins to 'recognize' that it is his or her labour that transforms the world. The object becomes conscious of potential power. Objectification, then, implies the potentiality for self-consciousness. The object talks back, rebels and overthrows the objectifier. The slave becomes the subject of history. In simpler language, the master knows that the slave can never really be absolutely objectified. He has an intuition of the slave's potential capacity to resist. He fears the slave's resentment, and knows that the only way to hold on to what he possesses is constantly to be on his guard. Although slaves 'cannot take the role of the subject', they nevertheless begin to suspect that the master is afraid of them. Why else does the master employ guards and overseers to police their labour? So, even though intersubjectivity has broken down between slave and master, this does not mean that they are not conscious of each other's power.

5   It is the coming to consciousness of the objectified or oppressed group that sets the alarm bells ringing for the 'objectifiers'. Once an oppressor concedes that the colonized or enslaved group is capable of resistance, then it becomes even more imperative to deny them status-worthiness. Now that feminism and the gay movement directly challenge 'hierarchic heterosexuality' in the political and cultural arenas, it is clear that its defences are being strengthened and reinforced by more sophisticated discourses and practices. Indeed, the 'discovery' of

heterosexualism has given the 'male epistemological stance' a cause.

The incorrigible propositions of gender now have a useful name, a name which is invoked whenever the family or marriage is threatened by other sexualities and practices. Heterosexualism is now being constructed and articulated in a very self-conscious and deliberate fashion. Recent texts by Scruton and Mount are examples of the systematic manner in which 'heterosexualism' is being theorized and defended (Mount, 1982; Scruton, 1986).

In very simple terms, this means that the objectifiers are frightened of the objectified. Nowhere is this better illustrated than in the consistent attempt to control and treat 'homosexuality'. Anti-gay attitudes are not peripheral to 'hierarchic heterosexuality' – they are at the very centre of its practice. Although we are witnessing the politicization of the gay movement, and we have seen some notable political victories in the area of gay rights, it is also evident that these victories have been partly responsible for a vicious counter-attack by the defenders of 'hierarchic heterosexualism'. The challenge that 'gay politics' presents to the assumptions taken for granted in official heterosexual discourse and practice is being met by the resuscitation of old stereotypes and moral panics. The current stigmatization of gay men as being responsible for AIDS echoes the language and stereotypes of racism. The virulence of the reaction is suspiciously like the National Socialist appropriation of anti-semitism. As one writer puts it:

Today the general mood is grim. Everyone is either melancholy or anxious, afraid not only of AIDS but the growing signs of hostility toward gay men and women. It is chilling when the *New York Times* purportedly in the interests of balanced journalism, publishes William F. Buckley in support of tattooing homosexual men and intravenous drug-users, while the word 'quarantine' quivers between the lines of the article. (I naively waited for letters of protest from both the Jewish and gay communities. Wouldn't Jews be disgusted by the parodic horror of the suggestion? (Kleinberg, 1987, p. 133)

The juxtaposition of anti-gay discourse and racism is not accidental. In both, there is an attempt to objectify and trivialize human intentionality. In the case of anti-semitism, especially in its Nazi form, the Jews were given a terrifying aura of power and sexuality. Not only were Jewish men the seducers of Aryan women, but they were also responsible for the defeat of Germany in the First World War, and for the revolutionary upsurge which followed. They were perceived as a threat to the very foundations of German nationhood. Jews were polluters of Aryan culture. The same kind of imagery is being used today by 'hierarchic heterosexuals'. Like anti-semitism, homophobia involves intense passion and feeling. It is not simply the snide remarks in the pub or the anti-gay joke of a television comedian, rather it is the contempt and hatred which gay men and women experience in all the interstices of everyday life. Like blacks and Jews, gay people are seen as dangerous, as an insult to traditional masculinity. Why such hatred and virulence?

One possible answer, is that 'hierarchic heterosexuals' understand at some subliminal level that all gender ascriptions and typification are tentative and fragile, and that, therefore, the only way to hold on to what they have is to use force and other coercive means. The universal acknowledgement that gender is a social construction would lead to the breakdown of the existing gender order. Moreover, such an acknowledgement would entail admitting that their own heterosexuality is suspect and flawed. To suspect that you are like those you hate and despise is tantamount to hating and despising yourself. 'Hierarchic heterosexuals' find it threatening to come to terms with these suspicions. In a sense, 'hierarchic heterosexualism' is built upon the idea of the unity of the male self, the 'seamless' self. It sees itself, as rational, transcendental and completely sure of its place in the world. Such a self cannot tolerate contradiction and ambiguity. To have doubts about one's sexuality and moral authority is to lose control of one's intentionality.

And, it is precisely at this level that gay politics has caused anxiety to 'hierarchic heterosexuals'. To demonstrate that masculinity is a construction which is located in social and historical practice, and also to question the myth of the valorized penis, is to undermine the authority of the seamless heterosexual self. In other words, it is the threat that gay politics and feminism poses to the power of 'hierarchic heterosexuals' that has unleashed their ferocious counter-attack at the legislative and societal levels (a case in point being the recent law passed in parliament to forbid the promotion of homosexuality in education). However, there is a danger in conceiving of this reaction as if it had something to do with the pathology of individual heterosexuals. It is not their pathology which is at issue here, rather it is the whole structure of gender oppression.

In this respect, the term homophobia may not be appropriate because of its association with mental illness. Racism is not about the pathology of prejudiced persons, neither is sexism. The oppression of gays cannot be conceived of as simply the homophobic reactions of this or that man. This argument is put powerfully by Kitzinger:

> The concept and operationalized definition of homophobia advances the cause of liberal humanism by appealing to individuocentric explanations of a sociopolitical phenomenon (blaming individuals who supposedly deviate from the rest of society in being prejudiced against homosexuals) ... The term derives from a psychology which has always reserved for itself the right to decide who is and who is not sick, and for which ... classifying homophobics as sick is far less threatening than any attempt to look at the issue in political terms. Psychology's achievement in popularizing the concept of homophobia, not only among its middle-class public generally but also in the gay, feminist and lesbian movements, represents a considerable success for liberal humanistic ideology. (Kitzinger, 1987, p. 61)

It also 'represents a considerable success' for 'hierarchic heterosexualism', in that it allows the male expert to establish the 'truth' about gay people and the pathological hostility towards them. If both homophobia and homosexuality are individual problems, then all that is needed is some kind of medical or psychiatric therapy to doctor them back to normality. This leaves the status quo intact.

6 The argument of this chapter (and the book) is that masculinism as an ideology universalizes 'man' as the 'maker' of history. It is male intentionality which conquers nature and pushes forward the limits of knowledge. Man is the 'subject' of history. More appositely, it is 'heterosexual man' who theorizes and knows about the world. The implication of this is that not everybody is perceived as being capable of intentionality. Objects have no subjectivity. Hence people without intentionality are not considered worthy of status; they have no dignity, no power. They are not persons. There is nothing new about this. The history of oppression is basically about the denial of status-worthiness to categories of people by those who have access to power. But what this history has glossed and ignored is the systematic objectification of women by men. The re-writing and re-appropriation of history by various feminist historians means that for the first time women are recovering their historicity as intentional beings.

The arrogance with which male writers cast their historical reconstructions is reminiscent of the way in which European historians discussed and analysed African history. Until recently, African history was written by white historians who, for the most part, denied that Africa had a history before the coming of European settlers. It was the 'discovery' of Africa by Europe that pushed it into history, just as the 'discovery' of America by Columbus gave it a history. The denial of history to the objectified, to the colonized, to the oppressed is one of the hallmarks of oppressive practice. Only those groups with a history have consciousness and intentionality.

Counter-intentionality

Accordingly, the recovery of historical consciousness by subordinate groups is seen as dangerous by their oppressors.

The truth is that intentionality can never be denied completely to others. While the dominant group may attempt to blot out the subjectivity and the feelings of those they exploit and oppress, they also implicitly acknowledge their potential for intentional opposition. Those millions who went to gas ovens in the Nazi concentration camps died not only because they were perceived as objects, but because they were seen as embodying an awesome counter-intentionality. It was the gas ovens which reduced them to the status of objects. It might be objected that this example is far too extreme. Surely there is no way in which the relationship between men and women, between heterosexuals and gays, can be described in these terms? Surely sexual objectification cannot be equivalent to the objectification of slaves and concentration camp inmates?

There are two points to be made about this. First, the history of the twentieth century is one of accelerated atrocity and genocide. After all, it is only 43 years since the end of the last war. War, genocide, starvation, poverty, pollution are very much on the international agenda. Secondly, despite the growth of ecological awareness, the natural world is being systematically appropriated in the name of economic rationality.

These are familiar themes. The point of referring to them is to illustrate the context in which objectification occurs. I suppose the classic example is the kind of discourse associated with the nuclear arms race and the nuclear energy industry. This discourse is couched in the language of rationality and objectivity. The nuclear scientist is the exemplar of the researcher who is dedicated to the disinterested search for truth. It is not my intention to replicate the pros and cons of the moral desirability of nuclear energy. (It seems self-evident that after Hiroshima there can be no moral arguments for its use.) My concern here is to argue that this discourse is a constituting dimension of 'hierarchic heterosexualism'. In this, I go along with the position of Easlea and others who have described how science, especially physics, articulates the interests and intentionalities of men (Easlea, 1981, 1983, 1987). The fact that physics is dominated by men needs no elaboration. What is relevant here is that the 'men who inhabit this scientific world particularly those who are successful in it – behave in culturally masculine ways. Indeed, as in other hierarchical male-dominated activities, getting to the top invariably entails aggressive, competitive behaviour' (Easlea, 1987, p. 198).

Doing physics involves competition in which the egos of men are put on the line. Getting the right results may often be overshadowed by winning the race against other men. This competitive edge to research is reinforced by the image of nature waiting to be mastered and penetrated by the scientist. Although a sizeable minority of nuclear physicists worry about the implications of their work, the majority do not.

> It is estimated that throughout the world some half million physical scientists work on weapons design and improvement. As the physicist Freeman Dyson has reported, not only is the world of the scientific warriors overwhelmingly male-dominated but he sees the competition between physicists in weapons creation allied to the (surely masculine) thrill of creating almost limitless destructive power, as being in large part responsible for the continuing qualitative escalation of the nuclear arms race. (Easlea, 1987, p. 200)

Easlea, of course, is not the first commentator to report on the masculine nature of physics, especially nuclear physics. The fact of the matter is, that men-as-scientists, as 'scientific warriors', not only compete with each other, but they do this in the context of objectifying and mastering the world. Nature is there to be tamed – it has secrets, hidden mysteries and depths, which can only be revealed by the objective methods of science. The hypostatization of nature as female is exemplified in the imagery of sexual penetration which is so typical of the rhetoric of physical science. To be sure, I am not suggesting that this is true of all nuclear physicists, but it certainly figures dramatically in the pronouncements and discourse of those public spokesmen who speak for 'science'. The penetration of nature is resonant of the imagery associated with valorized male sexuality. Just as pornographic representations of female sexuality are saturated with feelings of violence, so are the metaphors employed by cold-war militarists and 'scientific warriors' saturated with genital sexuality. Easlea mentions the terrible neologism coined by Herman Kahn 'wargasm'.

> And what conception of pleasure was foremost in Kahn's mind when he coined the term 'wargasm' – surely the most obscene word in the English language – to describe what he sees as the union between Eros and Thanatos that is nuclear holocaust? I find such comparisons and terminology almost beyond rational comment. Simone de Beauvoirs's accurate observation that 'the erotic vocabulary of males' has always been drawn from military terminology becomes totally inadequate. (Easlea, 1987, p. 200)

Whether Kahn has ever really thought out the full implications of this terrible concept, it remains true that to a lesser or greater extent concepts like this are entrenched in male consciousness. Put differently, it is 'hierarchic heterosexualism' which is entrenched in male consciousness. 'Hierarchic heterosexualism' is more than a discourse – it is also a practice in which differences between people are treated as if they had moral and ontological significance. It is men as administrators, as experts, as authorities, as generals, as nuclear scientists, as historians, as artists, as philosophers, as technicians, as psychologists, as sociologists, as politicians who legislate and decide how the world should be understood and governed. It is 'hierarchic heterosexualism' which embraces the conflation of valorized male sexuality and militarism. We live in a world in which the horrors of Hiroshima and Chernobyl are not seen for what they are, but as momentary setbacks in the forward march of science. When somebody like Kahn uses a term such as 'wargasm', it is seen as being perfectly legitimate because it is part and parcel of academic discourse. What it actually represents is the ultimate denial of human dignity to everybody living on this planet.

I realize that there is a great danger in seeing 'hierarchic heterosexualism' as though it were some kind of perverted hyper-intentionality which somehow has become lodged in the psyches of men. It is the social relations of gender and masculinity, that constitute the matrix in which certain kinds of intentionality are valued, and others are not.

7

Men, Reason and Crisis

One of the central difficulties in attempting to write about masculinity is that, as a topic, it did not really exist until feminists began to attack the presuppositions of traditional political and social theory. Talk about the 'crisis of masculinity' would be meaningless if women had not challenged the power of men in familial, economic and political contexts. In a sense, the obsessive interest that some men (myself included) have in masculinity is dependent, and parasitic on, the insights of feminist theory and practice. Perhaps, more than anything else, it is radical feminism which shocked the sensibilities of male academics and intellectuals. Some of us went along with 'liberal' and 'Marxist' feminism, but not radical feminism. Surely, to claim that 'all men were potential rapists' is simply to fall back on reductionism and essentialism? In defence, we tended to agree that this might be true of some men, men with deprived childhoods, men who were frustrated economically and sexually, but not all men.

However, although a number of radical feminist writers appear to espouse an essentialist position, this is not what is at issue. What is at issue is their insistence that it is men-in-general who are responsible for the oppression of women. The usual 'liberal' response to this is that we cannot talk of men-in-general, only individual men who behave in a variety of individual ways. All men start their lives possessing roughly the same kind of biological equipment, but it is individual men who are responsible for their actions. If a man rapes, than he is culpable, not his friends, his father or society. Accordingly, it is he who should be punished, medically treated or incarcerated in an institution. What horrifies men is the claim that most men behave like this, and that this is nowhere more evident than in the family. Rape is not something that only happens in the streets, rather it happens with brutal regularity in the marriage-bed. Violence against women usually occurs in the home. The evidence for all this is based upon the work of researchers such as Dobash and Dobash (1979). In addition, the evidence now being produced by researchers about the prevalence of father–daughter rape (Ward, 1984), and the general sexual harassment of women, is not readily assimilated into liberal images of what constitutes 'normal' sexual and gender relationships (Hanmer and Maynard, 1987).

The sheer scale of the documentation accumulating about male violence and sexual harassment does not make for comfortable reading, especially for those men who believe that in liberal Western democracies gender inequality is slowly disappearing. Yet, all these statistics and this research are not about abstractions. They refer to what men do. And because we tend to look for a reason which would allow us to explain men's behaviour, we draw the conclusion what they *do* must be connected to what they *are*. So this man's violence is attributable to excess hormonal activity; this man is a rapist because of a character defect. Alternatively, we may say that he does what he does because this is what he wants to do, what he desires. He intends to rape, despite the fact that certain consequences may flow from his actions. In both instances, we *interpret* his behaviour. We attribute his actions to some interior state. *Either* he could not help himself *or* he acted as a free agent. In both cases it is the individual who is seen as the source of behaviour. It is not patriarchy or heterosexualism, but the motives of individual men that are relevant.

The proposition that it is men-in-general who oppress women runs counter to all the established axioms of liberal individualism. But, more than this, it runs counter to the way in which political and cultural theory has been formulated and practised in the West. Men have never really seen themselves as a problem. Classes are a problem, nations are a problem, mental illness is a problem, education is a problem, but not 'men'. To be told that men are both oppressors *and* a problem is not something that men can easily live with.

But for which men is this a problem? There seems to be something very self-indulgent in talking about the crisis of masculinity when we may be referring to a very limited number of men, who may have read feminist texts, or who have feminist friends. To talk about a general crisis of masculinity would be to imply that men-in-general believe that their traditional powers and privileges are being systematically appropriated by women. True, in popular discourse this is a common theme. It certainly figures in media discussions about the feminization of men, but does this mean that there is a *real* crisis of masculinity which permeates the consciousness of the majority of Western men? Kimmel (1987, p. 123) maintains that: 'Definitions of masculinity are historically reactive to changing definitions of femininity.'

Masculinity only becomes problematic when changes in the social structure generate changes in institutions like the family. Thus, when capitalists used women as cheap labour, they altered the terms of personal relationships in the home. Men were threatened by women entering the labour market, and this led to a sharpening of gender differences and conflict. As men became increasingly conscious of women as potential rivals in the public sphere, they not only felt insecure, but they constructed new rationalizations for gender inequality. 'A woman's place is in the home' was the standard slogan of millions of men throughout the Western industrial world. Today the 'crisis of masculinity' is, by this token, much more severe because of the tremendous structural changes in advanced industrial societies. Moreover, the crisis is theorized and discussed in academic journals and texts; it is given reality in the media, and it is preached about in churches. Reasons for its magnitude have been attributed to the rise of feminism, the collapse of the nuclear family, and the consolidation of a hedonistic materialistic culture which celebrates the sovereignty of individual desire. More importantly, however, is the belief that women are not only beginning to dominate some sections of the labour market, but that they are also moving into positions of real power in government and industry.

The Crisis of Masculinity Thesis

In simple terms, the 'crisis of masculinity' thesis claims that when certain things happen in the economy and polity, this effects the family, which then precipitates a corresponding change in the status of women which, in turn, produces a reaction in men. Obviously, as stated, this thesis is far too mechanistic. It gives primacy to 'production' and ignores 'reproduction'. It assumes that gender relationships are constituted by the economy.

Both masculinity and femininity are relational terms. Masculinity has no meaning by itself – it is always defined in opposition to femininity. Both are rooted in what Kessler and McKenna call the 'incorrigible propositions of gender'. In chapter 2 it was noted that these 'propositions' are never neutral because they underpin the structure of 'hierarchic heterosexuality'. Thus, a crisis of masculinity is only a crisis in so far as the 'relations of gender' are perceived and experienced as being problematic by a significant proportion of men. Today, this is to assume that the kinds of discussions that inform the academic and feminist analysis of gender and male domination are generally understood, and that men-in-general are beginning to accept that extant gender relations give them unwarranted power over women. The optimism implicit in this assumption is illustrated by one commentator's belief that, in the United States at least, he can discern the emergence of a group of men who are committed to a 'humanistic' view of gender relations (Franklin, 1984, p. 208).

A humanist man is one who has constructed for himself the goal of sex role equality. Having rejected the outdated masculinist goal of male domination, humanist men also reject the strategies and techniques used by some men to maintain and support sex-role inequality. Instead, these men seem more likely to endorse an androgynous sex-role orientation, where both 'masculine' and

'feminine' traits are valued and exhibited in social interaction.
(Franklin, 1984, p. 212)

Franklin contrasts 'humanist man' with three other kinds of
men who co-exist in American society and, by extension, also
have their counterparts in other industrial societies.

First, there is Classical Man. Classical man is the male
chauvinist *par excellence* who believes that men and women
are not only different, but unequal as well. He is rigidly
heterosexual and blatantly homophobic. It is he who reacts
to feminism in the most stereotypical and hostile manner.

Secondly, there is Routinely Masculinist Man (Franklin,
1984, p. 209). This man acknowledges the possibility that
gender differences may be unfair and to his advantage, but
this is as far as it goes. There appears to be a contradiction
between what he does and what he says. To a large degree,
he typifies the married man who may routinely do the
washing up, but who never cleans the toilet. In other words,
he never puts himself on the line when it comes to
committing himself to giving up his privileges as a man. He
is like the white South African who makes 'liberal' anti-
racist statements, but ends up employing black servants at
the 'going rate'.

Thirdly, there is Anomic Man. This man is most affected
by his encounter with feminism. However, this encounter
has not led to an abandonment of his gender commitments.
Rather, it has led to acute gender identity crisis. Anomic
men are confused and anxious about their sexuality and
their role as breadwinners. It is these men who find 'identity
talk' relevant. They are continuously searching for a focus
for certainty and stability in a world which seems to have no
clearly demarcated role for the traditional 'masculine virtues'.

From the point of view of the 'crisis of masculinity' thesis
all four types are being subjected to considerable strain, but
it is only 'humanist man' who is capable of coming to terms
with the new circumstances arising out of the changing
balance of power between men and women in the last
decades of the twentieth century.

The trouble with the notion of a 'crisis of masculinity' is
that it tends to collapse into other 'crises'. There is a 'crisis of

capitalism', an accumulation crisis, a crisis of the individual. It is evident that there are a multiplicity of responses to feminism by men. Some ignore it, others systematically denigrate its arguments, others welcome its political implications. But are these responses symptomatic of some deep-seated malaise in men?

I take it that by crisis is meant some kind of 'turning-point' or 'discontinuity' in personal and social relationships. From the perspective of men-in-general, the concept 'crisis' involves the realization that their power and authority can no longer be taken for granted. If their power is challenged, then a dominant group is in a crisis situation. It begins to look around for explanations and rationalizations which allow it to understand and cope with the new situation. But, because of the escalation of the challenge by the subordinate group, it becomes increasingly difficult to provide a coherent image of itself as being in full control of events. The 'crisis of masculinity' then, is about the generalized feeling among men-in-general that they are no longer capable of fully controlling the world. They have lost their collective nerve, their self-assurance, their sense of certainty. They are 'uncertain' about their potency, their heterosexuality, their status-worthiness.

The problem as stated above is far too simplistic. First, it assumes that all men are in crisis. Secondly, it assumes that all men have the same sense of collective identity. There is a danger here of over-categorizing men. Not all men have the same interests, nor do they share collective identities. Furthermore, men are frequently in conflict with each other. If we accept that American men are divided into four types (and, of course, this is problematic), then it is evident that 'humanist men' cannot have the same interests as 'classical men'. What Franklin is emphasizing is that a number of masculinities co-exist within a given social dynamic. Some men are coping with this dynamic, others are not. True, there are a growing number of men who have changed their attitudes to women and gender inequality. There are also men who have consciously attempted to construct lifestyles which they hope are non-sexist and egalitarian. And there are others who have not made the slightest concession to feminism. Despite the proliferation of texts and media presentations of masculinity, it is these men who still control the world. Admitedly the 'macho' stereotype has become a figure of fun for some but, in the main, what Franklin calls 'classical man' is still in charge of the state, the economy and reproduction.

To be sure, as noted, masculinity is now a topic of analysis. It is seen as something which needs explanation and justification, and this is where biological and psychological accounts of masculinity come into play. Although social constructionist explanations about masculinity and gender are common currency among feminists and social scientists, this has not altered the commonsense versions of gender differences that underpin both popular and political practice. The 'incorrigible propositions of gender' remain the corner-stone on which social policy is built in all industrial societies. The nuclear family is still a sacrosanct institution, in spite of the evidence that it is a cardinal site of women's oppression.

What I am asserting here is that the current crisis of masculinity does not portend the end of male domination and masculinism. It may well be that what we are witnessing today is some kind of 'legitimation crisis'. The viciousness of the counter-attack against feminism and the gay movement by the New Right' is indicative of some kind of strain in masculinism. Male authority can no longer be presented as taken for granted – it has to be defended and rationalized by recourse to the most blatant sexual stereotyping.

Such a 'legitimation crisis' may be experienced differently by different groups of men. How concerned, for example, are male power-brokers about the feminist critique of men and patriarchy? How do they perceive the threat of gay politics? Do the powerful administrators of public corporations feel anxious about their masculinity? Do NATO generals spend sleepless nights worrying about the feminization of the armed forces? Do men who control the economy and the polity even acknowledge that their authority and power are under question? At one level, they obviously do not because they operate within the limits of the 'transcendental pretence' and its appeal to the 'natural'.

At another level, this picture of 'men-at-the-top' as being non-reflexive about their masculinity and power is belied by the kind of evidence coming from doctor's and psychiatric waiting-rooms. Although this evidence is contradictory, and often misleading, the indications are that 'men-at-the-top' are more likely to suffer from heart disease than women. They die earlier and, in general, find it more difficult to cope with stress. In the United States, according to Ehrenreich, the extraordinary rate at which male executives were keeling over with cardiac arrest led to American middle-class men becoming obsessed with physical fitness (Ehrenreich, 1983, pp. 142–3).

> Men who had been sluggish white-collar workers took up jogging, health foods, racquetball and aerobic exercises – and these exercises became the new insignia of class status ... The liberating project of self-transformation has come, increasingly, to include a program of physical rehabilitation, with the new male qualities of sensitivity and self-nurture now focused on sagging muscles and suspect arteries. (Ehrenreich, 1983, p. 143)

Ehrenreich focuses on American middle-class men running away from marriage and the breadwinner's role. Increasingly, these men found it difficult to meet the requirements of both roles without traumatic mental and physical consequences. Certainly, we know that American middle-class men resort to psychiatric counselling to a far greater extent than their European counterparts. Presumably, this a measure of their collective alienation and crisis. Indeed, some commentators go so far as to suggest that the 'male sex role' *per se* is dangerous to men's physical and psychological health (Franklin, 1984, p. 28).

We have already had occasion to look at some of the ambiguities in this area when we examined the problem of gender identity. Are we to assume that men cannot cope with life at the top? Or are we to believe that, just by being a man, there is a probability that some kind of crisis is inevitable?

General and Sub-crises

I am sure this is the case for *some* men. It would be the
height of presumption on my part to deny this. Yet, I find it
difficult to see this as being due to a general crisis of
masculinity. The notion of a general masculine crisis implies
the breakdown of 'heterosexualism' and the decline of men's
power and authority in the public sphere. This is not
happening. To be sure, the 'legitimacy' of male domination is
being questioned increasingly by women and some men, but
this has not led to a destabilization of the dominant mode.

Nevertheless, it would be inappropriate to dismiss such a
notion completely. While we might reject the idea of a
general crisis of masculinity, we nevertheless must acknowledge that the past 30 years or so have seen an unprecedented
attempt to undermine and understand the basis of male
domination. Although this attempt derives mainly from
feminist and gay sources, its influence has been profound.
Not a day passes when some official 'spokesman' does not
make some kind of reference to issues raised by these
sources. Recent public debates about abortion, gay rights,
rape, incest, child-battering, pornography, sexual harassment
and male violence have been profoundly effected by feminist
and gay discourse. To a certain extent, the defence of
heterosexualism mounted by the New Right is conducted in
terms of the discourse it despises. Before the advent of AIDS
there were signs that dominant and powerful masculinities
were beginning to show signs oi strain. Today, this has
changed because 'heterosexualism' is defended in the same
way as the family is defended.

Connell's concept of 'hegemonic masculinity' is relevant
here. The challenge mounted by the oppositional stance of
feminist and gay politics is being contained because dominant
male hierarchies rely on the support of a broad heterosexual
constituency which has begun to feel uneasy about this
challenge. While this support has been there for a considerable
time, what was unsettling to this constituencywas the sight
of thousands of gay people marching in the streets of San
Francisco, New York, London and Manchester. The political
influence of the gay movement, and the growing support for

the women's movement, forced a lot of men openly to assert their heterosexual commitments. They now *know* they are heterosexuals. But, ironically, this knowledge is premised on a misreading of the analysis of heterosexuality in feminist and gay literature. Instead of heterosexuality being perceived as a construction, it is construed as being natural and normal. The insights of feminist theory are incorporated into the official discourse of hegemonic masculinity. Not only should men not feel guilty about their 'heterosexuality', they should proclaim it. After all, it is natural. So, the defence of the gender order is being handled by legions of experts who reinforce their arguments with appeals to traditional morality and natural heterosexuality. This image of the natural is now being restated in Hollywood, and from the floor of the House of Commons.

I suspect that one of the reasons that a film like *Fatal Attraction* has been such a phenomenal box-office success is that it re-affirms the inviolability of the marriage-bond as the exemplary heterosexual relationship. The very health of Western society is seen to depend upon 'proper' sex within marriage. It is the 'other' woman who is treated as dangerous and subversive. As pictured, the 'Michael Douglas' figure is guilty of nothing more than a moment of indiscretion. The responsibility for the entire 'crisis' is blamed on the outsider. Ten years ago, this film would not have had such an impact because the terms of the debate about sexuality and gender were relatively more open-ended. Today, this has changed; the family and heterosexual relationships are being defended in clear, ringing tones.

In short, hegemonic masculinity is able to defuse crisis tendencies in the gender order by using counter and oppositional discourse for its own purposes. This is not to say that it defuses all crisis tendencies. There are local crises which have disturbing consequences for various groups of men. Some men find that 'unemployment' is a terrible threat to their image of themselves as autonomous. Others find their 'sexual potency' undermined by the alternatives posed by gay sexual practice. Others cannot cope with the demands put on them by a highly competitive economic and social system. Others cannot handle intimacy and emotion. Others find the very existence of the women's movement an insult to their masculinity.

So while hegemonic masculinism remains relatively intact, it nevertheless is faced with a host of sub-crises. It defuses some of these crises by absorbing and incorporating the voices of dissent into its own practice, but it cannot do this in every case. It cannot, for example, dissolve the anxieties of unemployed men. It cannot give men the traditional authority they once possessed as breadwinners. It cannot reassure the thousands of men who consult psychiatrists that their problems are temporary and ephemeral. It cannot guarantee the permanence of the present gender order.

Thus, while it is true to say that 'hegemonic masculinity' or 'hierarchic heterosexualism' remains dominant at both the public and private levels, it is also true that local crises of masculinity are not imaginary phenomena. Men who fail at work, in marriage, on the sportsfield, haunt the imagination of male writers. They also haunt the texts of those men who write about masculinity. 'Failure' is a highly loaded word. It is resonant of the loss of potency described so vividly in the clinical literature about masculinity.

Inevitably, in writing about masculinity, I am aware that my own masculinity has become a topic because I suspect, in some unformulated way, that my failure as a man, as a human being, is somehow related to the reality of the oppression of women. It is, as I noted earlier, remarkably self-indulgent to talk about the crisis of masculinity from the perspective of an oppressor. As a topic, masculinity becomes something which can be analysed, theorized and explained. For some of us its study is a means of expiation, of assuaging our guilt about our present privileged status. It is easy enough to blame our present discontents on 'hierarchic heterosexualism' or 'patriarchy'. We can lose ourselves in endless discussion about the macro-structural determinants of this or that crisis. And yet, to reiterate, these analyses and discussions are not about imaginary phenomena.

There are genuine crises of confidence which force some men into despair. In the late 1970s and 1980s, unemployment has shattered the self-respect of millions of men (and women) in most Western industrial societies. For these men the idea of the breadwinner's role is a travesty. Unemployed men see themselves as powerless and trivialized. The breadwinner's role (in theory) gives men a sense of identity of structural location. For most men in capitalist societies, their careers, their professions, their trades, their skilled and unskilled jobs are the prime focus of identity. Without work, they are rootless and disjointed (Ingham, 1984, pp. 26–30). The problem of unemployment is obviously not only a crisis for working-class men, although it effects them more than anyone else – it also has similar consequences for the male middle class. What is at stake here is not simply a diminishing of self-respect, but the realization that they are not in a position to demand 'respect' from women. Their authority in the home no longer has the legitimation of 'provider'.

Since most men have been brought up to see themselves as being responsible for the bread and butter of daily existence, they find it almost impossible to accommodate themselves to the sight of their wives going out to work to put food on the table. To be sure, the welfare state provides a last instance safety net between starvation and disintegration, but this compounds the problem. While unemployment is symptomatic of tensions and strains in capitalist economies, it also mirrors the tensions and strains in gender relations. Not only do unemployed men find it difficult to cope with their 'uselessness', but they have to come to terms with their wives. How they do this depends on a variety of factors, but what is certain is that violence is often deployed as a solution to their immediate difficulties. This is not to say that unemployment is directly responsible for the increase of violence against women and children; rather it is to emphasize the fact that violence is considered 'legitimate' in marriage. An employed man may come home every Friday night and batter his wife; an unemployed man may batter his wife three or four times a week. Unemployment does not cause the violence, it merely amplifies the violence already existing.

This would seem to suggest that men, whether they are unemployed or not, are subject to other kinds of pressures which impinge upon the lives of women. We have already examined some of the arguments and theories which claim that men resent and fear women because of their early experience of their mothers. Women-dominated child-rearing is blamed for the continuous reproduction of bruised male egos, which make it impossible for them to come to terms with feelings of tenderness and intimacy. The current escalation of violence in the family, the level of child abuse, the reports of father–daughter incest are attributed to the saliency of this mother–son relationship.

> The mother is also the 'first overwhelming adversary' of the will of the child, the first representative of authority that he or she 'confronts'. Thus the relationship with the mother within the family sets the emotional stage for our subsequent relationship with the variety of authorities we will encounter outside the family. The fear and loathing of women that the intolerable exercise of maternal power engenders becomes the unconscious basis for the acquiescence in, or even the affirmation of, first the authority of the father and then the authority of men as a whole. (Balbus, 1987, p. 115)

The question remains whether there is any relationship between mothering and domination. The position of Chodorow, Dinnerstein, Balbus and Flax is that this *is* the case. The current crisis of masculinity, therefore, is a heightening of tensions already existing within the gender order. From this perspective, there is a permanent crisis of masculinity *and* a permanent crisis of femininity. As long as child care is monopolized by women, they will be regarded as dangerous and as 'adversaries' by men. Thus, current talk about a male identity crisis is merely making explicit what has always been the case. Again, this is to presume that masculinity is a psychological problem which has its roots in childhood experience.

Iris Young has argued that there is a great deal of confusion and ambiguity in this entire discussion. What she suggests has happened is that 'gender differentiation' has collapsed into male domination. She argues that in principle 'a gender-differentiated society' could exist without there being any kind of patriarchal structure (Young, 1984, pp. 129–46). In other words, the fact that most societies tend to accept 'the incorrigible propositions of gender' as given, does not imply that patriarchy is inevitable. Male psychological problems are, by this token, not a function of gender differentiation, but of gender inequality. Men have identity crises only in contexts in which their rule is challenged, not because of an unconscious resentment of their mothers.

One of the recurring themes in the discussion of the male identity crisis is the problem of sexuality. Along with the breadwinner's role, the belief in the potency of the valorized penis has played a central part in male identity construction. But, as we observed earlier, male sexuality is historically constituted; there is no fixed aspect of sexual behaviour, feeling and meaning which would allow us to encapsulate it within a unitary framework. Today we are presented with a staggering number of possibilities for sexual behaviour. Traditional, classic, heterosexual men are faced with the reality of gay men and women who reject the claim that sexuality is naturally dichotomous. What was once considered to be necessary and right is now no longer the case for millions of men and women in the industrialized world. Now, whether this is a crisis for heterosexual men is a moot point. And if it is a crisis, is this because of the precariousness of their Oedipal resolutions?

As presented above, the unconscious is treated as if it is a completely non-social category. It is the home of anti-social desire, the kingdom of out of control instincts. Men with identity crises have no means of understanding their feelings and emotions. The effects of repression operate to polarize the social and desire. But, desire is itself socially constituted. Patriarchy is not a law of the unconscious – it is a law of society, just as heterosexuality is not intrinsic to the male and female body. Accordingly, if some men are experiencing an identity crisis, we cannot simply see this as some kind of personality malfunction. We cannot say that John, Peter, Paul and Donald are emotionally ill, without specifying the context which frames their illness. Men who talk about identity crises only do so in a context in which 'identity crisis' has become part and parcel of discourse. Who knew what an identity crisis was in the fifteenth century? We 'know' today because some of us have read Erikson, or we

have watched television programmes in which 'identity
crisis' is taken very seriously indeed. We have also been
exposed to countless discussions about the nature of sexuality
and the importance of 'proper' sex. We have been told that
desire is natural, and that its repression is unnatural. We
have been told that sexual potency is a sign of our manhood.
To be impotent is a reflection on our masculinity, on our
reality.

Why so many men believe this is the problem. How do
they become convinced that they are sick or deviant when
they do not conform to the master stereotype? One simple
answer is that they really are sick or neurotic. They cannot
cope with 'reality'. They have broken down like damaged
machines. They need some kind of therapy to restore them to
health. Their problems are medical and psychiatric. When a
man consults a psychiatrist about his impotence, he is not
imagining his symptoms. He believes that the psychiatrist
can help him solve his difficulty. If a large number of men
present themselves for treatment for impotence, then presumably they are all convinced that their symptoms are both
real and abnormal. And, no doubt, doctors and psychiatrists
accept that these men are impotent.

So, both therapist and patient operate on the assumption
that impotence is caused by some antecedent condition the
implication being that impotence is indicative of individual
failure. Somehow or other these men took the wrong turning,
made bad choices, found it impossible to relate to women.
Alternatively, their early socialization saddled them with
overwhelming inhibitions and repressions. From the point of
view of the therapist, each patient has a unique history
which has led, irrevocably, to his present predicament. The
same kind of logic is used in trying to account for rape. It is
this particular man who rapes, not that man. It is his
history, his psychological state, his testosterone level, his
desires which caused the rape. Thus, if a significant number
of men are impotent, and a significant number of men rape,
then this is not really relevant because, by definition, the
problem is an individual one, not social. All these men are
maladjusted, sick, abnormal. But, at the same time, they are
also considered to be immoral and evil. Both medical and

moral discourse emphasize the fall from grace of abnormal or evil men.

The Devaluation of the Social

There is, in other words, no such thing as a social crisis – it is individual men who have crises, not societies. Doctors and psychiatrists would argue, no doubt, that there have always been impotent men, and that some men have always raped. The difference between now and the past is that we now have better means to identify and classify forms of individual malfunction. Priests can also testify to the long history of individual sin. There is nothing new about male behaviour that has not been heard to in the privacy of confession. Behind these arguments is a commitment to the primacy of the individual. All social problems can be reduced to individual disposition and desire, the inference being that it is no use looking for social solutions to personal problems.

This tendency to underplay the significance of the social is a very dominant aspect of the counter-attack against feminism and the social sciences. One measure of this is the precarious position that disciplines like sociology find themselves in, when compared with the 1960s and 1970s. When Margaret Thatcher announces to the world that there is 'no such a thing as society', then we know that the dice are heavily loaded against any discipline which attempts to look for social explanations for social problems. While the notion of a general social crisis may be problematic, this does not rule out the fact that some groups, some populations, are in crisis some of the time.

I would want to argue that the notion of crisis simultaneously implies the personal and the political. I go along with Wright-Mills's assertion that public issues inevitably involve private issues. Individual life is political life – the personal is political. Very few male theorists and experts find his position congenial because they operate with implicit and explicit rules which divide the world into subjective and objective domains. Moreover, they operate with a concept of male intentionality and autonomy which does not recognize its own fragility and tentativeness, nor its historicity. So, until recently, it was highly improbable that they could ever be reflexive about gender and sexuality. Put differently, the personal is not seen as being dialectically related to the social – it is always seen as being something special and separate. Personal problems have nothing to do with power and domination, except in so far as power is seen as being an attribute of individual intentionality.

But, if there is an increase in male violence, in reported incidents of rape, in the amount of pornographic material distributed and sold in a society, can we realistically see this as being due to sudden changes in the personalities of men? On the other hand, if we locate these changes in the breakdown of old institutional frameworks – we may, for instance, trace them to the decline of the traditional patriarchal family and the influence of the mass media – then we have placed the locus of explanation on the social. We have recognized that individual intentionality is deeply entrenched in social processes. Male intentionality is implicated with female intentionality. What men want and do is always in relation to what women want and do. The discovery that some men are going through an 'identity crisis' is therefore not something which can be described independently of the current state of play is gender relations.

Accordingly, it is important to remember that male intentionality is political. It enters into gender relations from the vantage point of authority. Crises of masculinity erupt on the terrain of gender inequality. Whatever crises men are going through are experienced from the perspective of oppressors, not victims.

Many of the early writers on men, especially those who wrote for the popular press tended to describe men as passive victims of impersonal socializing forces, often in defensive reaction against overly voluntarist interpretations they found in some feminist writings. The male victimization thesis seemed to provide an escape from blaming men for the evils feminists identified. But with the denial of blame-worthiness often went the denial of responsibility ... Politically, the image of men as victims too sharply contradicted the in-charge image men had of themselves and therefore led to popular criticisms of writers on men, as well as the 'new men' themselves, as complaining 'wimps'. Academically, lacking a complementary group to identify as victimizers, the analysis was vague and glossed over too many issues, particularly issues of power. What was and is needed are analyses that show how men both form and are formed by their conditions, or, as Marx put it, how men make their own history, but not in circumstances of their own choosing. (Brod, 1987, pp. 12–13)

The 'victimization thesis' gave men an opportunity to deny their responsibility for oppression. It allowed men to be seen as being equally oppressed with women. In its extreme form it seemed to suggest that the man who attacked a woman was somehow a suitable case for treatment, more to be pitied than condemned. To a certain extent, this is how some of the arguments of Chodorow and Dinnerstein were used. If mothering was to blame for male domination then, in the final analysis, men are blameless.

The fact that 'men both form and are formed by their conditions' is self-evident, but its obviousness is one of the most difficult things to assimilate into male discourse. By this I mean that we are still obsessed with the distinction between the intending individual, and the objectivity of the outside world. The individual versus society is a theme returned to time and again in introductory sociology and political science courses. Even after our exposure to structuralism and post-structuralism, the individual remains right at the centre of discourse. This intending individual was usually a man. It was he, in the guise of hero, breadwinner, hunter, sportsman, intellectual innovator, who 'made' history. To come back to an earlier point masculinity is a relational construct. It only exists in relation to femininity. The terrain of gender differences is a contended terrain in which sexuality, power and authority are not fixed categories. So when we talk about patriarchy, masculinism or 'hierarchic heterosexuality', we are abstracting from a field of intentionalities and counter-intentionalities. We are looking at gender in the context of the balance of forces that are salient at any one time. Just as class relationships are not static, so are gender relationships. Male domination is not easily achieved – it meets resistance; there are notable local victories for women. It is a mistake to conceive of men as belonging to some homogeneous powerbloc without contradictions and crises. To repeat, not all men have the same interests, nor do they have the same status-worthiness.

In addition, gender relations are strongly implicated in other social relationships. Dominant masculinities penetrate class and race relationships. Until recently, there can be no doubt that white men ruled the world. They dominated trade and commerce; they colonized the Americas in the name of profit and religion. They 'raped' Africa and enslaved millions of black people. These are sweeping generalizations, but they are not inaccurate. We can translate them into generalizations about the outward expansion of European civilization, the voyages of discovery, capital accumulation, the dynamics of an emerging bourgeois class etc. but, even so, they are generalizations about the way in which sections of the white male bourgeoisie appropriated the world. Today, other groups of men participate in this domination. It is not only white middle-class men who appropriate productive and reproductive labour – this is now true for countries like Japan and many other 'developing' societies. In a sense, it could be said that masculinism was, and is, centrally involved in classism, racism and nationalism.

The way in which masculinism enters into nationalism is nowhere better exemplified than in the conduct and aftermath of war. It is the experience of victory or defeat that spawns the proliferation of metaphors of masculinity triumphant or in crisis. Take the Falklands War for example:

A war fought at considerable cost, with significant casualties, for a few bleak, scarcely populated islands with a lot of sheep, was enough to reverse the Conservative Party's slump in popularity and win them the 1983 general election. This was no mean feat – and it was largely due to the symbolic meanings attached to going to war. Churchillian phrases dripped from the mouths of the 'War Cabinet', as a sordid xenophobic enterprise was transformed into a paean to manhood, a celebration of the phallus draped in the Union Jack. Resurgent nationalism and a refurbished manhood were fused into one as the ships left port, the jets screamed overhead, and wives and sweethearts cried and waved goodbye. Everyone was in their place. We'd seen

the movie a hundred times: now it was time for the real thing.
(Metcalf, 1985, p. 13)

But there is another side to this coin. The 'official'
xenophobic masculinity of modern war is not the same thing
as the experience of frontline conditions. True, the First
World War had its 'heroes'. Thousands of men on both sides
received medals and were perceived as exemplifying selfless
courage; millions more were slaughtered in their trenches;
millions of others were maimed and incapacitated. The myth
of the transcendental male hero was shattered forever. Not
only was war dirty and disgusting, but it was pointless. If we
want to talk about a crisis of masculinity, then we can see
the origins of this crisis in the mud of Flanders and the
Russian Steppes.

And yet, the irony is that in 1939 the same armies
confronted each other. Men literally engaged in systematic
genocide, and the annihilation of centres of population. They
made war on civilian conurbations – saturation bombing
became normal strategic policy. And to end it all, we had
Hiroshima and Nagasaki. Today, politicians and strategic
planners can still contemplate the possibility of nuclear war
as being within the limits of human survival.

In this book I have been concerned primarily with looking
at the way in which men talk about and live their
masculinity. I made a distinction between masculinity and
masculinism, although this distinction is sometimes difficult
to maintain. I also borrowed concepts such as 'hierarchic
heterosexuality' and 'hegemonic masculinity' which seemed
to me to have the same kind of connotation, although, no
doubt, they have different theoretical significance for their
originators. Masculinism implies power, it entails hierarchy,
and it is also about the prescriptive heterosexuality in our
society. I argued that masculinism is not in a terminal crisis.
Both in its hierarchic and hegemonic forms, it dominates
gender relationships. In its most overt manifestation it can
be seen at work in what Hearn (1987) calls the mode of
reproduction. In this respect, although we can identify local
crises of masculinity such as unemployment and middle-
class sexual *angst*, we cannot identify the processes which

would allow us to say that masculinism is on the way out.
The interpenetration of masculinism, racism, nationalism
and classism means that, both at the national and international levels, the world is governed and controlled by
coteries of powerful men.

We have already had occasion to discuss the implications
of men's domination of the state and their control of the
means of public force and violence. We have noted the almost
exclusive preponderance of men in the military and nuclear
establishments. We note the same thing about trade unions,
the universities, the multinational corporations etc. A nice
summary of this kind of evidence can be found in Connell's
recent text (Connell, 1987, pp. 1–20). Furthermore, we
looked at the mode of reproduction, at the way in which men
not only appear to control its articulation at both the
administrative and political levels, but also how they benefit
generally from women's reproductive labour. In this respect,
it seems to me that Hearn's (1987) concept of 'human value'
encapsulates the manner in which women's sexual, child-
bearing and rearing services are appropriated by men-in-
general, and not only fathers.

The political and economic power of men today, in both the
productive and reproductive spheres, does not seem to
suggest that they are about to give up their privileges and
power. But this is not the whole story. Given enough time it
is more than likely that our generals, politicians and nuclear
scientists will end up destroying us all. It is at this level that
men demonstrate what Stanley sees as their 'potency capable
of world creation and destruction' (Stanley, 1978, p. 220). It
is at this level that masculinism becomes capable of self-
destruction. Stanley talks of the 'awesome power of human
intentionality'. What he is in fact really referring to is the
consolidation of this power in the hands of 'hierarchic
heterosexuals' who rule this world in the name of rationality
and objectivity.

The Spectre of Rational Man

The association of rationality with masculinity is a familiar
theme. On the whole men do not find this too problematic

but, inevitably, male philosophers get rather hot under the collar when accused of this (Lloyd, 1984, p. 109). There is something about 'reason' which they believe is genderless, not contaminated by emotion and passion. This is how rational men see themselves – it is how they are supposed to administer justice, and do science. To be rational in our society is to be impartial and objective – it implies a distancing of the observer from the object of his research, or policy. The canons of reason, objectivity and clarity are built into our educational practices, and into our scientific discourse. Yet, despite their commitment to reason, rational men are often strangely non-reflexive about the sources of their discourse. They fail to recognize their own ambiguities and contradictions. Their commitment to reason is a form of exclusion, a denial of certain kinds of experience.

What is excluded is the personal aspect of their discourse. Nowhere is this more evident than in the way they talk about war, especially nuclear war. The discussion about deterrence, for example, is often conducted without reference to the human consequences of a nuclear attack. Terms like 'mega-death' are bandied around as if they had no more significance than the poisoning of an ant colony. The peculiar thing about this is that it is their own death that they are talking about. It is as though reason is completely abstract. But reason cannot be disembodied. Even in its most instrumental form, it is always somebody's reason. The military strategists who simulate nuclear war are flesh and blood creatures, not computers. Their 'rationality' is embodied in the same way as their aggression is embodied. Both rationality and aggression represent an over-emphasis on specific kinds of intentionality, to the exclusion of others.

The question of intentionality remains largely unexplained in this final discussion. I come back to the point that it is men who 'do' certain things with their bodies. It is male discourse which is translated into action in wars, genocide and rape. The danger of this formulation is that it could be construed as another form of essentialism which allows biology in by the back door. To speak of male intentionality as though it is some trans-historical force is obviously nonsense. On the other hand, to conceive of patriarchy as not having anything to do with the interests and bodies of men is equally nonsensical. Patriarchy does not exist without men, just as capitalism does not exist without capitalists, or racism without racists.

This brings me back to the personal. As a man, am I responsible for patriarchy? Am I responsible for all men? As an author of a text on masculinity am I merely trying to assuage my own guilt? Some of my students have no doubts about the proper answers to these questions. A male academic writing about masculinity is simply another man attempting to write an 'authoritative' text. Masculinity, heterosexualism and gender become topics like any other topics. They are written about, analysed and set as exam questions. Male academics use feminism for their own purpose. They believe that if they read and comment upon this or that book or article, then they have contributed to the deconstruction of patriarchy. They fail to recognize that their discourse is itself a part of the problem. These students go on to argue that 'sympathetic' male academics should realize that what they say and write has nothing to do with the reality of gender inequality in and out of the academy. A similar point is made by Jardine in her critique in *Men in Feminism*. She writes:

> And what do feminists want? If you will forgive my directness, we do not want you to *mimic* us; we don't want your pathos or your guilt; and we don't even want your admiration (even if it's nice to get it once in a while). What we want, I would say what we need, is your *work*. We need you to get down to serious work, that involves struggle and pain. As guide to that work, I would like to remind you of a sentence by Helene Cixous – a sentence which, to my knowledge, has not been taken seriously by our allies at all! 'Men still have everything to say about their own sexuality'. *You still have everything to say about your own sexuality:* that's a challenge. (Jardine and Smith, 1987, p. 60)

Jardine argues that men-in-feminism have not even begun to take their bodies seriously. They write *about* their sexuality and *the* body, but they do not 'talk' their bodies: 'this would be talking your body, not talking *about* it. It is not essentialism; it is not metaphysics, and it is not/would not be representation. As Luce Irigaray put it, "The bodily in man is what metaphysics has never touched"' (Jardine and Smith, 1987, p. 61).

In a sense, those men who have used feminism as a theoretical tool have been no more able to comprehend their involvement in patriarchy, than those men who oppose feminism. Although 'they', 'I' and 'you' have perhaps agreed that there is a connection between sexuality and power, this has not really altered our everyday practice. To be sure, we have read Freud on sexuality, Lacan on desire and Foucault on discourse, and we believe that this gives us some kind of privileged insight into how our bodies are constituted by political and social practices, but we have not really come to terms with the way in which our bodies articulate power and hierarchy. We still have not taken the radical feminist discussion about rape seriously because we believe that rape is always an individual problem. Accordingly, we defend ourselves by saying that we reject all essentialist arguments. It is as though the accusation of essentialism immediately invalidates and neutralizes the feminist analysis. Indeed, a favourite ploy is to equate radical feminism with essentialism. But this is like equating Marxism with Stalinism. It deflects from the real issue, namely that it is men who rape, and not women.

As men, we have not really understood our bodies or put them in the foreground. We see them as fulfilling useful functions. They can be made to endure hardship, they can be extended to the full on the playing field, they can be disciplined for war, they can be used to intimidate others. They can be used to exemplify theories and statements about class, ethnicity and manhood. We believe that we 'own' our bodies. They are there to do our will and, at the same time, we discipline our desires, our feelings and needs. The male body is inhabited by a 'higher' intentionality, by the soul, the organizing ego. In short, the male body is a thing that is subject to the control of some master principle.

The implication here is that there is an essential dualism of spirit and matter, of body and mind which is central to the masculinist ethos. In the Middle Ages, this duality was legitimated by the church, and the belief in the intrinsic superiority of spirit over the materialist dross of everyday life. With the emergence of the new philosophy of Descartes, Leibniz and the triumph of Newtonian science, the duality of mind and matter, subjectivity and objectivity, the masculine and the feminine, came to be the common orthodoxy of academic and mundane discourse. Rational inquiry was now the means whereby men secured the domination of culture over nature. As an object of investigation, the human body was dissected, explored and subjected to every kind of chemical and physical test. Today this has gone much further. We are waiting for the genetic engineers to come up with techniques for the laboratory reproduction of human embryos. But what is completely missing from all this frenetic activity is any real understanding of how our bodies experience the world. Seidler puts this point strongly:

> As men have been closely identified with this rationalist tradition, they have often remained strangely ignorant of themselves, while rarely appreciating how this ignorance forms the character of their experience and relationships. It is as if they are left with little access to personal experience, so it can be hardly surprising if they feel drawn to intellectualist traditions, such as structuralism, which would seek to banish that very category of experience.
>
> Knowledge has become increasingly viewed as a commodity which can be accumulated and stored. It becomes a means of self-assertion within a competitive society in which men have constantly to prove their worth in relation to others. (Seidler, 1987, p. 85)

In a sense, therefore, masculinism in its abstract form celebrates the disembodiment of reason. Ideally, the world would be a much better place if we could somehow ignore and even cancel out our bodies. While this is common theme in science fiction, in the world we live in we *are* 'embodied'. We live our desires, intentions, our theories, our meanings. We experience pain and pleasure. Moreover, we share these feelings and experiences with other men and women, but we are not supposed to talk about them, except perhaps in the privacy of the consulting room or the confessional.

We have been taught that there is no place for the body and subjectivity in the public world. The body and its desires must be confined to the family, to the private sphere. It can be portrayed in the theatre, the cinema and on television, but it has no relevance in the corridors of power. Here abstract reason reigns. Decisions are made on the basis of rational rules and procedures. Our corporations are models of rationality in which there is no place for emotion and sentiment. Officially, sexuality does not exist in the board room or in the civil service. But masculinism is not only abstract. It is not simply a kind of instrumental rationality – it is also embodied in a complex of intentionalities.

Take the university as an example. Here reason is supposed to be the supreme value. The Western liberal university is theoretically built on the bedrock of open scholarship, supposedly available to all. They are supposed to be free of gender and race discrimination. Indeed, in the United States, some universities have positive discrimination policies. Be that as it may, the point I am making is what we all know, namely that the university is not a community of democratic scholars disinterestedly pursuing the quest for truth. Like other organizations, it is a morass of petty jealousies and betrayals. Those of us who make the grade, who get to the top of the academic pile, spend a great deal of our time denigrating the work of others. We compete with each other in ways which are no different from the cut-throat world of business. We resent the preferential treatment of some of our colleagues at the expense of our own claims. We spend countless hours gossiping about this or that person's 'private life'. In our dealings with students we pay lip-service to impartiality, but we continuously favour the 'intelligent' over the 'average'. Moreover, we resent some of their abilities. We see them as potential rivals in scholarship, as possible threats to our academic reputation.

Conclusion

Perhaps, more significantly, we have not recognized our masculinism, our commitment to gender inequality, our sexual objectification of women. The university is no different in this respect than any other institution, except that it glosses violence more successfully. Violence is often hidden behind a rhetorical smokescreen – it is couched in the language of academic 'one upmanship', but this is not a harmless little game – its aim is to hurt and diminish its object.

> A violent academic situation is not so much an experience of fisticuffs and flying chairs as one of diminishing other human beings with the use of sarcasm, raised voices, jokes, veiled insults, or the patronising put-down. There are many techniques for intimidating or silencing others, but examples of violence that are widely used in academic life for purposes of social control are verbal and vocal violence, and sexual harassment. (Ramazanoglu, 1987, p. 64)

What is true of the university is true of organizational life in general. Hearn and Parkin have documented the way in which sexuality is structured at the organizational level, how the most formal bureaucratic procedures are enmeshed with desire and 'hierarchic heterosexuality' (Hearn and Parkin, 1987). It is not only that organizational life is stratified in gender terms, it is also the framework in which men join together to objectify and trivialize women. Their claims to rationality and impartiality are invalidated by their practice of discrimination and sexual harassment. This is a theme which deserves further extended study. My concern here is to oppose the assertion that men are simply embodiments of abstract reason. They are also embodiments of desire. Both reason and desire co-exist uneasily in the male psyche, but they also co-exist in institutions.

The real crisis of masculinity is that men have come to believe that the distinction between reason and desire, the intellect and the body, the masculine and the feminine, is not only real, but necessary as well. The tragedy is that we have not really understood the connection between the personal and the political, between sexuality and power.

What we need to do is to stop listening to our own propaganda. We really have to listen to what women say, and not what we think they should say.

Bibliography

Abercrombie, Nicholas, Hill, Stephen and Turner, Brian S. 1980: *The Dominant Ideology Thesis*. London: Allen and Unwin.

Abercrombie, Nicholas, Hill, Stephen and Turner, Brian S. 1986: *Sovereign Individuals of Capitalism*. London: Allen and Unwin.

Altman, Dennis. 1982: *The Homosexualisation of America, the Americanisation of the Homosexual*. New York: St Martin's Press.

Arcana, Judith. 1983: *Every Mother's Son: the Role of Mothers in the Making of Men*. London: The Women's Press.

Archer, John and Lloyd, Barbara. 1985: *Sex and Gender*. Cambridge: Cambridge University Press.

Archer, J. and Westeman, K. 1981: 'Sex differences in the aggressive behaviour of school children', *British Journal of Social and Clinical Psychology*, 20: 31–6.

Arendt, Hannah. 1958: *The Human Condition*. Chicago: University of Chicago Press.

Balbus, Isaac D. 1982: *Marxism and Domination: a Neo-Hegelian, Feminist, Psychoanalytic Theory of Sexual, Political, and Technological Liberation*. New Jersey: Princeton University Press.

Balbus, Isaac D. 1987: 'Disciplining women: Michael Foucault and the power of feminist discourse.' In: Seyla Benhabib and Drucilla Cornell (eds) *Feminism as Critique: Essays on the Politics of Gender in Late- Capitalist Societies*. Cambridge: Polity Press.

Barrett, Michele and McIntosh, Mary. 1982: *The Anti-Social Family*. London: Verso.

Beechey, Veronica and Donald, James (eds) 1985: *Subjectivity and Social Relations*. Milton Keynes: Open University Press.

Benhabib, Seyla and Cornell, Drucilla (eds) 1987: *Feminism as Critique: Essays on the Politics of Gender in Late-Capitalist Societies*. Cambridge: Polity Press.

Bleier, Ruth. 1984: *Science and Gender: a Critique of Biology and its Theories on Women*. New York: Pergamon Press.

Bookchin, Murray. 1982: *The Ecology of Freedom: the Emergence and Dissolution of Hierarchy*. Palo Alto: Cheshire Books.

Boulding, Elise. 1976: *The Underside of History: a View of Women Through Time*. Boulder, Colorado: Westview Press.

Boxer, Marilyn J. and Quataert, Jean H. 1987: *Connecting Spheres: Women in the Western World, 1500 to the Present*. New York: Oxford University Press.

Bray, Alan. 1982. *Homosexuality in Renaissance England*. London: Gay Men's Press.

Brittan, Arthur and Maynard, Mary. 1984: *Sexism, Racism and Oppression*. Oxford: Blackwell.

Brod, Harry (ed.) 1987: *The Making of Masculinities: the New Men's Studies*. Boston: Allen and Unwin.

Brownmiller, Susan. 1975: *Against Our Will: Men, Women, and Rape*. New York: Bantam Books.

Bunch, Charlotte. 1975: 'Lesbians in revolt.' In: N. Myron and C. Bunch (eds) *Lesbianism and the Women's Movement*. Oakland, California: Diana Press.

Burstyn, V. 1983: 'Masculine dominance and the state.' In: R. Miliband and J. Saville (eds) *The Socialist Register 1983*. London: Merlin.

Caplan, Pat (ed.) 1987: *The Cultural Construction of Sexuality*. London: Tavistock Publications.

Carrigan, T., Connell, R. W. and Lee, J. 1985: 'Toward a new sociology of masculinity.' *Theory and Society*, 14: 551–604.

Chodorow, Nancy. 1978: *The Reproduction of Mothering: Psychoanalysis and the Sociology of Gender*. Berkeley and Los Angeles: University of California Press.

Chomsky, Noam and Foucault, Michel. 1974: 'Human nature: justice versus power.' In: F. Elders (ed.) *Reflexive Water*. London: Souvenir Press.

Cockburn, Cynthia. 1985: *Machinery of Dominance: Women, Men and Technical Know-how*. London: Pluto Press.

Connell, R. W. 1987: *Gender and Power: Society, the Person and Sexual Politics*. Cambridge: Polity Press.

Coveney, L., Jackson M., Jeffreys, S., Kaye, L. and Mahoney, P. (eds) 1984: *The Sexuality Papers: Male Sexuality and the Social Control of Women*. London: Hutchinson.

Coward, Rosalind. 1983: *Patriarchal Precedents: Sexuality and Social Relations*. London: Routledge and Kegan Paul.

Crompton, Rosemary and Mann, Michael (eds) 1986: *Gender and Stratification*. Cambridge: Polity Press.

Daly, Mary. 1978: *Gyn/Ecology: The Metaethics of Radical Feminism*. Boston: Beacon.

Davis, Angela Y. 1981: *Women, Race and Class*. New York: Random House.

De Beauvoir, Simone. 1972: *The Second Sex*. Harmondsworth: Penguin Books.

Delphy, Christine. 1977: *The Main Enemy*. London: Women's Research and Resources Centre Publications.

Delphy, Christine. 1984: *Close to Home: a Materialist Analysis of Women's Oppression*. London: Hutchinson.

Delphy, Christine and Leonard, Diana. 1986: 'Class analysis, gender analysis and the family.' In: Rosemary Crompton and Michael Mann (eds) *Gender and Stratification*. Cambridge: Polity Press.

Dinnerstein, Dorothy. 1987: *The Rocking of the Cradle and the Ruling of the World*. London: Women's Press.

Dobash, R. Emerson and Dobash, Russell. 1980: *Violence against Wives*. London: Open Books.

Dworkin, Andrea. 1981: *Pornography: Men Possessing Women*. London: The Women's Press.

Dworkin, Andrea. 1983: *Right Wing Women: the Politics of Domesticated Females*. London: The Women's Press.

Dyer, Richard. 1985: 'Male sexuality in the media.' In: Andy Metcalf and Martin Humphries (eds) *The Sexuality of Men*. London: Pluto Press.

Easlea, Brian. 1981: *Science and Sexual Oppression: Patriarchy's Confrontation with Women and Nature*. London: Weidenfeld and Nicolson.

Easlea, Brian. 1983: *Fathering the Unthinkable*. London: Pluto Press.

Easlea, Brian. 1987: 'Patriarchy, scientists, and nuclear warriors.' In: M. Kaufman (ed.) *Beyond Patriarchy: Essays by Men on Pleasure, Power and Change*. Toronto: Oxford University Press.

Easthope, Antony. 1986: *What a Man's Gotta Do: the Masculine Myth in Popular Culture*. London: Paladin.

Ehrenreich, Barbara. 1983: *The Hearts of Men: American Dreams and the Flight from Commitment*. London: Pluto Press.

Ehrenreich, Barbara and English, Deidre. 1979: *For Her Own Good: 150 Years of the Experts' Advice to Women*. London: Pluto Press.

Eisenstein, Zillah. 1979: 'Developing a theory of capitalist patriarchy and socialist feminism.' In: Eisenstein (ed). *Capitalist Patriarchy and Socialist Feminism*. New York: Monthly Review Press.

Elliot, Gil. 1972: *Twentieth Century Book of the Dead*. Harmondsworth: Penguin.

Engels, Friedrich. 1972: *The Origin of the Family, Private Property and the State*. London: Lawrence and Wishart.

Ferguson, Ann, Zita Jacqueline N. and Addelson, Kathryn Pyne. 1982: 'On compulsory heterosexuality and lesbian existence: defining the issues.' In (eds) N. O. Keohane, M. Z. Rosaldo, and B. C. Gelpi. *Feminist Theory: a Critique of Ideology*. Brighton: Harvester Press.

Fernbach, David. 1981: *The Spiral Path*. London: Gay Men's Press.

Filene, Peter. 1987: 'The secret's of men's histories.' In: Harry Brod (ed.) *The Making of Masculinities*. Boston: Allen and Unwin.

Foucault, Michel. 1970: *The Order of Things: an Archaeology of the*

Human Sciences. London: Tavistock.

Foucault, Michel. 1981: *The History of Sexuality: an Introduction*. Harmondsworth: Penguin.

Foucault, Michel. 1987: *The Use of Pleasure: the History of Sexuality*, vol. 2. Harmondsworth: Penguin.

Franklin II, Clyde, W. 1984: *The Changing Definition of Masculinity*. New York: Plenum Press.

Freud, Sigmund. 1975: *Civilization and its Discontents*. London: The Hogarth Press.

Freud, Sigmund. 1977: *On Sexuality*. Harmondsworth: Penguin.

Freud, Sigmund. 1986: *The Essentials of Psychoanalysis: the Definitive Collection of Sigmund Freud's Writing*. Selected by Anna Freud. Harmondsworth: Penguin.

Frye, Marilyn. 1983: *The Politics of Reality: Essays in Feminist Theory*. New York: The Crossing Press.

Gagnon, John H. and Simon, William. 1973: *Sexual Conduct: the Social Sources of Human Sexuality*. London: Hutchinson.

Gallagher, Catherine and Laqueur, Thomas (eds) 1987: *The Making of the Modern Body: Sexuality and Society in the Nineteenth Century*. Berkeley and Los Angeles: University of California Press.

Genovese, Eugene D. 1975: *Roll, Jordan, Roll*. London: André Deutsch.

Gerzon, M. 1982: *A Choice of Heroes. The Changing Face of American Manhood*. Boston Houghton Mifflin.

Gillis, John R. 1985: *For Better, For Worse: British Marriages, 1600 to the Present*. New York: Oxford University Press.

Goldthorpe, J. H. 1984: 'Women and class analysis: a reply to the replies.' *Sociology*, 18: 49–99.

Grimshaw, Jean. 1986: *Feminist Philosophers: Womens' Perspectives on Philosophical Traditions*. Brighton: Wheatsheaf.

Habermas, Jurgen. 1976: *Legitimation Crisis*. London: Heinemann.

Hanmer, Jalna and Maynard, Mary (eds) 1987: *Women, Violence and Social Control*. Basingstoke: Macmillan.

Hanscombe, Gillian E. and Humphries, Martin (eds) 1987: *Heterosexuality*. London: GMP Publishers.

Hargreaves, John. 1986: *Sport, Power and Culture*. Cambridge: Polity Press.

Hartmann, Heidi. 1981: 'The unhappy marriage of Marxism and feminism: towards a more progressive union. In: Lydie Sargent (ed.) *Women and Revolution*. London: Pluto Press.

Hartsock, Nancy C. M. 1985: *Money, Sex, and Power: toward a Feminist Historical Materialism*. Boston: North Eastern University Press.

Hearn, Jeff. 1987: *The Gender of Oppression: Men, Masculinity, and the Critique of Marxism*. Brighton: Wheatsheaf.

Hearn, Jeff and Parkin, Wendy. 1987: *'Sex' at 'Work': the Power and*

Paradox of Organisation Sexuality. Brighton: Wheatsheaf.

Heath, Stephen. 1982: *The Sexual Fix.* London: Macmillan.

Herzfeld, Michael. 1985: *The Poetics of Manhood: Contest and Identity in a Cretan Mountain Village.* New Jersey: Princeton University Press.

Hey, Valerie. 1986: *Patriarchy and Pub Culture.* London: Tavistock.

Hite, Shere. 1981: *The Hite Report on Male Sexuality.* New York: Knopf.

Hoch, Paul. 1979: *White Hero, Black Beast: Racism, Sexism and the Mask of Masculinity.* London: Pluto Press.

Hodson, Phillip. 1984: *Men: an Investigation into the Emotional Male.* London: BBC Publications.

Horkheimer, Max. 1941: 'The end of reason.' In: A. Arato and E. Gebhardt (eds) 1978: *The Essential Frankfurt School Reader.* Oxford: Basil Blackwell.

Illich, Ivan. 1983: *Gender.* London: Marion Boyars.

Ingham, Mary. 1984: *Men: the Male Myth Exposed.* London: Century Publishing.

Jackson, Margaret. 1984: 'Sexology and the social construction of male sexuality (Havelock Ellis).' In: L. Coveney, M. Jackson, S. Jeffreys and P. Mahony (eds) *The Sexuality Papers.* London: Hutchinson.

Jackson, Margaret. 1987: '"Facts of life" or the eroticization of women's oppression? Sexology and the social construction of heterosexuality.' In: Pat Caplan (ed.) *The Cultural Construction of Sexuality.* London: Tavistock.

Jaggar, Alison M. 1983: *Feminist Politics and Human Nature.* Brighton: Harvester.

Jardine, Alice and Smith, Paul (eds) 1987: *Men in Feminism.* New York and London: Methuen.

Kappeler, Susanne. 1986: *The Pornography of Representation.* Cambridge: Polity Press.

Kaufman, Michael (ed.) 1987: *Beyond Patriarchy: Essays by Men on Pleasure, Power, and Change.* Toronto: Oxford University Press.

Keohane, Nannerl O., Rosaldo, Michelle Z. and Gelpi, Barbara C. (eds) 1982: *Feminist Theory: a Critique of Ideology.* Brighton: Harvester.

Kessler, Suzanne J. and McKenna, Wendy. 1978: *Gender: an Ethnomethodological Approach.* Chicago: University of Chicago Press.

Kidd, Bruce. 1987: 'Sports and masculinity.' In: Michael Kaufman (ed.) *Beyond Patriarchy: Essays by Men on Pleasure, Power and Change.* Toronto: Oxford University Press.

Kimmel, Michael S. 1987: 'The contemporary "crisis" of masculinity in historical perspective.' In: Harry Brod (ed.) *The Making of Masculinities.* Boston: Allen and Unwin.

Kitzinger, Celia. 1987: *The Social Construction of Lesbianism.* London: Sage Publications.

Kleinberg, Seymour. 1987: 'The new masculinity of gay men, and beyond.' In Michael Kaufman (ed.) *Beyond Patriarchy: Essays by Men on Pleasure, Power and Change*. Toronto: Oxford University Press.

Lacan, Jacques. 1977: *Écrits*. London: Tavistock.

Lacan, Jacques. 1979: *The Four Fundamental Concepts of Psychoanalysis*. Harmondsworth: Penguin.

Lerner, Gerda. 1986: *The Creation of Patriarchy*. New York: Oxford University Press.

Levi-Strauss, Claude. 1969: *Elementary Structures of Kinship*. Boston: Beacon Press.

Lewis, Charlie and O'Brien, Margaret (eds) 1987: *Reassessing Fatherhood: New Observations on Fathers and the Modern Family*. London: Sage Publications.

Lipman-Blumen, Jean. 1984: *Gender Roles and Power*. New Jersey: Prentice-Hall.

Lloyd, Genevieve. 1984: *The Man of Reason: 'Male' and 'Female' in Western Philosophy*. London: Methuen.

Lockwood, David. 1986: 'Class, status and gender.' In Rosemary Crompton and Michael Mann (eds) *Gender and Stratification*. Cambridge: Polity Press.

Maccoby, E. E. and Jacklin, C. N. 1974: *The Psychology of Sex Differences*. Stanford: Stanford University Press.

Maccoby, Eleanor, E. 1980: *Social Development: Psychological Growth and the Parent–Child Relationship*. New York: Harcourt Brace Jovanovich.

MacKinnon, Catharine A. 1982: 'Feminism, marxism, method and the state: an agenda for theory.' In: Nannerl O. Keohane, Michelle Z. Rosaldo and Barbara C. Gelpi (eds) *Feminist Theory: a Critique of Ideology*. Brighton: Harvester.

MacKinnon, Catharine A. 1987: *Feminism Unmodified: Discourses on Life and Law*. Cambridge: Harvard University Press.

Mangan, J. A. 1981: *Atheticism in the Victorian and Edwardian Public School*. Cambridge: Cambridge University Press.

Mann, Michael. 1986a: *The Sources of Social Power. Volume 1: A History of Power from the Beginning to AD 1760*. Cambridge: Cambridge University Press.

Mann, Michael. 1986b: 'A crisis in stratification theory.' In: Rosemary Crompton and Michael Mann (eds) *Gender and Stratification*. Cambridge: Polity Press.

Marcuse, Herbert. 1955: *Eros and Civilization*. Boston: Beacon Press.

Marx, Karl. 1977: *Capital*, vol. 1. London: Lawrence and Wishart.

Marx, Karl and Engels, Friedrich. 1970: *The German Ideology*. London: Lawrence and Wishart.

McKee, Lorna and Bell, Colin. 1985: 'Marital and family relations in times of male unemployment.' In: B. Roberts, R. Finnegan, and D.

Gallie (eds) *New Approaches to Economic Life*. Manchester: Manchester University.

Mellen, Joan. 1978: *Big Bad Wolves: Masculinity in the American Film*. London: Elm Tree Books.

Merchant, Carolyn. 1980: *The Death of Nature: Women, Ecology and the Scientific Revolution*. London: Wildwood House.

Metcalfe, Andy and Humphries, Martin (eds) 1985: *The Sexuality of Men*. London: Pluto Press.

Mieli, Mario. 1980: *Homosexuality and Liberation*. London: Gay Men's Press.

Moi, Toril. 1985: *Sexual/Textual Politics*. London: Methuen.

Moi, Toril. 1987: *French Feminist Thought: a Reader*. Oxford: Basil Blackwell.

Morgan, D. H. J. 1985: *The Family, Politics and Social Theory*. London: Routledge and Kegan Paul.

Morgan, D. H. J. 1987: 'Masculinity and violence.' In: Jalna Hanmer and Mary Maynard (eds) *Women, Violence and Social Control*. Basingstoke: Macmillan.

Mort, Frank. 1987: *Dangerous Sexualities: Medico-Moral Politics in England since 1830*. London: Routledge and Kegan Paul.

Mount, Ferdinand. 1982: *The Subversive Family*. London: Jonathan Cape.

Moye, Andy. 1985: 'Pornography.' In: Andy Metcalfe and Martin Humphries (eds) *The Sexuality of Men*. London: Pluto Press.

Nicholson, Linda J. 1986: *Gender and History*. New York: Columbia University Press.

O'Brien, Mary. 1981: *The Politics of Reproduction*. London: Routledge and Kegan Paul.

Parsons, Talcott and Bales, Robert. 1955: *Family, Socialization and Interaction Process*. New York: The Free Press.

Passmore, John. 1970: *The Perfectibility of Man*. London: Gerald Duckworth.

Pleck, Joseph H. 1981: *The Myth of Masculinity*. Cambridge, Massachusetts: MIT Press.

Plummer, Kenneth (ed.) *The Making of the Modern Homosexual*. London: 1981.

Ramazanoglu, Caroline. 1987: 'Sex and violence in academic life or you can keep a good woman down.' In: Jalna Hanmer and Mary Maynard (eds) *Women, Violence and Social Control*. Basingstoke: Macmillan.

Reynaud, Emmanuel. 1983: *Holy Virility: the Social Construction of Masculinity*. London: Pluto Press.

Rich, Adrienne. 1977: *Of Woman Born: Motherhood as Experience and Institution*. London: Virago.

Rich, Adrienne. 1980: 'Compulsory heterosexuality and lesbian existence.', *Signs*, 5: 631–600.

Rieff, Philip. 1979: *Freud: The mind of the Moralist*. Chicago: University of Chicago Press.

Roberts, Yvonne. 1984: *Man Enough: Men of 35 Speak Out*. London: Chatto and Windus.

Rose, Jacqueline. 1986: *Sexuality in the Field of Vision*. London: Verso.

Rubin, Gayle. 1984: 'Thinking sex: notes for a radical theory of the politics of sexuality.' In: Carole S. Vance (ed.) *Pleasure and Danger: Exploring Female Sexuality*. Boston: Routledge and Kegan Paul.

Sahlins, M. D. 1976: *The Use and Abuse of Biology*. London: Tavistock.

Sanday, Peggy Reeves. 1981: *Female Power and Male Dominance: on the Origins of Sexual Inequality*. Cambridge: Cambridge University Press.

Sargent, Lydie (ed.) 1981: *Women and Revolution: a Discussion of the Unhappy Marriage of Marxism and Feminism*. London: Pluto Press.

Sayers, Janet. 1986: *Sexual Contradication: Psychology, Psychoanalysis, and Feminism*. London: Tavistock.

Sayers, Janet, Evans, Mary and Redclift, Nanneke (eds) 1987: *Engels Revisited: New Feminist Essays*. London: Tavistock.

Schwartz, Barry. 1986: *The Battle for Human Nature: Science, Morality and Modern Life*. New York: W. W. Norton.

Schwendinger, Julia R. and Schwendinger, Herman. 1983: *Rape and Inequality*. Beverley Hills: Sage Publications.

Schwenger, P. 1984: *Phallic Critiques*. London: Routledge and Kegan Paul.

Scruton, Roger. 1986: *Sexual Desire*. London: Weidenfeld and Nicolson.

Seidler, Victor J. 1987: 'Reason, desire, and male sexuality.' In: Pat Caplan (ed.) *The Cultural Construction of Sexuality*. London: Tavistock.

Shahar, Shulamaith. 1983: *The Fourth Estate*. London: Methuen.

Shorter, Edward. 1975: *The Making of the Modern Family*. London: Fontana/Collins.

Snodgrass, Jon (ed.) 1977: *For Men Against Sexism*. Albion: Times Change Press.

Solomon, Kenneth. 1982: 'The masculine gender role: description.' In: K. Solomon and N. B. Levy (eds) *Men in Transition*. New York: Plenum Press.

Solomon, Kenneth and Levy, Norman B. (eds) 1982: *Men in Transition*. New York: Plenum Press.

Solomon, Robert C. 1980: *History and Human Nature: a Philosophical Review of European History and Culture, 1750-1850*. Brighton: Harvester.

Stacey, Margaret. 1986: 'Gender and stratification: one central issue or two.' In: Rosemary Crompton and Michael Mann (eds) *Gender and Stratification*. Cambridge: Polity Press.

Stanley, Manfred. 1978: *The Technological Conscience: Survival and Dignity in an Age of Expertise*. Chicago: University of Chicago Press.

Sydie, R. A. 1987: *Natural Women, Cultured Men: a Feminist Perspective on Sociological Theory*. Milton Keynes: Open University Press.

Theweleit, Klaus. 1987: *Male Fantasies*. Cambridge: Polity Press.

Tolson, Andrew. 1977: *The Limits of Masculinity*. London: Tavistock.

Trebilcot, Joyce. 1984: *Mothering: Essays in Feminist Theory*. New Jersey: Rowman and Allanhead.

Turkle, S. 1978: *Psychoanalytic Politics: Freud's French Revolution*. London: Burnett.

Vance, Carole S. (ed.) 1984: *Pleasure and Danger: Exploring Female Sexuality*. Boston: Routledge and Kegan Paul.

Vetterling-Braggin, Mary (ed.) 1982: *'Femininity', 'Masculinity' and 'Androgyny': a Modern Philosophical Discussion*. New Jersey: Littlefield Adams.

Vogel, Lise. 1983: *Marxism and the Oppression of Women: toward a Unitary Theory*. New Jersey: Pluto Press.

Walby, Sylvia. 1986: *Patriarchy at Work*. Cambridge: Polity Press.

Ward, E. 1984: *Father–Daughter Rape*. London: The Women's Press.

Weedon, Chris. 1987: *Feminist Practice and Poststructuralist Theory*. Oxford: Basil Blackwell.

Weeks, Jeffrey. 1977: *Coming Out: Homosexual Politics in Britain from the Nineteenth Century to the Present*. London: Quartet.

Weeks, Jeffrey. 1981: *Sex, Politics and Society: the Regulation of Sexuality Since 1800*. London: Longman.

Weeks, Jeffrey. 1985: *Sexuality and its Discontents*. London: Routledge and Kegan Paul.

Weeks, Jeffrey. 1986: *Sexuality*. London: Tavistock.

Weeks, Jeffrey. 1987: 'Questions of identity.' In: Pat Caplan (ed.) *The Cultural Construction of Sexuality*. London: Tavistock.

Wong, Martin R. 1982: 'Psychoanalytic-development theory and the development of male gender identity.' In: Kenneth Solomon and Norman B. Levy (eds) *Men in Transition*. New York: Plenum Press.

Young, Iris Marion. 1984: 'Is male gender identity the cause of male domination?' In: Joyce Trebilcot (ed.) *Mothering: Essays in Feminist Theory*. New Jersey: Rowman and Allanhead.

Index

aggression
    as innate, 79–83, 179
    and socialization, 7, 83–4
    and sociobiology, 7–8
AIDS, 64, 129, 171, 186
alienation, 68–9
anti-gay attitudes, 171–2
Archer, J., 8

Balbus, Isaac D., 125, 190
Bales, Robert, 138
Barrett, Michele, 136
Bleier, Ruth, 9, 63, 78, 83
body,
    gendering of, 123–4
    and male intentionality,
        199–203
Bookchin, Murray, 89, 92
Boulding, Elise, 91
Boxer, Marilyn J., 133
breadwinner, the
    as privileged, 113–18
Brod, Harry, 195
Brownmiller, Susan, 83

capitalism, 85, 91, 92, 95, 98,
    119
Carrigan, T., 127, 128
categorization
    danger of, 139–41
Chodorow, Nancy, 29, 31, 33, 190,
    195

Chomsky, Noam, 145–6, 160, 161–2
claim
    of attribution, 145
    of truth, 145–6
class
    and gender, 109–12
    and hierarchy, 91
    Marxist view, 126, 143, 167
    men as a, 5, 17, 108–13, 115,
        116
competition, 16, 77, 78, 79–80, 85,
    87, 99
    and scarcity, 85–6, 87–92
Connell, R.W., 23–4, 44, 70, 74, 83,
    127, 128, 140, 198
critical theory
    and men-as-theorists, 166–7
culture
    and nature, 103
    see also public and private

De Beauvoir, Simone, 32, 103
Delphy, Christine, 17, 113, 115, 137
differences
    as rationale for inequality,
        125–6, 177
dignity
    constitutive approach, 154–5
    definitional approach, 155–7
    and human intentionality,
        156–7
    phenomenological approach,
        153–4

problem of, 152–9
and status-worthiness, 156–7, 174
Dinnerstein, Dorothy, 29, 31–2, 33, 190, 195
discourse
of human nature, 146, 147, 152
of humanism, 146–7
and male power, 130–1, 138, 147–52
of 'presence', 149–50, 151
reverse, 130–1, 168–9
true, 147–52, 168
Dobash, R. Emerson, 179
Dobash, Russell, 179
Dworkin, Andrea, 164–6, 167
Dyer, Richard, 31, 59–60

Easlea, Brian, 31, 34, 175–7
economic
man, 100–2, 104
sex, 93–4; *see also* Illich
egalitarianism
complementary, 91–2, 122
Ehrenreich, Barbara, 2, 49, 185
Eisenstein, Zillah, 99
Elliot, Gil, 81
Engels, Friedrich, 16, 86–7, 88, 104, 111, 126
English, Deirdre, 49

family
and economy, 97, 133
as haven, 134
and the new right, 64–5
and patriarchal authority, 134–6
and private property, 86
as site of women's oppression, 113, 131, 184
and social order, 112
fascism, 159–60
fatherhood, 97–8, 100, 114
discovery of, 120–2

female sexuality, 49, 55, 125
feminism, 173, 178, 183
radical, 178–9, 201
Foucault, Michel, 48, 50, 51–2, 54–5, 76, 130, 143–6, 148, 149–50, 160, 161–2, 168
fragmentation thesis, 133, 136
Franklin II, Clyde W., 182–3, 185
Freud, Sigmund, 29, 47, 48, 49, 50, 53, 55, 70, 72, 75, 148, 168

Gagnon, John H., 61
Garfinkel, Harold
and incorrigible propositions, 43
gay politics, 171–3
gender
attributions, 38–9, 40
dichotomous view of, 14–15, 39, 61, 127, 138
and dualism, 15–16
incorrigible propositions, 42–3, 65, 127, 144, 168, 171, 181, 184, 191
social constructionist view, 39, 172, 173, 184
social relations of, 2–3, 181
and sociological theory, 138
gender identity
and biological differences, 21
and fatherhood, 28, 32–3
and masculine crisis, 25–36
mother-son relationships, 29–36, 190–1
and psychoanalysis, 28
and reality construction, 36–41
and sexual division of labour, 22
and socialization, 19–24
and stage irreversibility, 39–40
gender inequality, 43, 109–10
Genovese, Eugene D., 164
Goldthorpe, J.H., 112
Grimshaw, Jean, 34

Hanmer, Jalna, 179
Hargreaves, John, 163
Hartmann, Heidi, 99
Hearn, Jeff, 18, 118, 120–1, 123,
    124, 126, 127, 141, 198
heroism
    the male appropriation of,
        162–3
heterosexualism, 139–41, 167,
    170–1, 186
heterosexuality, 60, 61, 64, 98, 131
    compulsory, 62, 127, 128, 139
    hierarchic, 18, 75, 76, 127, 128,
        139, 158, 168, 170, 172, 173,
        177, 181, 188, 204
    and the state, 127–32
Hobbes, Thomas, 79, 80
Hodson, Phillip, 57
homophobia, 172, 173–4
    and humanistic ideology, 173–4
homosexuality, 65, 98, 141, 168
    and sexual identity, 129
Horkheimer, Max, 134, 135–6
human nature
    and economic rationality,
        100–2
    as essence, 151–2
    and masculinity, 6–11
human value, 123–4, 198
    see also reproduction
humanism
    as ideology, 1434
    as patriarchal ideology, 144–5

identity work, 36–7
Illich, Ivan, 93–4, 97, 104
Ingham, Mary, 189

Jacklin, C.N., 8
Jackson, Margaret, 57, 58
Jaggar, Alison M., 86–7
Jardine, Alice, 200

Kappeler, Susanne, 67, 169
Kessler, Suzanne J., 20, 37–8, 181

Kitzinger, Celia, 173
Kleinberg, Seymour, 171

Lacan, Jacques, 71–3, 75, 146
law of the father, 71–3
Lee, J., 127, 128
Leonard, Diana, 113, 115
Lerner, Gerda, 92, 103, 110, 121,
    122–3
lesbianism, 65, 141
Levi-Strauss, Claude, 87–9
Lewis, Charlie, 114
Lipman-Blumen, Jean, 7
Lockwood, David, 111–12

Maccoby, E.E., 8
McIntosh, Mary, 136
McKenna, Wendy, 20, 37–8, 181
MacKinnon, Catharine, 19, 125,
    144
male
    identity crises, 191–2
    sex role, 23–6
    sexual narratives, 57–60
    sexual scripts, 60–2
male epistemological stance, 144,
    148, 170
male sexuality
    as autonomous, 46
    and the hydraulic model, 47–9
    as innate, 10
    as privileged, 54–7, 72
    valorization of, 55
    and violence, 11–13
man-the-breadwinner, 84–5
man-the-hunter thesis, 77–80
Mann, Michael, 106
Marcuse, Herbert, 50, 52, 134, 167
market relations, 92–5, 101
Marx, Karl, 46, 87, 89, 91, 126, 143,
    167
Marxism, 34, 93, 116, 118, 123, 138,
    168, 201
masculinism
    as dominant ideology, 3–6

as ideology, 4, 125, 148, 158, 167, 174, 197–8, 202
and nationalism, 196–7
masculinity
crisis of, 180, 181–5
hegemonic, 127, 128–9, 139, 140–1, 168, 186–8
and impotence, 192–3
local, 3–4, 139, 188–9
and rationality, 198–204
as relational, 181, 195–6
and testosterone, 9
and war, 80–2, 196–8
Maynard, Mary, 179
men-in-general
as oppressors, 179–80, 181
Merchant, Carolyn, 95–6, 97, 104
mode of production
domestic, 112–13, 137
industrial, 112, 137
Moi, Toril, 144–5
Morgan, D.H.J., 8, 98, 100
Mount, Ferdinand, 171
Moye, Andy, 67

Nazism, 139–40, 156, 159–60
nihilism, 158–9
non-trivilization imperative, 156–9
see also Stanley, Manfred

objectification
and female sexuality, 62, 66–70, 95
and master-slave relationship, 164, 170
and pornography, 66–8, 164–6, 169
and resistance, 170–1, 174–5
object-relations theory, 31, 41
O'Brien, Margaret, 114
O'Brien, Mary, 119–20, 121, 135, 141
Oedipus complex, 29, 47, 70, 191

Parsons, Talcott, 138

Passmore, John, 152–3, 157
patriarchy, 95, 104, 124, 191
in agrarian societies, 105
as autonomous, 16–17, 105–6
and capitalism, 99, 125
and class, 16, 88, 116–17
and individual responsibility, 200–1
as male domination, 106
and motherhood, 32
and private property, 85–6, 104
penis
as phallus, 56, 72, 73
valorized, 56–7, 62, 66, 173, 191
Pleck, Joseph H., 25–8
power
and gender, 44–5
production, primacy of, 117–18
psychoanalysis, 55, 167
public and private, 30, 133–9, 193–4
and culture and nature, 136–7

Quataert, Jean H., 133

racism, 96, 102, 125, 173
and anti-gay discourse, 171–2
Ramazanoglu, Caroline, 204
rape, 51, 54, 59, 68, 74, 83, 95, 102, 164–5, 167, 179, 194, 201
rationality
instrumental, 96
and men-as-scientists, 175–7
reductionism
and biological explanations, 13
and mother-child relationships, 34–5
and psychological primacy, 13–14
Reich, Wilhelm, 50, 134
repression, 48, 50, 52–3, 65, 69
basic, 52
as embodiment, 50, 73–6

as insertion into the symbolic, 71–3
surplus, 52
vulgar, 70–1
reproduction
and male domination, 119–23, 126, 137, 198
and production, 118–23, 126
reproductive labour power, 124–6
Reynaud, Emmanuel, 46–7
Rich, Adrienne, 39, 63, 127
Rieff, Phillip, 52–3
Rubin, Gayle, 131

Sahlins, M.D., 17
scarcity
and domination, 89–92
Schwartz, Barry, 100
Scruton, Roger, 171
Seidler, Victor J., 50–1, 202
self, the
as phallic, 144–5
sexual division of labour, 31, 85, 94, 126, 137
sexuality
as discourse, 48, 50–4
and violence, 11–14, 164–6
Shahar, Shulamaith, 127
Shorter, Edward, 134
Simon, William, 61
Smith, Adam, 79
social Darwinism, 78–9, 80, 101
social, the
and its devaluation, 193–4
sociobiology, 6–9, 82
Solomon, Kenneth, 23
Solomon, Robert C., 142–4, 167
South Africa, 110, 113, 164
Stacey, Margaret, 116

Stanley, Manfred, 153–8, 166, 198
state, the
as abstraction, 132
liberal view of, 131–2
Marxist view of, 132
and violence, 132
structuralism and post-structuralism
and male discourse, 148–9
see also discourse
Sydie, R.A., 138
symbolic order, 72–3
see also Lacan

Tolson, Andrew, 84
transcendental pretence, 142–3, 148, 158, 167, 184
Turkle, S., 148

unconscious
as a non-social category, 192
as the 'other', 151
unemployment
and breadwinners role, 188–9

vernacular gender, 94
see also Illich
victimization thesis, 194–5

Ward, E., 179
Weedon, Chris, 72, 149
Weeks, Jeffrey, 12, 48, 50, 58, 61, 129
Westeman, K., 8
women
and employment, 110–11
in feudal society, 127
work and labour, 85–6

Young, Iris, 190